Stanley
Matthews

Stanley Matthews

The Authorized Biography

**DAVID
MILLER**

PAVILION
MICHAEL JOSEPH

First published in Great Britain in 1989 by
PAVILION BOOKS LIMITED
196 Shaftesbury Avenue, London WC2H 8JL
in association with Michael Joseph Limited
27 Wrights Lane, Kensington, London W8 5TZ

Designed by Tom Sawyer

A CIP catalogue record for this book is
available from the British Library

ISBN 1–85145–161–7

10 9 8 7 6 5 4 3 2 1

Phototypeset by Input Typesetting Ltd., London
Printed and bound in Great Britain by Biddles Limited

CONTENTS

FOREWORD

*F*OR more than thirty years, which is an exceptional duration for a professional sportsman, Stanley Matthews gave to football a touch of special, individual magic all his own. He was appreciated as much by the supporters of the opposition as by those of his own club, at Stoke and then at Blackpool and then back again with Stoke – which is a tribute to his unfailing gift for entertainment. We loved him when he came to Yorkshire, and would eagerly go to see him play, even though he was weaving his spell for our rivals from the Potteries or from Lancashire. We were delighted when he helped England defeat the Scots, or the Italians or Brazilians, and such was the fascination of his dribbling skills that even the Scottish crowds were obliged to praise him also.

Stanley Matthews was a symbol of the country which gave football to the world, and internationally a symbol of English sportsmanship in the days when that was a quality acknowledged world-wide. He was a national figure of whom we were all proud, and I was delighted for him to receive his knighthood – in the early days of my Premiership – while still playing at the remarkable age of fifty, just before his retirement in 1965. We shall not forget the many happy hours which Stanley gave to millions (even before the era of television). We remember him as a humble and modest hero who had a particular affinity with the ordinary man.

Lord Wilson of Rievaulx

PREFACE

To explain to someone nowadays the impact that Stanley Matthews had on the game is difficult. I was fortunate, in that I bridged the end of the Stanley Matthews era and the modern times of Pelé and Beckenbauer, and have seen all the contemporary stars such as Platini, Zico and Gullitt. So I am able to give an honest comparison. In the context of great players, going back as far as I can remember, Stanley Matthews is probably the greatest of all.

Just after the war, when I was beginning to evaluate players, his aura pervaded the whole of football. As a little lad, I used to go with my brother Jack and sit on the track at St James Park to watch Newcastle, and of course our interest was in the best players. It wasn't so much a matter of when were they going to be there as when was Matthews coming? That was the highlight of the season. I was impressed by many of the players at that time: Lofthouse, Franklin, Mannion, Shackleton, the Spurs team which won the championship in 1951. Yet never was more of an impression made on me than by Matthews. I couldn't take my eyes off him, the feeling that I was actually breathing the same air as he was.

In those days, there was a particular mystique when visiting teams came out on the field and you first saw them. They didn't warm up earlier, the way they do now, which I think detracts from the drama. Just the sight of Matthews coming out on the pitch gave you a feeling of the magic of the man. People would travel, in the days when it was really difficult, hundreds of miles to see him. And if, when they got there, it was announced he was not playing everyone would groan and be really depressed. That was the impact he had on the game.

What did he do? The skill was mesmerizing. He frightened full-backs to death. Every week, the left-back of the team that Stoke or Blackpool were playing on Saturday would have an article in the local paper, sometimes in the national papers, about how he was going to play against the master. That itself is an exceptional tribute to a man. The full-back would say, 'I'm going to keep my eye on the ball and not on Matthews' or 'I'm going to stop him getting the ball', but no system ever worked. Stan had the ability to use both feet, inside and outside. The way he destroyed defenders was almost embarrassing.

I remember the occasion when my uncle Jackie Millburn first played for England, against Ireland at Old Trafford. Jack and I couldn't get there so the next week we went to see the Movietone news reel at the cinema. We got there late, and sat through *The Red Shoes*, which was marvellous, but then had to ask not to be thrown out, because it was not a continuous performance, so that we could stay and see the newsreel in the next show. We were proud when we saw Uncle Jack running out, but what I remember most is seeing Stan sending the full-back running literally ten yards the wrong way. I felt sorry for the man.

Stan knew exactly when, and where, to go. People could *never* tackle him, and no one could touch him for speed over ten yards. Even late in his career, when he was nearing fifty, he still had his magic, and I am sorry I only played against him a couple of times or so. Whenever he reached the dead-ball line, his crosses were pinpoint accurate, right through the whole of his career.

His magic is hard to describe to people who never saw him. He was as great an attacker as there's ever been. Today, there'd be busloads travelling all over the country to see him. As a professional, I don't use the term genius lightly, but Stanley was a genius. Stan Mortensen likes to tell one of his stories about an England match when Matthews and Finney were both playing. Matthews centred, and Morty's header went thundering into the net. Morty gave Stan a thumbs-up sign. Later in the game, Finney centred, and another Mortensen header flew into the net, but there was no signal afterwards. Tom later asked him why he didn't receive the thumbs-up sign. Morty told him that it was because Stan had crossed the ball with the lace facing away from him. I half like to think it could be true.

Bobby Charlton OBE

ACKNOWLEDGEMENTS

*O*F the many people who have helped with this biography, I would like to thank those who so willingly gave their recollections of a unique man: George Male, Stan Cullis, Joe Mercer, Sir Matt Busby, Raich Carter, Ted Drake, Tommy Lawton, Hans Jacob, Peter Buxton, Neil Franklin, George Hardwick, Ron Burgess, Johnny Aston, George Birks, Tut Whalley, Colin Melbourne, Tom Finney, Billy Wright, Stan Mortensen, Sir Walter Winterbottom, Nat Lofthouse, Jimmy Armfield, Bill Perry, Jackie Mudie, Bobby Charlton, Geoffrey Green, Joe Pannaye, Bobby Cowell, Ralph Banks, Jupp Durwall, Werner Liebrich, Helmut Schoen, Harry Haddock, Mihaly Lantos, Didi, Ray Wilson, Tony Waddington, John Barrett and Jimmy McIlroy, in particular, and others too numerous to list. I have had extensive help from Stanley's brothers, Jack and Ronnie, and their wives, from Stanley's daughter Jean, and from his long-standing friend Charlie Chester. Above all, there has been Stanley's own enthusiasm and assistance in the project over two and a half years, which has been invaluably informative. Frances Carman and Jane Butterworth were indispensable audio-typists, Steve Dobell an interested and sensitive editor, and Peter Buxton a permanent source of experienced reference. I am grateful to *The Times* for permission to reproduce Geoffrey Green's report of Brazil's defeat by England in 1956.

Stanley and I much appreciate the enthusiasm of Lord Wilson of Rievaulx and of Bobby Charlton in writing, respectively, the Foreword and Preface.

D.M.

INTRODUCTION

*L*ET homage be rendered to the various sports, and in particular to football. For, still more than the king of sports, football is the king of games. All the great games of man are games with a ball, be they tennis, pelota or billiards. In our life, the ball is that thing which most easily escapes from the laws of life. This is its most useful quality. It has, on earth, the extra-territorial quality of some force which has not been fully tamed. It is in no way related to the concept of the animal being, which is that of constriction; and, like a satellite of the globe whose laws it obeys without zest yet with flashing defiance, it has the virtue of being nothing down here but a ball. Football owes its universality to the fact that it can give the ball its maximum effect. The football team is the pelota wall, suddenly become intelligent, the billiard cloth suddenly endowed with genius. Beyond its own principle, that of resilience, of independence, the team implants to the ball the motor of eleven shrewd minds and eleven imaginations. If the hands have been barred from the game, it is because their intrusion would make the ball no longer a ball, the player no longer a player. The hands are cheats, they have been given exclusively to two cheating animals, to the man and monkey. The ball will not permit any cheating, but only effects that are sublime...*'*

JEAN GIRAUDOUX

*J*EAN Giraudoux was a French novelist, playwright and sporting enthusiast, who died in 1942 having written some of the most popular of theatrical comedies, and being at the same time an expert in the Basque game of pelota; or chistera, as the French call it. He was a disciple of de Coubertin, the founder of the modern Olympic Games, with a profound belief in the value of sport to man's morality. His commentaries on sport are sufficient to convince even the intelligentsia that games, and especially football, are far more than merely muscle and sweat: that they engage the mind and can generate moments of poetic beauty and subtlety. This biography is an attempt to tell, through the recollections of Sir Stanley Matthews' colleagues and contemporaries, and though his own reminiscences and a few of mine, the story of his eventful and exceptional lifetime in football, in which so often he brought beauty to the prosaic.

Stanley will be seventy-five on 1 February 1990. He became legendary, in the colloquial sense, because in his early days, before television penetrated every home and laid open the intimate skills of every sporting hero, he was legendary in the literal sense: an acknowledgement of his genius being passed from person to person, second- and third-hand by word of mouth, or by newspapers, so that a tide of folk-hero worship grew among millions who had never, in fact, set eyes upon him. Those were the days when to have seen the King, even to have been to London, was regarded as an event. To see any sporting hero in person, you mostly had to take the opportunity on those few occasions when he or she visited your town. Here was a contemporary Musketeer, who, during the depression of the Thirties, brought a sense of freedom and adventure; who suggested that all obstacles were surmountable, that the diligent could overcome the aggressor, who satisfied a common yearning for simple pleasure. The secret of Stanley's ability to win such unqualified devotion from the public lay in his seeming frailty, his shy, unassuming modesty; yet simultaneously in his magician's spell over the opposition. There was about his battles with the full-back the aura of Peter Pan and Captain Hook, with the gleeful crowd knowing beforehand, like a pantomime audience, who was going to win. So we cheered and laughed at the capitulation of left-backs like children in thrall at the approaching ticking clock of Barrie's crocodile. In Stanley rested all our fears and all our hopes.

When I was a small boy growing up in war-time, he entered my consciousness along with other mythological heroes that were part of education, such as Nelson, Livingstone and Captain Scott. When I was about twelve, and he thirty-two and just transferred from Stoke to Blackpool, I wrote to him: the only time in my youth I ever requested an autograph. Back came the neatly signed Blackpool match programme, and suddenly, with that signature, he took on tangible proportions. Now I knew him, personally. Not only had he superhuman ability with a ball, but he was an ordinary fellow, for here was his name in his own pen and ink. For several years, as a winger, I had tried to understand what it must be like to be him; pretended in my fantasy moments, on a deserted school playing field after returning from church on Sunday morning, that I *was* him; just as, with a friend in summer, we used to play day-long two-man Test matches, he Australia and I England, impersonating in turn Lindwall and Compton or Hassett and Wright.

Yet as I became increasingly familiar with the galaxy of sporting figures from Owens and Louis to Wooderson and Hobbs, Stanley had a particular and different position. It was as though, and as yet I had not seen him, he was somehow indestructible, imperishable. There was about him this feeling already that he would continue playing indefinitely, and I think it was because his performance was beyond the physical. He was an athlete, yet not athletic. Because he hardly ever spoke or, that I was then aware, showed any emotion, there was an abstract quality about him, and he imperceptibly became part of one's general contemporary cultural back-cloth, with Housman, Eliot and Kern, Frank Whittle, Manny Shinwell and Max Beaverbrook. He was always *there*. An institution. You knew from conversation, from listening to aunts, that this is what he was to many of my era, including women, who knew nothing of sport but were conscious of Matthews, of those mystical qualities that transported spectators everywhere into paroxyms of delight.

I listened to wireless commentaries on Stanley losing two Cup Finals before, at last, I saw him. Living on the Surrey-Hampshire border at Hindhead, my nearest First Division clubs were, equi-distant, Fulham and Portsmouth. At fifteen, attending a schoolboy coaching course at Acton, where I first met Walter Winterbottom, the England team manager, and Bertie Mee – a physiotherapist who later became Arsenal's manager – I had seen Alf Ramsey and Eddie Baily passing a football as I had never seen it passed before, while standing on the terraces at Craven Cottage. The next year, I managed to persuade my father to take me to see Blackpool's first match, as I remember, after losing the Cup Final to Newcastle, when they played Portsmouth at Fratton Park. And there on the pitch were twenty-one players: and Matthews. He was like no other player I have seen before or since, and

I have seen them all in my time. With even the greatest players, such as Pelé, Cruyff and Di Stefano, there was an awareness of their muscular effort, even in those sublime moments when they were on a quite separate plane to the opposition. With Stanley, it was as though he had placed the ball under a spell, whereby from the moment he received it he no longer needed to pay attention to it, as he began that mesmerizing stroll towards the left-back. In exactly the same way as the left-back, you ceased to watch the ball and watched him; for both of you a drug, and for the full-back fatal. Stanley hovered, not on the ground but seemingly just above it, like a dragonfly – there one moment, gone the next. And standing there among a 50,000 crowd at Fratton Park, struggling to see between adult shoulders, I recognized something unique, though without properly understanding it, and came away feeling as if I had caught a glimpse of Richard Coeur de Leon himself.

I saw Stanley off and on for the next thirteen years, yet that was only the last third of his career; possibly, according to some, the least exceptional of the three – pre-war, war-time, and post-war. I was to see some of the most famous of all his matches at Wembley for Blackpool or England: against Bolton Wanderers, Hungary, West Germany, Brazil, and onwards into that last remarkable swansong back at Stoke. Generation after generation went to see Stanley; not to watch a match, but just to see him. We went because we knew that we would afterwards feel the better for it. As the years passed, the skill remained unwithered, the hypnotism unrelenting, the public adulation unrestrained. My own years of fitness as a senior amateur player came and departed within that last third of his playing span; and there he was, still going, at an age when some can contemplate nothing more strenuous than mowing the lawn and certainly cannot run for the bus. Still he epitomized, unostentatiously, the most fundamental virtues of sport, the essential reason why we play games: that they teach us equally to be modest in victory and magnanimous in defeat, morally to turn the other cheek, to respect the rules and our adversaries, to place joyfulness above profit. Though it was never his calculated objective, but an example born of his background and upbringing, Stanley was a paragon of sportsmanship. He was, in the words of George Male, his pre-war contemporary with Arsenal and England, a professional playing as an amateur. Therein lay part of his charm.

The span of his career, from Baldwin to the Beatles, is a story that, in the telling, it is difficult not to believe an exaggeration. It is truly the stuff of fiction, and to have seen him play was one of the privileges of our time. 'Why does the whole football world and many outside that world look for Matthews whenever he plays?' J. P. W. Mallalieu asked. Like the organ-grinder's tune, he drew to him all manner of people. There is the story of an appearance in Dublin, against the Republic at Dalymount Park. Sitting in the stand are a priest and a typical Irish punter of the kind more normally associated with the racecourse. Stanley gets the ball, and is off the mark, past the full-back.

'Faader, Faader, did you see t'at? T' speed o' the man!'

The priest nods sagely. 'Speed was always his forte,' he says.

'Forte? Forte? T' man's fifty, Faader, forheaven'sake.'

No other player in English football, young or old, ever carried such an atmosphere with him.

Near the Victoria Football Ground in Stoke there is a churchyard: the tombstones are said to belong to the full-backs that Matthews has destroyed. Once, playing at Chelsea with Blackpool in the mid-1950s, his team was 2–1 down and on the receiving end of some rough treatment. McFarland, the left-back, had put his knee in Stanley's thigh; and after giving him a long, hard look, Stanley had limped off the field. Some of the crowd had chanted 'Are you finished, Stan?' Ten minutes later, following treatment, he was back on the field. Jimmy Armfield, his own right-back, asked him if he was all right, with his thigh heavily strapped. 'Yes, keep knocking it in quick,' Stanley replied. There were twenty minutes to go, during which time McFarland was twisting and turning until his boots nearly fell off. Blackpool won 4–2. For the last goal, Stanley ran through from an inside-right position, beat two men, and tapped the ball past the goalkeeper. The grandstand crowd rose to its feet.

Professional footballers came to learn never to expect the hand shake of friendship from Stanley if they had deliberately fouled him. That was the world of the hypocrite. Neither would Stanley shake hands before a match – though always afterwards – because good wishes before a game are insincere. Stanley was on the field to win. In order to win, he had perfected his game over long, lonely afternoons, when he would go back to the Victoria Ground on his own, take out half a dozen balls, place pieces of paper around the penalty area, and practise centring until he could drop a ball on any of them at will. 'Only three other players, in my experience, had as great a sense of theatre – Alfredo Di Stefano, Alex James, and Pelé,' wrote Geoffrey Green of *The Times*, who witnessed the whole period of Stanley's exceptional career.

Credibility extended beyond sport. In the programme for his Testimonial match in 1965, Lady Violet Apsley wrote: 'He has been, and still is, a wonderful ambassador of British trade. Throughout the world he stands for British quality and integrity.' Stanley believed in giving value for money. It is his opinion that the current freedom of contract, which allows star players to wander from club to club extorting the highest fees they can demand through their agents, is unfair on the clubs and unfair on football. There was an occasion when Stoke were on tour in Turkey, with the condition that Stanley would play; but he had a septic toe on his right foot. So he cut a hole in his soft boot to ease the pressure, and played the whole match exclusively using his left foot. Versatility had always been there. When England put eight goals past Northern Ireland in 1938, Frank Coles of the *Daily Telegraph* wrote:

> The Stoke City right-winger gave a superb display, one which has never been bettered in the long history of international football, and can very rarely have been equalled by the giants of the past. We have known Matthews as a fine player, sure in his control of the ball, and beautifully balanced on his feet, for a long time now. This afternoon he reached the pinnacle, and at the close the crowd rose as one man to salute the player whose wizardry had held them fascinated.

Jack Matthews, Stanley's father who was a professional boxer, had fought until he was forty. 'It's genes, isn't it?' Stanley's elder brother, Jack, says. 'He'll still be out running at breakfast time when he's eighty, like he has all his life.' Ronnie, his younger brother, thinks that it was the character of their parents that gave Stanley his dedication: that with his ability and without self-discipline he would never have been the same. Peter Buxton, a journalist in Stoke who knows the family well, says: 'His father was kind but very firm, while his mother was one of the gentlest people you could meet. All the brothers have their mother's nature, and Jean, Stanley's daughter, has it more than most.'

Such was his magnetism on the pitch that many of the current records for attendance were established when Stanley was playing: 149,547, the British record, at Hampden Park in 1937; and the records at Maine Road, the home of Manchester City, and Stamford Bridge. In 1934, in six consecutive matches including a cup replay, Stoke were watched by 399,874 people, an average of over 66,000, including the Maine Road record of 84,568. Thirty years apart, Stanley won Second Division championship medals with Stoke at the ages of eighteen and forty-eight. When he played against Denmark in the World Cup in 1957, he had made eighty-four England appearances, including thirty war-time matches, and when he played for Stoke against Fulham in 1965, aged fifty, he was the oldest to have played in the Football League. He is the oldest to have scored in the FA Cup. Of the eighty-four matches with England, they won fifty-one, drew fifteen, and lost eighteen, scoring 245 goals. The only player with an international span to compare with Stanley's twenty-three years is Peter Shilton, who currently has been playing in goal for England during eighteen years.

Yet fame neither penetrated nor affected him any more than sunshine coming through a bedroom window. He observed it, never really understood it, and, with originality, ignored it. Colin Melbourne, sculptor of the statue of Stanley that now stands in a Hanley pedestrian precinct, says that Stanley was the only sitter he has ever had who was wholly without vanity. 'When it was over,' Melbourne says, 'it was as though it was nothing to do with him.' Jackie Mudie, a Scottish colleague with both Blackpool and Stoke, says: 'He has a sincere lack of understanding of his greatness. Even today, in retirement, I don't think he realizes how big he is. If he pushed himself, he could still make a lot of money.'

Charlie Chester, a close friend, came to know him as well as anyone, though it took many years. 'There was a time when he wouldn't go out in public,' Chester recalls. 'At a Scouts' function in the Potteries, back in the Forties, I had to persuade him to say a few words. He was so reticent. He would never talk after a match, never criticize. And he was so proper. He didn't like to swear, and if there was any mention of sex on television, he would make his young daughter leave the room.' Jean remembers him being very strict, and a bit of a prude. If there were scenes of childbirth at the cinema or on television, her father would start talking, or turn off the television. Jimmy McIlroy, an Irish international colleague, recalls that it was only in later years that Stanley became less offended by blue jokes in the hurly-burly of the changing-room. Through his shyness, he would often become confused in public about people's names. At a fiftieth birthday party in his honour at the Grosvenor House Hotel in London, a surprise 'This is Your Life' programme was planned. Over the public address system came a voice: 'Hello, Stanley, this is Eamonn Andrews.' 'Hello, Andrew,' replied a bashful Stanley.

In his single-minded pursuit of healthiness he became almost a fetishist. George Hardwick, first post-war England captain, recalls that Stanley took pills by the score. 'He was a near hypochondriac,' Hardwick says. 'We'd share a room, and the bathroom shelf would be crowded with boxes, and I'd say "Stan, leave me enough room for my toothbrush".' Nat Lofthouse, the Bolton and England centre-forward, has seen Stanley take bread rolls at lunchtime, open them, and pull out all the dough, eating nothing but the crust. Peter Buxton recalls: 'Sometimes, when he was manager at Port Vale, I'd go to have lunch with him on a Tuesday, and Stan would be rubbing his hands, saying "I'm looking forward to this!" And he'd sit and hungrily eat a salad. I would ask whether he'd not had breakfast, and Stanley would say "I've had nothing since Saturday." He believed in weekend fasting. His family complained he ate like a rabbit, endless salads.'

Yet, though his colleagues would good-humouredly joke about his almost neurotic preoccupation with maintaining his fitness through careful diet and stringent exercise, their praises ring down the years like a peal of cathedral bells. Stanley Cullis, an England captain before the war, whose own experience spans every great player since 1925, says:

I've never seen *any* better player than Stanley, in his rôle. He was the most perfectly balanced player of all, and balance is the essence of any great games player. Opposing teams disintegrated because of the panic he created. He wouldn't say it, but he knew the effect he had on them. He put players out of the game for the sheer entertainment of it, and he enjoyed it, though I don't think it was an obsession.

Mihaly Lantos, the left-back of Hungary who faced Stanley in one of the most famous of all matches, considers that no player has ever dribbled in such a way, and that only Garrincha of Brazil came close to equalling him. Harry Haddock, a Scotland full-back in the World Cup of 1958, who was torn apart by Stanley at Wembley in 1955, remembers: 'That match was perfection. He did things with the ball that were undreamed of, that players now being paid £3,000 a week cannot even imagine. Players will forever attempt to attain his standard. There'll not be another in a hundred years. If he was playing today they would get treble the gates.'

Few of his colleagues were envious, and those that were mostly were lesser players. The good players, though they might rib him for his mannerisms, had an admiration that amounted to awe. Tommy Lawton, possibly the best known of all England centre-forwards, says simply: 'He was the greatest player that ever kicked a ball', and closes his eyes at the pleasure of the recollection. Nat Lofthouse, another of England's formidable goal-scorers, acknowledges the value to himself of such a winger:

Stanley could cross or chip a ball from anywhere to within a yard of you. [Lofthouse says]. He was marvellous. We not only admired him, but respected him, because he was modest as well as brave. When he got clogged by some full-back, the most he would say afterwards was: 'He wasn't nice at all, was he?' If I pulled his leg beforehand, he'd warn me: 'Watch it, or you won't get any goals today.' He made it so easy for us.

It was modesty that endeared him to the crowds and fellow players alike. Ray Wilson, the Huddersfield and England left-back who played against both Matthews and Garrincha, says he would rather the game was remembered for such as Matthews, Tom Finney and Bobby Charlton than for the likes of some of those around today. Finney, much of whose own career was spent in direct and friendly rivalry with Stanley for the same position in England's team, says: 'I loved to watch him.

He was superb. He always rose to the occasion, he really did, and the bigger it was the more he liked it. He was the greatest ball-player in our era, and he showed no mercy, took every advantage of it. That's essential to a player's make-up.'

Billy Wright, another England captain, recalls that over fifteen yards, even at the age of thirty-five, Stanley could leave standing the late and much loved Jackie Milburn, an England centre-forward and a former Powderhall sprinter. Jimmy McIlroy says that the secret of the magic of Matthews was *timing*:

I remember once [McIlroy says], in an international at Windsor Park, that I was determined to get the ball, and was convinced Stanley had over-played it as he moved towards me, that the ball was mine. I went to block it: our feet passed in opposite directions, his with the ball. I felt a fool. He had phenomenal speed over five yards, there was no one to touch him. Yet no matter how fast he did anything, he was always under control and had something to spare. George Best had this. Cowdrey had it against fast bowlers. Keegan didn't. When Keegan was at top speed, you could *see* he was flat out. Stanley would pull his hair out watching John Barnes today. It's so easy to go past a full-back on the inside, and in the old days a winger who came inside was often gutless. There's so much more space inside. The hard way is going outside, and Stan was still doing it easily when he was fifty.

Team managers, often in anxiety, recognized the magnitude of the threat Stanley posed to any team. It was a relief to have him on your side. 'You can't deceive the public, whether it's 500 or 50,000,' says Tony Waddington, his manager at Stoke. 'Stanley's reputation was based on a genuine, absolute ability, which he could summon at any time. He ruined five-a-side practice matches. Nobody could get the ball from him.' Walter Winterbottom, who was England's first appointed team manager, from 1946 to 1962, thinks that the appeal to the crowd was not Stanley's speed, but the reverse:

Stanley sidled up to his opponents, tormented them, and it was part of the show for the public that the full-back was expected to try to knock the ball out of the ground [Winterbottom says]. Stan would torture one opponent, and then there'd be two of them on him. In the Thirties, wingers were expected to be fast, direct runners, but Stan had the slow approach, and played cat-and-mouse. I don't know if he'd survive today. In our time, you'd get sent off for the sort of tackles from behind we see nowadays.

Arthur Ellis, an English referee who officiated around the globe and took charge of the World Cup Final of 1954, was the man in the middle for Stanley's testimonial match of 1965. He said at the time: 'Over the years, I've seen him tripped, charged in the back, flattened in the mud, almost have his shirt pulled off. Yet I've never heard him say a wrong word or retaliate in any way. If there were twenty-two Matthewses on the pitch, I would be out of a job,'

If shyness contributed to Stanley's politeness, never wishing to be conspicuous or to cause a scene, it also could create a false impression that he was unsociable, particularly because he did not drink. He grew up during times of depression, and, on the strict guidance of his father, his first trip after he had received his initial £10 wage in 1932 was to the Post Office. The principle of financial prudence was established early in his life; but there was more to his carefulness than any wish not to squander his money. The Stoke City environment that he joined in 1930 was one in which, according to one of his contemporaries, players trained largely on ale and women. Stanley grew to hate the smell of beer and pubs, a dislike well justified by one particular event.

At an away match when he was still a teenager, several of his colleagues sneaked out of the hotel late one evening before a match, and smuggled back several quart-bottles of beer, returning to the room which Stanley shared with another player, and where he was seemingly asleep. There being no glasses from which to drink the beer, the other players retrieved the chamber-pot from beneath the bed, poured the contents down the hand-basin, and proceeded to drink from the unwashed chamber-pot while Stanley, with half an eye open, lay there sick with nausea.

Yet however much the roisterous or clubbable players such as Stan Mortensen or Lofthouse might pull Stanley's leg about his carefulness, close friends know his generosity. Peter Buxton says:

To say that he was mean would be nonsense. I never saw a mean thing about him in my life, and such talk as there was of this was mostly jealousy. He was plagued with invitations to appear in charity matches because of his public appeal, and would often say, 'You'll have to see my agent.' He never had one. He was trying to side-step the invitations without seeming rude, but people thought he was asking for a hundred pounds. Each of us on the committee for his Testimonial received an engraved silver tea service. This so-called mean man said to Waddington, when he rejoined Stoke, 'Pay me what you think I'm worth', and left Waddington to write out a contract. He could have asked for three times more than he received. At Port Vale, he was there by nine in the morning, and never drew a salary for three years. When he left Port Vale, he offered to stay and coach the youngsters for nothing.

When Jackie Mudie first arrived in Blackpool at the end of the war, he was an apprentice painter-decorator, and at one time was engaged on painting the Romford Hotel, owned by Stanley. At the same time Mudie was playing part-time for Blackpool. When Stanley learned of this, he told Mudie to see the chef at breakfast time, and have what he wished any morning. Mudie's wife, Brenda, recalls that Stanley never came to their house without bringing something for the children. When Stoke were on tour and Stanley received a fee for a foreign newspaper article, it would be shared among the players; and Lofthouse himself recalls that when Stanley received personal social invitations on tour, he would insist that all his colleagues were invited as well. 'He was all for team spirit,' Lofthouse says.

George Birks, a founder member of the Stoke Supporters Club, recalls the day that Manchester United brought with them a blind boy to a match at the Victoria Ground, and sent the boy's autograph book to Stanley in the Stoke dressing-room. It came back, signed, and with a five-pound note folded inside. Without it being known, Stanley contributes substantial sums to old people's homes in the Potteries, and his provision on occasion for his brothers and their families has been uncalculating. I have to say that in all my experience of professional footballers, he is one of the few who has always been ready to pick up the bill in a restaurant, when it was going to be paid out of his own pocket and not signed on the club's account. Stanley gently deflects any accusations, and does not let them bother him. 'Whenever I was asked to appear in charity matches,' he says, 'I'd tell people to wait and see what the takings were like. If they were poor, I'd ask for my travel expenses; if they were good, then maybe £20, or, if it was near the Cup Final, £100. I've seen it written that I've demanded £500. I never *demanded* anything.'

His demands were almost exclusively of himself. Behind that slightly austere exterior, which so easily unfolds into warmth and relaxation in private surroundings, there lies a relentless self-discipline. Without quite knowing what perfection was, Stanley wanted to be perfect at his game; and to this end he gave, for over fifty years, an exclusiveness of effort and concentration that shut off from him so many of life's alternative pleasures: a sacrifice which those who lack a vision of objective are less prepared to make.

SM: The excitement was the business of getting ready, through the week. There was a battle to be won, and there was the thrill of getting on to the field beforehand. That was *the* moment. I never knew who the referee was, I never looked to find out. I had great concentration, and once the match began, every other thought was excluded. Yet I never reflected afterwards on whether I had given a good performance.

How do you *know*, in a team game, whether you've played well? I only knew when I played badly. I was never conscious of being famous. It was only when, years later, I travelled to Australia, Africa and America that I began to realize the kind of reputation I had.

Could Stanley have been today the success he was twenty, thirty and forty years ago? Would he have been allowed to develop? Jimmy McIlroy had an instinctive appreciation of what Stanley was: to him, to the team, and to the public. He doubts if Stanley would have *wanted* to play today. 'He wouldn't be allowed now to train as an individual, to work on his own at sprints and breathing exercises and jogging,' McIlroy says. 'Now, he'd be regimented, they would demand circuit training. There's no way he would do that. *Mentally*, he couldn't exist today. But skill-wise? He'd be a sensation.'

Sometime before the Second World War, on an occasion when Stanley was dropped by the England selectors, the first of a dozen or more times such misjudgement would happen, Henry Rose, of the *Daily Express*, received the following telegram from an Irishman:

ENGLAND SELECTORS RIGHT FOR ONCE.
ENGLAND TEAM NOT IN THE SAME CLASS AS MATTHEWS

1. BOYHOOD

'CRICKET has produced many national heroes – mortals touched with divinity. It was not Gloucester or Sussex or Surrey that we went to see. We went to see Grace and Ranji and C.B. Fry and Hobbs, just as today we go to see Hutton, not Yorkshire. Even if we never saw them at all, we knew them. Their art, their achievements, their idiosyncracies were our personal possession, a part of our personal and affectionate pride. But until now football has produced no such heroes. There have, of course, been great footballers – Billy Meredith, Steve Bloomer, 'Billy' Dean, Alex James – but they were not household names or personalities.

Now, at last, a footballer has become a national hero, not placed on a pedestal in some distant temple but imagined, with Grace and Ranji and Fry and Hobbs, into all our living-rooms at home. Stanley Matthews' successes have become our joy and his failures our sorrow. His name has become a magic which for the moment can still a child or stir an old man, which even on the bitterest day can draw nearly all of us from our firesides. Yet there is nothing remarkable about him. There is no oddity about his dress, except perhaps that the laces in his boots look new and always are new: for Matthews' feet and Matthews' boots must be as one, and new laces play a part in ensuring that end. Otherwise you'll notice only that as he comes on the field his head is not down contemplatively, but forward, expectantly. '

J.P.W. MALLALIEU, *Sporting Days*

*J*ACK Matthews, a barber with his own premises in Market Street in Hanley, one of the Five Towns of the Potteries, epitomized Victorian generations and those immediately following: hard working, self-disciplined, undemonstrative. Family unity and loyalty were everything; financial independence was both an objective and a virtue. Affection, which was deep, tended to be unspoken. Jack treated his four sons with that slightly patrician discipline that was typical of the time. The sons respected him, and remember him lovingly for all his air of severity.

It was an age when you were expected to be self-sufficient. When Stanley, the third of four sons, was born on 1 February 1915, Ada, his mother, was at home on her own, and lay with him peacefully on the bed until someone returned to give assistance. The boy was, she later told one of her daughters-in-law, the most beautiful of her sons at birth. Ada was a good-looking and a warm woman, who mostly kept her thoughts to herself while tending to the five men in her life.

Most Sunday mornings, Jack would walk the five and a half miles, and back, from Hanley to Werrington, where his wife was born and where a spinster sister had a shop. On many Sundays, his wife and one or more of the sons would accompany him. Walking was a customary and accepted feature of day-to-day existence, and it certainly contributed to the fitness of the Matthews family.

The family's life in residential, terraced Seymour Street, where Stanley was born, was dominated by the affairs of the barber's shop. This was open from eight in the morning until, most days, nine in the evening. Even on Christmas Day, following a handsome spread of traditional Christmas fare, Jack would proceed to Market Street by two in the afternoon to shave those of his Jewish customers who wished to attend. His elder two sons, Jack and Arthur, were required, from an early age, to assist him in the shop; both subsequently opened their own premises in the same trade, remaining in the Potteries throughout their career. Matthews senior came to be regarded as a stalwart citizen of Hanley, a man of his time. When, on one occasion, he engaged in conversation with an American and discovered that the visitor had been overcharged at a department store, he accompanied him back to the shop and insisted on the man being given a refund.

Jack Matthews' reputation in the Potteries was notably enhanced by his achievements in the boxing ring. In a fighting career that began late, he had some 350 bouts, many of them over twenty rounds of three minutes, and he was only defeated nine times. A featherweight, he was particularly quick on his feet, a characteristic inherited to a fine degree by Stanley. His self-discipline in his preparation for the ring was remarkable, and this too was something which he would hand down to the boy who would surpass most sporting standards. At around eight in the evening, Jack would leave his shop for the remaining hour in the care of either of his two elder sons, and go to the gymnasium at Etruria where he would train with a number of sparring partners for two or three hours. Having walked the two miles home to Seymour Street, he would then be up again by six, to go for a five-mile run before opening the shop again at breakfast time. He took Thursday afternoon off, apart from which it was rare for Ada to see him other than on Sundays.

Mrs Matthews was a quiet but resourceful woman. Mavis, the wife of Ronnie, her fourth son, recalls that 'she enjoyed going to the races, and had a fine sense of humour. She was half the size of Jack, and had every meal off a six-inch plate – not enough to keep a snail alive. But very modern in her outlook. She was a fantastic cook. She didn't know how – just mixed the handfuls together,'

Ada conceded to Jack's boxing with, in the opinion of her son Jack, an unstated anxiety; though a regular winning purse of twenty or fifty guineas, many times the average weekly wage of a working man in those days, must have been a substantial compensation towards the family's welfare. She would sit at home waiting for her husband's return in the evening after a fight. When he had won, he would walk in and often place some sovereigns on the kitchen table. On those occasions when he had lost, she would know: because his kitbag with his shorts and towel and shoes would be slung through the door on to the floor in advance of his presence.

Two of Jack senior's brothers, Charlie and George, and both of his elder boys were competent boxers. Charlie was similar in physique and appearance, and occasionally, when Jack was due for what promised to be a less than demanding bout, he would say to Charlie: 'If you fancy £25, why don't you go down to the ring tonight and take my place?' . . . which Charlie would gratefully do. They trained together and their styles were similar.

George, by all accounts, might have been the most outstanding of the three. But during the First World War he was machine-gunned when storming the barbed-wire from the trenches at the Somme; was retrieved half-dead, and had a leg amputated. His days as a flyweight were over. A year or two after the war the following letter appeared in the *Staffordshire Sentinel*:

Sir, I hope all the sporting gentlemen of a thoroughly sporting county will give my suggestion a little thought. I had the good fortune to meet

Young Nipper Matthews the other day, minus a leg, surrendered gladly in the late war. Now, as you no doubt know, prior to the war this boy's future looked rosy indeed. A champion's belt was within reach. And now: well, poverty. What I suggest is that some influential gentleman promotes a boxing entertainment to give him a start in life. Jim Driscoll, Basham, Wells or Becket would be only too pleased to help. And he is deserving of it. I've always found him a sportsman and a thorough little gentleman in all respects, and I am ready to give my contribution as a tribute to a deserving case.   Yours, etc.

George was assisted during his difficulties, of course, by Jack and Ada – 'A decent man, Jack was, easy to talk to, someone who'd always say what he thought, always forthright', in the words of George Birks, an accountant who would later become a founder member of the Stoke City Supporters' Club. Jack, who himself served with the North Staffordshires for three years, might well have become the national featherweight title-holder, but for the interruption of the war. His progress had developed in his early twenties; and not long after the opening of his shop in Hanley he made his first mark in the sport outside the immediate vicinity of the Potteries. Jack McNiff, a local promoter, had seen Matthews in training and fancied him to beat an up-and-coming fighter called Chambers, who was being promoted in Manchester. When McNiff visited the City Athletic Club in Manchester to offer the challenge, the matchmaker of the club was reluctant to accept, never having heard of the Hanley barber. McNiff therefore promised that if Matthews failed to put up a good performance, he would foot the purse money and expenses. Jack senior, following some intense training in the evenings with Charlie, duly arrived in Manchester for the fight. Outside the hall, he met Tim Coleman, another Potteries fighter, who had walked the six miles from Oldham to watch the fight; and who upon invitation agreed to act as second with Charlie. Chambers had previously established a strong reputation, but so good was the footwork of Matthews that he was soon tormenting his opponent, easily evading his furious swings. In the fifth round, Matthews put him down for the count. 'I've watched him wide-eyed in training,' says Jack, his second son, who is eighty-two and now contentedly retired in Stoke-on-Trent. 'I've seen him clear six chairs in the row with a standing jump. He had tremendous speed in the ring.'

It was in May 1912, when already twenty-nine that Jack Matthews became a candidate for a national title when he scored a sensational victory at the National Sporting Club in London. He had been waiting some time for the opportunity to get on the card at the NSC, but on the night in question he only stepped in as substitute against George Mackness of Kettering. Albert Hough of Salford failed to put in an appearance, and Matthews, though having had twelve teeth removed earlier in the week, immediately volunteered to replace him.

Boxing magazine reported: 'This was a fight which can never have been excelled as a real, right-down tearing, thrilling slam in the whole history of the game.' Over four extraordinary rounds, Mackness was knocked down six times and Matthews eleven times before the finish in the fourth. Such had been the excitement in the second round that the time-keeper allowed the round to run almost five minutes; during which time Matthews was knocked down eight times. However, such was his courage and fitness that he was back on his feet for the third, in which he was down again three times, though twice flooring Mackness. Ring-siders could hardly believe it when both men came out for a fourth round seemingly as fresh as ever, though Matthews now appeared the weaker of the two. Yet after exchanging a dozen or more blows, Matthews connected with a right which put his opponent down for the full count. Onlookers were on their feet, waving their programmes and shouting 'Bravo!', while Mackness's seconds dragged their unconscious fighter to the corner and thrust his head into a bucket of cold water. The following morning the *Daily Express* reported, under the headline 'Unknown Boxer's Win':

How a boxer can rise from obscurity to instant success was demonstrated at the National Sport Club last night. Jack Matthews, from Hanley in Staffordshire, had asked to be given a trial at Headquarters, and his request was granted. It was his first appearance, and Mackness started a big favourite. Matthews upset all the calculations. In the very first round he proved he was the better boxer. While he had a little trouble [!] through overconfidence in the second round, he recovered, and in the fourth, feinting with a left, he drew Mackness to him and sent a right crashing to the point of his chin, knocking Mackness out. Matthews will now be a star at the NSC until someone can be found who can beat him.

On 21 May, *Sporting Budget* wrote:

He's only a barber, gentlemen, and he comes from Staffordshire: the moustache is just to convince you that he has no homicidal tendencies. They let him out of the Black Country for a trial, but it was Mackness of Kettering that had the trial. And now, we will turn him loose and, who knows, perhaps there will be more features punched by the scrapping whirlwind from the Potteries. Gentlemen, how little we knew that in that dark district there was a light that shines so bright.

Matthews is believed to be the last professional boxer to have appeared in the ring with a waxed moustache.

The correspondent of *Boxing World* said that it had been a bout full of science as well as hard knocks, and that he had not witnessed such an exciting encounter for fifteen years. 'At one moment the ring-side betting on Matthews was 2 to 1, the next moment it would 3 to 1 against him.' Jack junior recalls that there was nothing in the world his father was frightened of, other than dogs. And it is his opinion that George might well have become the better of the two. 'I used to sit and watch George take off his artificial leg when he was living at home with mother, and it used to make me weep to think that here he was with his life ruined, and there was Haig with an earldom.' Jack senior continued fighting after the war for five years until he was forty; and still withstanding twenty-round bouts. There would be no doubt in later years from where his third son had inherited his exceptional and long lasting endurance.

One of Jack's later fights was against Tommy Harrison – who subsequently became European bantamweight champion – in front of a full house of 8,000 at the Port Vale football ground, for a £100 purse. It was the opinion of Jack junior that his father won easily; but the referee, possibly swayed in the way referees are by the greater reputation of the other man, gave it as a draw. As Jack junior was leaving the stadium, he met his mother, with young Stanley toddling at her side, coming to find out the result: something she rarely did. Perhaps she was more than usually concerned: it had been a twenty-round fight. 'How did it go?' she asked, seemingly trembling within.

In one of his last fights, one of the most poignant demonstrations of his skill, Jack Matthews fought 'Cast Iron' Hague of Oldham, a fighter of less than half his age, and the winner already of over one hundred contests who had never yet been knocked out. At the end of twenty rounds, C. H. Blackburn of Liverpool, the referee, gave his decision in favour of Matthews, a verdict received with great acclaim at the Staffordshire Sporting Club. Hague fought desperately throughout and proved he had a punch in both hands, but was rarely able to connect. The enduring ringcraft of Matthews, and the superb use of his left hand, brought a victory which roundly confirmed a popularity that would remain with him for the rest of his life.

The record in the ring of men such as Jack Matthews, who lived healthily until his early sixties, when he was suddenly struck down by cancer of the stomach, was proof that the noble art is by no means necessarily damaging to the health. There is, alive and well in New-castle-under-Lyme today, at the age of seventy-six, a contemporary of Stanley's, Tut Whalley, a renowned flyweight who fought 378 bouts. Tut was scheduled for a world title fight in America in 1939 that never took place because of the outbreak of war. Visit him in the redbrick house he bought for a few hundred pounds with his winnings when he was newly married, and he will soon be on his feet, in a boxer's pose, Cagney-style, recounting the halcyon years.

You couldn't go wrong in those days [Whalley says], there was so much boxing everywhere. I once fought twice in one day. I never suffered any real damage. The problem nowadays is that they don't teach them anything, fighters have no idea how to get out of the way. In all my time fighting over eleven years I only had one black eye, and that was when I was in the RAF and from playing cricket. Today's fighters only compete twice a year, that's the trouble, they don't fight often enough. I started in '27 when I was fourteen. The British Boxing Board of Control was not founded until '29. I once had eight fights in twelve days.

Tut trained over a stable, where he admits the smell used to be terrible, but it was the only place available. And that was why, he says, he survived: because he was mentally and physically supremely fit, running twelve miles at six in the morning and then training in the gym twice a day. He fought for the British flyweight title in 1934 in Dundee, and was disqualified in the eighth round. He fought and beat nine champions from different nations, until he was matched against Jackie Jurich of the United States for the world title. Tut started fighting as a boy with bare hands to fend off the bullies in his street, with his sister holding his jacket. When he was fifteen he cycled eighteen miles in the snow to Congleton for a fight, and when he got there they wouldn't let him in at first because they claimed he was too young. He fought an opponent half as tall again, knocked him out, and earned twelve shillings and sixpence (62p).

At the age of nine Tut was hanging from the rafters at the Palais de Danse in Hanley when Tommy Harrison fought Charles Ledoux of France – from the same stable as Carpentier – for the European bantamweight title. In the same week, he was playing football against Stanley's school, Wellington Road, though not against Stanley, who was two years younger. When, on one occasion later, he went to watch Stanley in a Cup replay against Sheffield United at Bramall Lane, he jumped to get a better view at one moment, and such was the pressure of the crowd that for five minutes he was pinned two feet off the ground.

Maybe with the instinct of an outstanding sportsman, father Matthews recognized very early that there was something particular about young Stanley. When Stanley was only four he bought him a pair of running spikes, and had him training in Finney Gardens. Though, in a quiet way, Jack showed an enthusiasm about this third son which had been denied the two older boys, perhaps this was good judgement; or maybe it was partly the contemporary practice that the eldest were expected to contribute to the family income from the moment they left school. Jack junior wonders, without resentment, whether Stanley would have received the same degree of encouragement and indulgence had he not been the third child to arrive. Jack, as the first son, had to leave school at thirteen to become an office boy and also to assist in his father's shop. Nine years older than Stanley, he spent much of his boyhood spare time pushing his younger brother round in a pram. Yet Jack, who boxed until he was twenty-five, admits that he himself was less than diligent at training, and this no doubt was reflected in the father's shrewd attitude towards his boys' respective talents.

Every August an athletic meeting was staged at the Victoria Ground in Stoke, which included a junior handicap event. It had soon been evident that Stanley was as fast a whippet, and at five his father entered him in the August meeting. When they arrived at the Victoria Ground, however, so tearful was the small boy, so pronounced already his shyness in the public eye, that his father relented and took him home. The next year, however, aged six, Stanley had begun to acquire a confidence from a degree of knowledge of his ability. Running in the hundred yards handicap, for boys under fifteen attending elementary school in the borough of Stoke or Newcastle, and having a handicap of 45 yards, he won his heat; and then the final, ahead of R. M. Hardie, and S. Hughes, by 'many yards' in eleven seconds. Jack, running off five yards, could get nowhere near him: in the expectation of which, father had made himself a tidy sum with the bookmakers.

The handicaps for the August meeting were published a week beforehand and father had taken his two boys down to Finney Gardens for a trial run. Having established to his own satisfaction that Stanley would be unbeatable on the day, he duly placed a substantial wager, and returned home on the Saturday evening in a jubilant mood. Stanley, for his reward, had received two goldfish in a bowl from a local pet shop – what might be termed payment in kind – but unfortunately the fish survived no more than a few days.

The meeting was a significant local event that drew competitors from around the country. On the occasion of the first public appearance of a name that would later captivate the imagination of millions, A. G. Hill, who was 800m and 1,500m gold medallist at the Olympic Games in Antwerp the previous year, was among the competitors, while Howard Baker, renowned high jumper and goalkeeper for the Corinthians football club, was only prevented from arriving by the breakdown of his car. The lengthiest section of the report of the day's races in the *Sentinel* was the listing of the day's officials: referee, judges, time-keepers, umpires, starter, starter's stewards, programme stewards, prize stewards, telegraph stewards, megaphone stewards, lady competitor stewards, competitors' stewards, clerks of the course (captain and vice captain), general clerks, St. John's Ambulance superintendant, medical attendant, and secretary. Thereafter followed the list of winners.

Stanley continued to run in these races until he was fourteen, during which time he won four first prizes and a second. In his final year he won from scratch. Ronnie, his younger brother, recounts that in the build-up to these races, his father would give young Stanley a daily massage. A further reflection on the fact that the father may have advisedly favoured his third son was that Jack would have much preferred to run in the mile, but was not allowed by his father to do so: a realist, his father considered that the main prize to go for was the hundred metres. Stanley, for his efforts, won himself a silver watch.

It was from the experience of these races that Stanley learned one of the tricks of the trade which he would later apply to his addictive training. His elder brother, in an attempt to deceive the handicappers – a commonplace piece of gamesmanship – would run in preliminary races with lead plates in the soles of his shoes. 'Anyone could tell at a glance if you weren't trying your hardest,' Jack says. As a professional footballer, Stanley would walk around on a Saturday morning with lead in his shoes, so that when the time came to put on his boots at three o'clock he would feel as though he were walking on air.

Seymour Street is today little changed from the period seventy-odd years ago, when Stanley had his first pair of spikes: circumspect, solid, dark red and grey brick houses in a uniform terrace, with a low three-foot garden wall no more than a yard or so from the front door. Nowadays one or two are garishly – or fashionably? – re-faced in chequered cream and rust-red imitation stone cladding. On the corner still stands The Highland Laddie public house, with its pool room formerly graced by billiard tables; and round the corner is the old Wellington Road School, with its iron railings, tarmac playground and sombre navy blue painted doors and window frames. It was here that Stanley played his first formal football. A few yards on from the school, in Waterloo Street, stands the corner house where, for the better part of a century, a succession of proprietors have sold, through the window from the kitchen range, the mouthwatering oatcakes and pastries, for which Stanley and his friends would in ritual queue on a Saturday morning, come rain or shine. The current owner is a Mr Fowler. In seventy years Stanley's shyness has not diminished. When, recently, he stopped at the shop in his car with a friend, it was the friend and not he who went to buy the oatcakes: wrongly giving Mr Fowler the impression that this was an attitude of self-importance, rather than a reluctance, as it was, to present himself for public scrutiny.·

Near to Seymour Street, and now no longer there, used to be a patch of rough ground upon which the local boys played from dawn to dusk, and after that by gaslight, if their mothers allowed them to stay out that late. It was known as 'Meakins' square', alongside the local pottery. 'You had to keep your balance or you would be cut to pieces,' Jack says, 'because it was covered in old bits of broken pottery – pitches and shards as they were known in the trade.' He has a scar on his knee to prove it.

From the age of three, Stanley would stand behind goal at 'Meakins'' to get a kick at the ball, his understanding of which was uncanny almost from the time he could first run. Such was his extraordinary dexterity with the ball that when he was no more than six or seven, men on their way home from work would make a detour of half a mile, so as to pass by this piece of rough playground to witness a child already doing things that dazzled the experienced eye. With a ball at his feet, he was no longer shy: the way he still was when, at twelve, his father sent him to enquire about an offer to join the cricket club at Longton. Stanley's first success at Wellington Road School was at cricket, where he kept wicket for the team that won the Hanley Shield. Yet when, having walked the two miles or so to Longton, he saw all the players practising at nets in white trousers, he was too embarrassed to introduce himself, and walked home again. His father said nothing.

Hours were spent kicking and dribbling a rag ball or a tennis ball; if not at 'Meakins'' then along the pavement of Seymour Street bouncing the ball up against that low garden wall. 'I was playing all the time.' Stanley says. 'My mother couldn't understand what I was doing, but a ball fascinated me. My mother thought I was an idler, but I'm certain my ball control can be traced back to a tennis ball and practising against the garden wall until I could do with it almost what I liked. Even Arthur, my elder brother, who was rather serious and looked upon me as a bit of a nuisance, would say that I had trained the ball to obey me. I used to use kitchen chairs as opponents, dodging between them, and turning to shoot suddenly into an imaginary goal.'

When he was still in the infants form for seven- and eight-year-olds, Stanley was already playing for the school team among thirteen-year-olds. When the local education authorities came to hear of this, the school was given instructions to leave him out of the team, because it was thought he was jeopardizing his education. By the age of eight, his dribbling skill was so accomplished, Jack recalls, that on those days when it was too wet to play on 'Meakins'', a special kind of game was played, confined to the pavement, 'and Stan would sometimes dribble past ten or twelve people in a row.' Gladys Brain, who died in 1988 at the age of eighty-eight and had lived in the next road to Seymour Street, at one time managing The Highland Laddie, used to recall that she would see Stanley kicking a ball, or indeed anything, all day.

The games master under whose influence Stanley came at Wellington Road was Mr James Slack. Unlike the tens of thousands of schoolmasters who today see themselves as being lesser versions of Sir Alf Ramsey, and push their pupils at an early age towards inhibiting tactical formations and stereotypes, Mr Slack was a master with vision and imagination. When Stanley, at the age of eleven, moved out of the junior into the senior school, Mr Slack had this prodigy playing as goal-scorer; at centre-half. 'It seems that I was a tall boy for my age,' Stan says. 'It was therefore thought best for me to be what was primarily an attacking defender, though one afternoon, when we were 2–1 down at half-time, I moved to centre-forward and scored eight goals. We won 13–2 and Mr Terry, the headmaster, gave me a sixpence.' That was in the English Schools Shield against Altrincham. On another occasion, from the centre-half position, he scored eleven goals in an 18–0 defeat of Cannon Street School.

It was after such goal-scoring feats that Mr Slack began to have the idea that this rare and strange young player might be best as a winger, and it was at outside-right that he was chosen to play for the North against the South in an England Schoolboys' trial.

By now, with the growing evidence of his talent for the game, Stanley was being made to rise by his father at six in the morning for exercises and deep breathing at the open window, summer and winter, a habit that has remained with him. 'At fourteen, I had to do chest expanding, skipping, and to walk round the block. If father said get up, you got up. Yet I enjoyed it.' The *Sentinel* reported, on a match between Hanley and Flintshire, in the third round of the English School Shield when Stanley was thirteen: 'Matthews was a prominent figure for the home side and after a good run on the wing he beat Catherall with a shot which entered the net off the foot of the upright.' Hanley won 5–3.

Though he seldom spoke much about the game, either at home or at school, Stanley protested mildly when selected at outside-right for the North v. South trial in Nuneaton, but was told, as you were in those days, to get on with it. The move proved a success, and in quick succession, two months after his fourteenth birthday in 1929, he appeared for England against The Rest at Kettering and then for England against Wales at Bournemouth. He scored at Kettering, 'but apparently I didn't play so well at Bournemouth and was dropped for the match against Scotland.' He was reluctant in those days to be watched by his family when playing for the school, though when he returned from Bournemouth his father was waiting for him at the station. The newspaper reports from Kettering had suggested that England's chief danger had come from the wingers, Matthews and Hooper of West Ham, but he was unable to sustain that impression with the selectors at Bournemouth.

'I preferred not to have my father watching me.' Stanley says. 'It seemed better to me. Not like today, when you have parents all along the touchline shouting at their children, what they should or shouldn't do, when they themselves haven't the first idea. Where would I have been with a father shouting at me all the time?' In fact, Jack Matthews had been to the trial at Kettering, leaving Arthur to look after the shop, but had not told Stanley.

At this stage, Stanley had no idea about becoming a professional footballer. When he left school, he went at first to be a bricklayer's apprentice, and was acquiring some skill at the trade; at the same time, like his brothers before him, he would also assist his father at the barber's shop in the evenings, lathering the customers in preparation for a cut-throat shave. It seems certain, however, that unknown to Stanley there had already been contact between Tom Mather, the manager of Stoke City, and his father. The ability of such a schoolboy prodigy as he would not have passed unnoticed. Whatever the background, Jack Matthews had a sudden change of mind, and decided that Stanley should devote his fifteenth year to improving his physique, paying him pocket money to continue assisting in the shop. 'One day, when I was there in Market Street, a small man with a bowler hat came in, and asked to see my father when he was finished. He turned to me, and said in a friendly kind of way, "Hello, Stan." One of my brothers told me it was Mr Mather, and after that he visited the shop every few days in his effort to get me to join the ground staff at Stoke.'

Blissfully unaware of the bees gathering around the honey, Stanley busied himself, strengthening his body, playing between times for Stoke St Peter's – which was in effect the nursery club for Stoke City, though he may well have been unaware of this – and watching the home games of Port Vale, the club with whom his heart lay. 'I much preferred the Hanley club, and worshipped Bob Connelly, their centre-half, who was the stalwart for many years. I believe there was some talk, when I first left school, that Aston Villa wanted me, and certainly Port Vale had asked my father for an option on my services,' Stanley says, 'but father decided I was to go to Stoke.'

When the day of his fifteenth birthday arrived in 1930, it was, typically, Jack junior who was directed to take his brother down to the Victoria Ground to sign apprentice forms for Stoke City. 'I had to close down *my* shop, putting up a notice 'Back in an Hour'', Jack smiles.

For the following two years young Stanley made the same journey on foot four times a day: past the oatcake shop, along Waterloo Street, left at the Rising Sun, right at Hanley Pottery, down Derby Street and Regent Road, through Hanley Park, across Avenue Road, into Boughey Road, down past the station, round St Peter's parish church and along Lonsdale Road to the Stoke ground. No bus fare, except when it was snowing, though occasionally his mother, reminding him to take his raincoat when it was wet, would slip him the bus fare out of sympathy.

2. EMERGENCE

ʹLₐₛₜ weekend Stanley Matthews came to town. And of the twenty-odd thousand citizens who went to the match at White Hart Lane, some ten thousand went to see Stanley Matthews. I was one of that ten thousand, and it was the first time in my life that I ever went to see an individual footballer. Teams and matches are my interest in football: I have no use for verbal edifices.

In the Potteries, they tell me, it was a nuisance when Stanley Matthews had one of his off days and Stoke did not win on a Saturday, because all the factory works found their hands out of heart and idle at least till Wednesday. So you see the effect on humanity of a gentle-voiced, medium-sized, pussy-footed, match-winning outside-right with the sovereign quality of style.

Style, like all aesthetic terms, has various meanings. Here it signifies what elsewhere we call charm. Once there was a party in Nigel Bruce's villa in Hollywood. Also present were Aubrey Smith, Herbert Marshall, David Niven, P.G. Wodehouse and myself. And the subject of long and lively discussion was the quality they call 'oomph'. All these scores and scores of beauties around, yet among them all, only here and there was 'oomph'. And why? The conclusion was that the quality is one of life's mysteries.

In humble parallel, far be it from me to explain the mystery in the games player which we call style. Stanley Matthews has firm, not broad shoulders, a distinct tapering to the waist, and strong, easy hips. Finely muscled, shapely thighs and legs. Very flexible ankles and small, strong, tactile feet. Even sitting in the changing-room he suggests quality of movement. Quality is there as he walks on to the turf like Agag, delicately. None of your tramp, tramp, tramp, the boys are marching. No walking upstairs but a precious lift and swing from the hips and a softly placed foot. And a forward poise of the hips, with the torso incipiently in front of them, well over the foot. It is delicacy and subtlety of minute appropriate adjustment of body to every intended movement that gives him his swift elastic start from standstill, his elusiveness and his uncanny accuracy. For the rest, he has a peculiar sensibility to his surroundings, the who-where-what of the moment, and a peculiar availability, immediate and sure, of his perceptions.*ʹ*

C.B. FRY, *Daily Mail*

*G*EORGE Male, who was a cornerstone at full-back of the defences of Arsenal and England in the Thirties, signed professional for Arsenal on his nineteenth birthday, three months after Stanley Matthews, four years Male's junior, had signed as an apprentice for Stoke in 1930. George was the strong, silent type; someone who observed much and spoke only when he had something to say – a characteristic which would be welcome in the modern era, when too many people on radio and television talk interminably when they have nothing to say. George was symptomatic of his era. 'I signed as a professional, but played as an amateur,' he says, with fond recollection of the glorious years at Highbury, where they won five League championships in eight seasons, three in a row from 1933 to 1935, under the legendary Herbert Chapman. Male won four championship medals, and played in six championship seasons, including 1947–48. It is typical of his nature that when he retired he donated his medals to Denis Hill-Wood, the Arsenal chairman, as a souvenir for the club. Hill-Wood had played with him in amateur football at Clapton.

As a boy, George had been, like Stanley, an attacking centre-half: that was where almost all good players fancied playing, as indeed they still should today if only there was a proper understanding of the role of *libero*, the free-playing sweeper. As a senior, George played with Clapton at the Spotted Dog ground in East London. His first appearance for them was at centre-forward, and he scored six goals out of seven against Wycombe Wanderers. Signing for Arsenal, he found himself deputizing in his first season at left-back when somebody was injured – and Chapman decided to keep him at full-back. 'I'd signed for him in Lyons tea-shop at Forest Gate,' George recalls. 'He was a marvellous bloke – kidded you along a bit, though only for your own good. He had a great influence on me, apart from converting me to full-back. He ruled the roost at Highbury, even the chairman couldn't come into the dressing-room before a match. Yet we were all still playing for the love of the game.'

Not that there was much else to play for. In those days a professional received a £4 minimum wage and £8 maximum, with a £1 winning bonus, which remained £1 even if you won two matches in a week. George's first FA Cup match as a professional was at left-half . . . in the final of 1932 against Newcastle, which they lost 2–1. Alex James was injured, and though he was with the squad that trained at Brighton,

Tom Whittaker ruled him out following a fitness test. Bastin moved inside from the wing, Bob John went to outside-left and Male to left-half. The other three forwards were Hulme, Jack and Lambert. John scored Arsenal's goal, the first. Newcastle equalized when the ball was pulled back after crossing the goal-line, with the referee thirty yards away. 'The defence all eased up, including me,' George says.

For the better part of ten years George played opposite Stanley in the First Division and regularly immediately behind him in the national team. He saw him from both viewpoints:

I can vouch for you, he had the beating of anybody [George says]. I'd try to force him to go on to the outside, where you think it's safe. You think you have him there, but you're conned, and you haven't. He's so quick, his control is so perfect, and the only way to stop him is to get the ball before he does. I always thought he could have been an even better player at inside-forward, but he gave the spectators great excitement, especially in the way he went directly in on defenders, challenging them. The way he committed defenders meant that there were always spaces elsewhere for his colleagues.

Prior to the Second World War, sport was something which was still happily without argument or controversy for most of the time. Arsenal may have been annoyed about the equalizing goal at Wembley, yet there was no prolonged row about it. Football was to a surprising degree unquestioning, almost wholly encased in tradition and habit. There is the story of Palethorpe, a successful centre-forward with Reading, who, before Stanley's debut, was transferred to Stoke. He bought himself a house several miles away from the ground, and after some weeks there was concern that his form had disappeared. He was sluggish. No longer was he scoring the goals that had been so prevalent with Reading. It was then discovered not only that he was cycling five or six miles each day when attending training, but that he was travelling by bicycle to League matches on a Saturday, whatever the weather. He was immediately instructed that he should travel by bus! No such luxury as a taxi in those days. Thereafter, his goal-scoring touch returned.

With a reticence that is unimaginable today, people did not publicly discuss their affairs the way they do now.

SM: You didn't talk about your work. When I played my first game as an amateur apprenticed to Stoke, I came home and told mother we had won 2–1, and she just said, 'Well done, your tea's ready' – and that was it. Nothing more. There was a little club in Wellington Road, or maybe St Luke's Road, with table tennis and snooker. I'd say to mother I was going round to the club, and she would say, 'Don't be late, be back by nine-thirty.' When I got home again, Dad would be there, but we wouldn't really talk about anything. We rarely discussed matches, and it was the same down at the club. Nobody ever talked about tactics. My job as an apprentice was to be down there early and to put out the jerseys and the training gear.

When the first team had a match, I had to wait for the visitors to arrive and help their trainer carry in the hamper with the kit, and after the match see that the baths were run and the water was warm. I wasn't expected to do anything more than listen; it wasn't my position to talk. One morning I went into the dressing-room and said 'Good morning'. and the senior players threw me into the bath with my clothes on just to teach me a lesson. Yet I firmly believe in the value of youngsters listening. I remember Billy Meredith once coming into the dressing-room after a match and saying to me, 'Always listen to the older players', and it was sound advice.

One of the unusual aspects of Stanley's upbringing was that, prior to becoming an apprentice, he had watched hardly any senior football, other than his occasional visit to Port Vale, so that his game was wholly uninfluenced by any of the acknowledged stars of the day. His style was spontaneous. He does remember going by bus with the reserves to Goodison Park when he was sixteen, and seeing Dean and James.

SM: Those were the days when Arsenal were Arsenal. I remember James feinting, sending opponents the wrong way, his shorts baggy on such a small player, and those telling long passes. Dean was amazing with his headers, and Cliff Britton would find him so accurately with his crosses from right-half.

It was a great experience to see Hughie Gallagher at Stoke when I was fifteen, but I must honestly say that at that age I couldn't understand much of the game, tactically speaking. Gallagher was outstanding, and he killed us in a cup-tie. I played once against the great Pongo Waring of Aston Villa, in the Staffordshire Cup. On one occasion in that match, I beat the full-back, went round the goalkeeper, side-footed the ball . . . and hit the post. The ground was lumpy. Waring came up to me and said gruffly, 'You've got a big head.' Young players were not expected to try to be clever. On another occasion, I played up against the England full-back Warnie Cresswell when he turned out with Everton's reserves, but I can't say I remember much about him.

You regularly encountered well-known players in the reserves, and I remember once that Villa had nine internationals in their reserve team. There was no security in the game in those days, when clubs would have forty or more professionals. You never knew if you would be retained for the next season, even if you had played thirty or forty first-team matches that season. Yet in a way that was a good thing; it kept you on your mark. Nowadays, one good game and you are a star overnight. Play badly, and you're still in the squad.

It was a humdrum life off the field. Married players mostly lived two or three hundred yards from the ground in digs.There was no staying in hotels. Stanley's life as an apprentice was uneventful. His entertainment was to go to the cinema, where there were reduced prices for club players, or to go to the public baths. Training at the club, like much of professional football, was largely unimaginative. Managers, who spent most of their time sitting, city-suited with watch chains at waistcoat pocket, reserved their imagination for team selection. It was headline news if a team was unchanged for more than two weeks in succession. A team could win 3–0 twice running and an individual player who had an off day would lose his place. Training was mostly a matter of running round the pitch. There was seldom practice with a ball.

SM: We attended a gymnasium next to the club to do bodywork. Round the pitch, we used to do at least twenty sprints a day. I was the only one who used spikes, from the experience of my youthful sprinting days. And all the time I was very keen on practising my dribbling. This had always come naturally to me, but to bring it to perfection I used to knock stakes in the ground and weave my way around them. I practised this for hours at a time, until I could go at speed through these stakes in all directions without touching any of them. Another thing that experience of matches taught me was that a winger who had only one body swerve to get past an opponent would have success only for a short time. Once his opponent realized what was happening, he very soon had the edge on the winger. I was blessed with a two-way body swerve, which made it difficult for my opponent to know which way I would go, and it was at this stage of my career that I set about making this two-way swerve as good as possible.

On 26 September, 1930, the *Sentinel* had reported, under the head-line 'New Player's Debut':

Another interesting change is being made by the introduction of the very useful outside-right and schoolboy international, S. Matthews. This player has been doing great things in private trials, and has been training with the City team for the past eighteen months . . . The attraction at the Victoria Ground today, where the Central League XI oppose Burnley, will be the appearance of the latest City recruit and amateur J. McDaid, who has recently come to England after playing in Ireland with Drumcondra.

> STOKE CITY: Beswick; Beachill, Dawson; Robertson, Jackson, Scrimshaw; S. Matthews, Mawson, Wilson, J. McDaid, Hales.

The following day, in its account of Stoke's 2–1 victory over Burnley – 'Burnley Mastered In Keen Game' – the *Sentinel* wrote: 'Matthews frequently gained the applause of the crowd by some very pretty movements, but his inside-forwards seemed to have left their shooting boots at home.' Already discussion was beginning to stir in this provincial town. The Potteries was not a place where excitement was in any way expected. Football, though an established part of the social fabric, was no more than a regular event, like the changing of summer to autumn. George Birks, an habitué of the Victoria Ground, recalls:

Everyone in the Stoke team was known by his first name, or his nickname. The spectators knew the players. We would stand or sit side by side with them on the bus on the way to the match. There was the friendly humour of familiarity. If someone yelled at Steele, 'Shoot, Freddie', another would yell, 'Why not shoot the lot?' If there were visiting spectators, there would be the occasional argument, and the occasional punch would be thrown, but afterwards you'd all end up in the pub together, and a rival would say laughingly, 'I gave you a good one, didn't I?' And you'd buy each other a drink. Yet if there were obscenities at the match, with women present, others would tell the offenders to shut up.

Birks was born eight years before Matthews, and was afflicted with polio at the age of four. An uncle carried him, with his calipers, to his first senior match when he was thirteen, and from then on throughout his teenage years he attended whenever he could get transport.

Then in 1930, along came this young boy [Birks says]. There had been a lot of talk about a schoolboy who had played at centre-half, and some of the older people had already said it was silly to play such a player in defence, that he was a 'natural'. I saw him early on in the Thirties, he was marvellously clever, but there was some opinion that he wouldn't make use of it. Yet gradually people came to realize that he could provide for others. We didn't see his best in those first years at Stoke, not the Matthews that became a legend. We saw a lot of brilliant football from him, but it was only later that he became a world beater.

Stanley played two games in the reserve side at the age of fifteen, and in 1931–32, aged sixteen, he played 22 matches. He was, of course, still an amateur, and it was a generous gesture by the other players to give him two shillings each out of their £1 bonus whenever they won, which would mean that he had an extra pound to take home. This doubled his wage of £1 a week as a member of the ground staff; his duties including licking the stamps in Tom Mather's office. His performances on the field were beginning to draw the attention of other clubs, and while he was still sixteen, Huddersfield offered £1,000 for his signature, which they were to increase to a formal bid of £5,000 after his very first game when he had signed professional in 1932.

The tension surrounding Mather, Stoke's manager, as Stanley approached his seventeenth birthday, was considerable. He knew that many clubs were vying for the signature of a boy who, it was already clear, was to become an exceptional player.

SM: The weeks prior to my birthday were hectic for Mather. He became a familiar figure in our house, and he visited my father's shop whenever he could find an excuse for a shave, a haircut, or anything that would give him the opportunity to convince my father what great plans Stoke had for me. He was really desperate, and confided that my signature meant so much to the club that if he failed to get it he would be sacked. In the two or three days before my birthday, Arthur Sherwin, the chairman, and Mather went to great lengths to safeguard their interest. There was always someone keeping watch to see if any other club managers or representatives visited our home, or Dad's shop. Mr Sherwin himself took up guard in the pub opposite the shop, where he could see who was coming and going.

Mather would later recall, in an interview for the *Empire News* Sunday paper:

I knew, and far too many other managers knew, that Stan was no ordinary footballer. From his schooldays, under the guidance of his teachers Jimmy Slack and Bill Hawkins, until he left school and joined me in the office, it was obvious he was going to become a genius. Stoke could not afford to lose such a prize. Never have I known more anxious days than those preceding the lad's seventeenth birthday. I drew up a plan of campaign to repel invaders. Mr Sherwin took up a position at the window of the pub on the other side of the road, and I had sentries on the road where he lived. This vigil was kept until ten-thirty on the morning of 1 February, when I entered the barber's shop, wished Stan many happy returns, and got him to sign on the dotted line. For his rapid development in first-class League football credit is due to Harry Sellars and Billy Spencer, the two players I usually put up against Stan in private practice games. I used to tell them to let him develop his footwork and not to hit him for six. I remember Harry coming to me one day and saying: 'You remember telling me not to hit young Matthews? Well, believe me, I can't get near him.' Harry was not the only defender who has found that out.

Stanley signed for £5 a week in the season and £3 in the summer, and upon the insistent instruction of his father paid half of this into a savings bank account, together with the £10 signing-on fee, and the other half to his mother towards the housekeeping. It was a careful life lived by the Matthews family.

Six weeks after signing professional, Stanley made his first-team debut, away to Bury in the League. Two injuries created vacancies, and Stoke, winning 1–0, gained revenge for defeat a month earlier in the FA Cup. The winning goal came in a strange manner a minute from the end of the match. Bussy, Stoke's inside-right, crossed the ball and Mills, the Bury goalkeeper, came off his line and attempted to *head* the ball clear. Mills succeeded only in heading the ball to Maloney, Stoke's left-winger, who struck it into an empty net. Stanley made no great impact on the match, though a week later he made his home debut in the 2–0 win over Barnsley. For this match he had been moved to outside-left, and a headed goal by him was disallowed for off-side. It was not until the following season, however, that he made regular first-team appearances. The season 1933–34 was, in fact, his best ever in the scoring of goals, with fifteen; eleven of them in the League. His fifteen first-team appearances earned him a medal in the season in which Stoke gained promotion to the First Division. The directors gave each of the players a three-piece suit; and Stanley, without as yet his own home, gave it to his mother, who kept it hanging in a wardrobe until the day she died.

Although not as yet a regular in the Stoke team, he was sufficiently noticed to be selected, in March 1934, for an England trial, playing for The Rest against England at Roker Park, Sunderland. His inside-forward partner in this match was, for the first time, Horatio Carter, known to all as Raich, and likewise a player of prodigious talent. Carter was one of those marvellous instinctive players of the first half of the century who, having developed spontaneously, was scornful of coaching. In Carter's opinion, then and later when he became a manager, and even to the present day in retirement in Berkley in Yorkshire, you were either a player or you weren't. Short, yet one of the most perfect strikers of the ball with his left foot that there has ever been – comparable to Puskas of Hungary – Carter had been told by Leicester as a seventeen-year-old 'to go back home and grow up'. Great was their loss when he became the jewel of the Sunderland side that would win the League championship in 1936 and the Cup the following year.

Carter had, and has, splendidly heroic attitudes towards the game. 'Give me a good forward line,' he says, 'and to hell with the defence!' He insists that at Derby, where he joined that other superb inside-forward of Ireland, Peter Doherty, after the war, they never had any discussion of tactics. If you were as intelligent as Carter and Doherty, he implies, why should you need to talk about the game? Coaching, he opined, was a load of rubbish: a view in which, I would respectfully hasten to add, he is sadly misled. But that is another story, and it did not prevent him creating a bewitching partnership with Matthews before, during and after the war. Of the trial at Roker Park in 1934, Nomad of the *Daily Express* wrote:

Matthews was one of the star performers of the match. He showed magnificent ball control, and Roughton's close tackles failed nine times out of ten because the Stoke winger knew the moment to stop the ball dead and come on the inside of the Huddersfield man. His play throughout was quite a feature and he and Carter made a storming right wing.

The Rest won 7–1 against an England side containing many of the then regulars such as Copping, Westwood and Bastin. Frank Carruthers wrote in the *Daily Mail* that 'the Stoke outside-right, although only nineteen, played with the calmness of a fully experienced man'; while the *Daily Mirror* thought that 'his baffling body-swerve made Roughton look like a second rater.' The celebrated Ivan Sharpe said in the *Daily Dispatch*: 'The right wing was a triumphant combination, and both Matthews and Carter, who got four goals, appear to have come to stay.'

Stanley remained detached, unaffected by the praise. He recollects that he had no emotion about his club debut at Bury, and was neither distressed nor motivated by the fact that he did not play regularly until the following season. Maybe it was an emotional inhibition created in part by the attitude of his father. Certainly that is the opinion of his younger brother Ronnie, while Jack recalls that Stanley reacted with concern only at having played badly. 'When Stan missed a chance against Manchester City in the Cup in 1934, he worried about it all weekend, because Stoke had lost,' Jack recalls. Stanley's mood, though one of restrained emotion, was more a matter, on the pitch, of disciplined concentration. He had learned from an early age never to be provoked by the opposition's comments or fouling, and his concentration was such that he remained largely unaware of the crowd. Nor was he bothered by referees.

SM: I never looked in the programme for the referee's name, or remembered that this or that referee had done something or other three months ago. I just went out on the pitch. If I'd been kicked in one match, it didn't run on in my mind in the next . . .

He was worried only by conscience, of having let the public down if the team lost. After a defeat at home, he would linger in the bath, and then get Harry Cummings, the head groundsman, to go and peer through the fence to see if the crowd had gone and whether it was all clear to make his retreat. He had a conscience, too, about the failure of professional footballers to organize their own collective welfare and insurance. James Fay, the secretary of the Professional Footballers' Association, used to visit the club every other month, and as an apprentice it had been Stanley's duty to take him a mug of tea. 'Young Stanley, you don't know anything about professionalism,' Fay would say. 'You ought to join the PFA, because one day it will be powerful. If you join, for a shilling a week, you will receive £500 if you are put out of the game by injury,' Fay told him. It was the club captain's job to collect the subscriptions, though Stanley remembers that membership was disorganized, and that nobody really wished to be bothered with collecting the small change. Yet the security was handsome, at a time when a cartilage operation could put you out of the game for four months and maybe permanently. Stanley's first cartilage operation would not be until he was seventy-one.

It was during the first regular season in the first team that he began to realize, without any advice, that there was a need for variation in his tactical style.

SM: More and more, I was already a marked man, so I couldn't just stay upfield waiting for the ball. I hit on the ruse of coming back deeper to give myself more room. It paid off, because full-backs wouldn't come as far forward as they do today, and until after the war it was unknown for a rival winger to mark another defensively.

There was disappointment, following the trial at Roker Park, when Stanley learned that, while Carter had been selected to play at inside-right against Scotland, Crooks of Derby had been preferred to him on the wing. Crooks and Carter were selected for the touring party that summer to Hungary and Czechoslovakia, in which there was the warning signal for English football of a 2–1 defeat in Budapest, and another by the same score in Prague. Perhaps on account of those results,

Matthews, excitedly grabbing an evening paper one afternoon in Stoke after training, found himself selected for England in their first match of the new season against Wales at Cardiff. Not waiting to collect his change, Stanley hurried to his father's shop with the news. Subsequently, the formal notice of selection arrived from the FA offices in Lancaster Gate: 'Dear Matthews, you have been selected . . .'

This was no less than he had had reason to hope; ten days previously, he had played outstandingly for the Football League in their 6–1 victory against the Irish League in Belfast, during which he had scored. He had run rings round the Belfast Celtic full-back Fulton, and the knowledgable Charles Buchan, former Sunderland and England forward, had reported in the *News Chronicle*: 'In a spritely forward line, Matthews stood out as the most accomplished player afield. He made certain of his England place.' Preparing in the dressing-room at Ninian Park for the match against Wales, Stanley received a sporting visit from John, the Welsh goalkeeper, who had recently moved from Stoke to Preston North End and now wished him well. Matthews repaid the compliment by running through the Welsh defence in the first minute of the second half, when England were already two in front, to drive the ball wide of John for the third goal. England won 4–0, with the first and last from Tilson of Manchester City and the second from his club colleague, Brook, on the left-wing. Yet it must be said that it was a less than auspicious performance by England's young right-winger, never mind that he was selected six weeks later for the following match against Italy at Highbury. He felt at this stage a relative stranger, for there was no talk before the match, no discussion of tactics. For all his own assertion in later years, with which one must disagree, of the unimportance of tactical planning, Stanley had had little opportunity to say more than hello to his partner for the afternoon in Cardiff, Ray Bowden of Arsenal. These are his recollections of his colleagues on that first international outing:

HARRY HIBBS (*Birmingham*): 'A small goalkeeper, similar to Hodgkinson of Sheffield United in later years, very agile, with good anticipation of shots; rarely if ever came off his line for crosses. It was the continental goalkeepers more than the British who blazed the trail for coming off the line, even as far as the edge of the penalty area.' TOM COOPER (*Derby*): 'A good tackler, but a bit of a hoofer.' EDDIE HAPGOOD (*Arsenal*): 'Could give and take a pass; a classic player, one of the first footballing full-backs.' CLIFF BRITTON (*Everton*): 'Threw a long ball, had a very good right foot and centred to the goal-mouth quite a lot. Accurate, and a good marker of his inside-forward.' JACK BARKER (*Derby*): 'A tremendous centre-half, who was excellent at finding his wingers with the ball, in the same manner as Franklin and Cullis.' JACK BRAY

(*Manchester City*): 'A workman of a wing-half who would run and tackle all day.' RAY BOWDEN (*Arsenal*): 'A lightweight inside-forward with some nice touches.' FRED TILSON (*Manchester City*): 'Always on the move, but not in the same class as Dean or Lawton.' RAY WESTWOOD (*Bolton*): 'Strong as a horse, would dribble through from the half-way line and shoot from twenty yards.' ERIC BROOK (*Manchester City*): 'A good crosser of the ball, who would never let up and gave you everything.'

The match against Italy saw the first international appearance of that great-hearted centre-forward Ted Drake, as third choice. Tilson was injured, then also his deputy Hunt, and so Drake was called up at the last moment: as the seventh representative in the side of the all-powerful Arsenal club. The only 'outsiders' were Britton, Barker, Matthews and Brook. Drake was three years older than Stanley, and had made his debut for Arsenal that year after being transferred from Southampton. He holds the all-time record of seven goals in a match, against Aston Villa, and is regarded by everyone who ever met him as one of the most genuine players and managers the game has known. What Drake remembers about Matthews is that he was always available:

He never hid, he was always there, wanting the ball [Drake says]. He had fantastic awareness, he could read the shape of the play with a single glance, and pick the best positioned colleague to give the ball to. I never saw him lob-it-and-hope. As soon as Stan had the ball, I'd go for the *near* post, not the far post as people tend to suppose. On the near post, where Stan was so accurate, I could go for the glancing header.

Characteristically, what Ted misses when he watches the game these days is the companionability. He would always reckon to exchange greetings at the start and finish of a match with his opponent, however hard the pair of them might go. He may not have felt the same after the Italy match, in which he had to be carried off, and which was one of the dirtiest international matches yet played.

Italy were the recently crowned winners of the second World Cup, but that was a matter of supreme indifference to the insular and off-hand English, who had withdrawn from FIFA in 1928 over the question of broken-time payments for amateurs in the Olympic Games. Few professionals within English football were aware of the advance of the game across the Channel and in South America - never mind the two summer defeats – and a continuing succession of home victories, including, notably, that against the outstanding Austrian team by 4–3 at Stamford Bridge in 1932, was perpetuating the tide of ignorance. When a penalty by Brook in the first minute was saved brilliantly by Ceresoli, and when Brook made amends for that nine minutes later, hammering in a cross from Matthews, there seemed no cause for the calm of English self-satisfaction to be disturbed: even less so when Brook scored his second two minutes later. A third goal, quickly scored by Drake when he knocked in the rebound after his first shot had been parried, had Italy on the ropes. The England team was in splendid form, but the effect of this was to cause the world champions to lose their tempers. Soon Hapgood, England's captain, had to leave the field, after being smashed in the face by an Italian elbow; and although he gamely returned to the fray fifteen minutes later, England's poise had gone and the Italians were, according to Hapgood in his memoirs, *Football Ambassador*, 'kicking everybody and everything in sight.'

Italy had themselves been reduced to ten men when their captain, Monti, the Juventus centre-half, had to leave the field after breaking a bone in his foot, but the Italians had much the better of the second half and in the space of two minutes pulled back with two fine goals by Meazza, their centre-forward. Moss, the Arsenal goalkeeper, had to be at his best to prevent Italy drawing level, even though Hapgood, for all his handicap, never shirked a tackle. Since the First World War, Belgium, Spain, France, and Austria had all failed even to achieve a draw in England. Italy had held England to 1–1 in Rome when they had met the year before the World Cup. Now they were determined not to surrender their mantle of world champions.

SM: I was only nineteen, and it was one of the roughest games of my life. The incident when Hapgood had his nose broken and was taken off rattled most of our players, and it was fortunate that in Brook and Copping, our left-winger and left-half, we had a couple of tough nuts. They were able to respond with the honest shoulder charge, but it was a bad moment for us when young Ted (Drake) was also carried off just before half-time, having scored that valuable third goal. In the dressing room Tom Whittaker, the trainer, insisted that we should go out for the second half and continue to try to play football. I felt relieved, because to have played the Italians at their own game would have led to a blood-bath. It took me a while to get back to my normal game after that match, and I was dropped from the first four international matches the following year. I was quite glad to be out of the news for a while.

The home newspapers were severe in their criticism of the Italians. Frank Carruthers of the *Daily Mail* wrote: 'From the point of view of football as I understand it, I shall hope to forget the match,' under the headline 'Should These Games Be Played?' There were gravely conflicting views, Carruthers said with justification, of interpretation by the two countries of what was right and wrong within the laws of the game. 'It is impossible to reconcile the British and Continental point of view.'

Fifty years later the position has hardly changed. Such credit as there was on this afternoon was awarded primarily to the two goalkeepers, Moss and Ceresoli. The report in *The Times* seemed to fit nicely the following morning alongside its other two sporting accounts: of coursing and hunting. The report, 'from our Association Football correspondent', concluded a trifle pompously: 'The verdict is that England is still supreme in a game essentially our own.' Such myopia would continue for almost another twenty years. However, it became apparent in the weeks following the Highbury match that the Italians had been under the inducement of large financial rewards from Mussolini, including an Alfa Romeo car for each man if they won and, even more attractive, exemption from military service.

The teams on that ignoble day had been:

ENGLAND: Moss (*Arsenal*); Male (*Arsenal*), Hapgood (*Arsenal*, capt.); Britton (*Everton*), Barker (*Derby*), Copping (*Arsenal*); Matthews (*Stoke*), Bowden (*Arsenal*), Drake (*Arsenal*), Bastin (*Arsenal*), Brook (*Manchester City*).
ITALY: Ceresoli (*Ambrosiana*); Monzeglio (*Bologna*), Allemandi (*Ambrosiana*); Ferraris (*Lazio*), Monti (*Juventus*, capt.), Bertolini (*Juventus*); Guaita (*Roma*), Serantoni (*Ambrosiana*), Meazza (*Ambrosiana*), Ferrari (*Juventus*), Orsi (*Juventus*).

Earlier that year, Stanley had married Betty Vallance, whose father was the Stoke City trainer and under whose guidance he had spent much time during his two years as an apprentice. Betty was two years older than Stanley, and an enthusiastic golfer. It was on a golfing holiday in Scotland, together with Jimmy Vallance, that they had first come to know each other, and after a year's engagement they were married at the club house of the Bonnyton Golf Club near Glasgow: the course where Rudolph Hess would land, near the fifth hole, on his bizarre flight in 1941. When the young Matthewses purchased their first house that year, Betty had to sign the mortgage papers because Stanley, under twenty-one, was legally too young.

In the late autumn of 1935, Stanley had a lucky break. Birkett, the Middlesborough right-winger, chosen for England against Germany at Tottenham, had to drop out with injury the previous Saturday. The Germans, incidentally, are thought to have been the first European team to travel to an away match by air, landing in London at Croydon.

They brought with them problems of a different kind. In 1930, they had shown themselves to be a strong football nation, holding England to a 3–3 draw in Berlin, Hofmann scoring a hat-trick and Jack gaining a late equalizer for England. In 1935, international feeling was running strongly against Hitler because of his intervention in Spain. In Britain, the TUC in particular were annoyed that German and Italian support for General Franco had enabled him to get the better of the Republicans. Demonstrations were organized by the TUC outside the ground in Tottenham, and there were fourteen arrests for insulting behaviour. The Germans brought ten thousand spectators to White Hart Lane, and their behaviour was exemplary. Sir Charles Clegg, the chairman of the FA, was irritated by the demonstrations, and unwisely saw fit to criticize the TUC in his speech at the banquet following England's 3–0 victory, apologizing to German officials. Sir Walter Citrine, replying on behalf of the TUC, later stated: 'So far as the remarks about perverting football into politics are concerned, the trouble is that Sir Charles Clegg does not bother to inform himself of the nature of sport in Germany. If he did so he would realize that football there is part of the Nazi German regime.'

Neither side was wholly correct, and Sir Stanley Rous, in his autobiography *Football Worlds*, later wrote:

For me this was an object lesson in the dangers of taking political standpoints about sport. If the government of the day does not stop a match, how can sporting bodies grade the character and politics of another country? By nice historical inversion, Russia is now the country that looks on sport as a means of furthering its political aims, and is often blatant in its political manipulation of sport. Yet the TUC is hardly likely to take the same view about Russia as it did about Germany.

Matthews' father and two older brothers, anxious to see him repair a reputation which had been dented a year before, borrowed an old car to drive to London from Hanley, but it was to prove a disappointing trip.

SM: There were two reasons why I failed that day. The first was Muenzenberg, Germany's left-back, who was too quick and experienced for me. The second was that I made a terrible miss early in the game, when I had the ball on my own about fourteen yards out from the goal. I felt sure I would score, but kicked the turf. It was early in the game, and you could hear the crowd groan almost with one voice. This destroyed my confidence. Muenzenberg wasn't a particularly good full-back, but I still lacked experience, and allowed him to mark me closely, not making any attempt to move away from him. It was different when I played up against him two and a half years later.

The *Manchester Guardian* reported: 'Matthews failed as badly as he did against Italy, and Carter was not much better.' Yet the key to England's alleged failure of winning by only three goals lay in Germany's adroit tactics of playing with five defenders, and the confidence of Hans Jacob, their tall goalkeeper.

Now sedately retired at eighty-one in Regensberg in Bavaria, though still assisting his daughter in the running of the family travel agency, Jacob is a benign old man with happy memories of his international career. He won 38 caps, the first of them against Norway in 1930. His model was Heiner Stuhlfarth, of Nuremberg, whom he used to travel to watch, and he subsequently played against him four times for his own club in Regensberg.

We had a very bumpy flight from Frankfurt to Croydon [Jacob recalls]. We arrived two days before the match, but had not done any special training before that, other than on our own at home. Our trainer was Dr Nerz, a university sports professor, who was in charge of the team from 1920 to 1936. The man we talked most about beforehand, in our tactical planning, was Bastin, your outside-left, whom we knew to be very dangerous. Matthews, on the day, was dribbling too much, was too individualistic. Camsell, the England centre-forward, was very good with his head, but my main problem was Westwood, always roaring in to charge me with his shoulder. The Swedish referee, Olssen, did almost nothing to stop him, but I was able to protect myself. [Jacob smiles knowingly. He is still a large and imposing man.]

Camsell put England in front two minutes before half-time, and Jacob was annoyed with himself for failing to get down to a shot from twelve yards that was quite close to his legs. At half-time, he relates, Nerz told his team to continue playing in the same way. There was already that established vein of German tactical confidence, which has served them so well over the years: keep at it, and something will happen. But not this time. Camsell scored a second, and Bastin the third; and the *Manchester Guardian* said that magnificent goalkeeping had saved the Germans from worse.

It was, however, a dispirited Stanley who returned to Stoke; to the point of apologizing to colleagues in the dressing-room before training for his inadequate display. After lunch, he returned, as so often, alone to the ground to practise with half a dozen balls until it was dusk. He felt better. He gathered up the balls and headed back to the dressing-room.

SM: In the gathering gloom I thought I could see someone standing in the tunnel entrance. It was my father. I hadn't seen him since before the international, though I knew he had been at the match, and I felt I had let him down. I said, 'Hello Dad, what are you doing here?' He took two of the balls from me and said: 'Betty called and asked your mother and me round for tea, so I told them to go along and I would come here and pick you up and walk home with you.' I asked him how he knew I would be there. He said, 'Because I know what you are going through at the moment.'

He waited for me outside while I changed, and as we walked home I asked him what he thought of my performance the day before. He said, 'I'm not bothered about what happened yesterday, or worried about what you do the day after tomorrow in Stoke's next match. In any trade you must serve an apprenticeship, and during those years you make mistakes. In your job things are different, there are no basic rules, you don't work under anybody, you're on your own all the time and you learn by experience and by watching the strengths and mistakes of others. But there is one thing you must learn, and that is never to try to correct a physical mistake by a physical effort without first getting your mental outlook right. When you missed that open goal yesterday, it didn't alter you in the physical sense but it destroyed your mental outlook. You let the full-back sense you knew he was the master, and that was fatal. You should have thought things out and tried other methods, and not for one instant should you have admitted that he was better than you, because if you do that you surrender your confidence. If you ever meet this situation again, don't give up; try this, try that, never admit defeat, and with your abilities you will one day reach the top – and stay there. I've never said so before, but I'm sure you have it in you to be one of the best footballers this country has ever seen. If you go on to the field on Saturday in the state of mind you were in this afternoon, you may ruin yourself for life. Forget what the papers say, and what people say. Remember that crowds are fickle, that they love a winning team, and that they love a footballer who gives them what they have paid to see. Pure football. But don't in the future ever let your mistakes upset your mental balance.'

They were wise words from a man who had fought in the ring with intelligence and guile until he was forty.

3. GENIUS

'*W*HAT shall we remember? First, as he runs out on the field, our feeling of surprise. Here he is again, the incomparable master of English football, the man of talent and reputation – and how little aware of it he seems. As we stand near the touch-line, waiting for the kick-off, he is only a few yards from us. His face is spare; his skin is neither ruddy nor brown, as you might expect of an athlete, but pale, tight over his cheekbones and forehead, with a high smooth forehead with the thin hair drawn well back. His eyebrows are raised, and his eyes hooded; he has an almost Chinese impassivity. He holds himself nervously, with a kind of brittle stiffness, his hands closed and his arms slightly bent. He tries his legs, shifting his weight from one to the other – but carefully; as if he were taking an inventory of his muscles, confirming that he has overlooked nothing in his methodical preparations. There is a tension in him, a restrained anxiety. For all his experience and confidence, he suggests the serious excitement of a schoolboy who hopes he will do well.

As the whistle goes, the ball moves upfield, he jogs forward with that same careful movement, wasting no energy, but with his cool eyes shifting, watching intently. He is a little behind the rest of the forward line, with a clear space ahead of him, when the ball comes to him for the first time – as he likes it, straight to his feet. The ball comes fast, but he stops it dead as it reaches him. It is already perfectly controlled as he turns and, at little more than a fast walk, takes it towards the full-back. The back, like every other in the game, has heard all about Matthews. He knows that he likes to beat his man by going outside him; he knows that if he rushes his tackle, Matthews will be round him; so he stays near the touch-line, watches and retreats. Matthews continues, in his leisurely way, to bring the ball to him; retreat becomes dangerous. The back holds his ground. Another man comes across in support, Matthews is now very close; the back is within a stride of the ball. Matthews sways to the left.

In that second, with a kind of desperate clarity, we can read the back's mind. It comes to him in a flash that this time Matthews *is* going inside. The ball is held in the curl of Matthews' right foot, and that lean, wonderfully balanced figure has swayed so far to the left that it is almost too late to catch him. But not quite: he is a quick strong back, and he goes across in a swift lunge. There is no one there. Matthews is gone, on the outside again, flying past him, already yards beyond him, imperturbable as ever; slowing down now to his jog trot as he shows the ball, obligingly, to the next crouching defender. The speed of that sudden sprint, over those few yards, is amazing and it is his essential secret. Without it, with all his other gifts, Matthews could still outwit and wrong-foot his opponents, but he would not leave them grotesquely and completely beaten, staggering off balance, or sitting helplessly, facing the wrong way. He has done so, again and again, to the best defenders in the world...'

MAURICE EDELSTON AND TERANCE DELANEY, *Masters of Soccer*

*T*HE relationship of those two incomparable players, Carter and Matthews, was not dissimilar to that of Walter Matthau and George Burns in the film comedy *The Sunshine Boys*: intimate, dependent, yet simultaneously faintly jealous and antagonistic to an amusing degree. How good was Stanley? 'Well, you could see he could do a bit,' Raich will say, imperceptibly grudging. When intermittently they meet, stimulated by each other's presence and the recollection of great days and great victories, Raich likes to preen himself with reminiscences. Stanley becomes embarrassed. When they attended a recent function, Stanley pleaded with Raich beforehand not to go on about the old times; and they were hardly past the commissionaire when Raich was off, at the first handshake. 'You should have been there when we . . .'

Raich knows in his heart, as we all do, that in sheer technique he himself was the equivalent of any English player there has ever been, but Stanley's fame undoubtedly got under Raich's skin. 'In *those* days, as an inside-forward, you were expected to supply your winger and the centre-forward, and to support your wing-half, you were expected to be the jack of all trades,' Raich complains. 'An inside-forward was expected to change his game to accommodate a Matthews or a Finney. They didn't need *you*.' Here is your definitive dispute on publicity-billing between one legitimate Hollywood star and another, for Raich on his day was perfection indeed. It is as though he begrudged Stanley the service of his own genius. 'Normally, to progress in a movement, you expect a return pass. With Stan, he was off on his own, beating the wing-half or full-back and then crossing it. You're getting a rest, but you're not in the *game*. The trouble playing with Stan is that he gets the credit. You give him the ball, he beats his man, centres, and Lawton heads a goal. They forget all about *you*.'

Yet his acknowledgement of the other man is ultimately unrestrained. 'He was a good bloke, good company, modest. He had *total* control of the ball. I remember one incident at Maine Road when he was pinned down by the corner flag, with a defender a yard away. With barely a touch he was round the defender and the ball was gone, it was amazing.' Yet another lingering resentment Raich has is towards the modern light balls. 'If we'd played with them, I'd have knocked them in from the half-way line.' And if you saw him play, with that rifle-shot in his left boot, you believe him.

In Carter's day, the game, like life itself, was more prosaic; tastes were simple. It was the era of Woodbines, and a footballer's ambitions did not extend beyond the optimistic expectation that he might retire from the game to run a small newsagent's. There was no socializing, no nightclubs, though as ever there was plenty of gambling, even on restricted wages. A working man's wage was maybe £2 a week; a head teacher would be on £300 a year, the chief of the city police on maybe £400. Yet this would not prevent there being £50 or more on the table during a game of cards among players on a long train journey. If a wealthy businessman in town found his daughter going out with a footballer, as likely as not she would be struck out of his will. The social elixir of the professional life was a game of snooker. Players travelled to matches by bus: few had cars, and not that many could drive. They were indistinguishable, off the field, from spectators.

Walter Winterbottom, who was to become, after the war, the first official England team manager, was for a while beforehand a part-time inhabitant of this player's world, playing with Manchester United while he simultaneously studied physical education at Oldham and then Carnegie College in Leeds, where he subsequently joined the staff. 'I played against Stanley once,' Winterbottom relates. 'Freddie Steel had to go off, and Matthews moved to centre-forward. I was terrified. I stood off, so as not to make the mistake of committing myself, and fortunately, with Stoke down to ten men, we managed to control him.' The game, then, Winterbottom remembers, was at most clubs unimaginative:

The managers didn't manage, they signed the cheques [Walter recalls]. It was player power. The older players decided the tactics. Goalkeepers rarely came off their line, so Dixie Dean was able to head goals standing only two or three yards out. Full-backs pivoted around the centre-half, so that the winger on the opposite side to where the play was had plenty of space in front of him, hence the value of the long cross-field ball by inside-forwards. The game was nearly all long balls, and an only loosely created midfield: 'final' passes were laid on from the centre circle. Nobody had worked out even simple things, like the fact that a wing-half, by moving towards the centre of the field, could pull the opposing inside-forward with him and force the opposition to play the ball out to the wing: when the winger was not as dangerous as Matthews!

Excluded, following the match against Germany, for the whole of 1936, Stanley was recalled to the England team for the first game of 1937 against Scotland at Hampden Park. It was a notable day for Stoke, because the club provided three of the forwards: Matthews and Johnson on the wings and Steele in the middle. It also produced a crowd of 149,547, the biggest in British history, apart from the first FA Cup

Final at Wembley in 1923 between Bolton and West Ham, when the gates were stormed and over 150,000 crowded inside. It was Stanley's first game at Hampden, and he was warned of the ordeal by his Scottish father-in-law. More to the point, he was up against an outstanding full-back in Andy Beattie of Preston, who was also making his Hampden debut. Yet Matthews, during that year's absence, had indeed become mentally stronger, and in spite of that intimidating Hampden roar he was able from time to time to silence the terraces by his mastery of Beattie. England led by the only goal at half-time, Steele having scored after forty minutes. The disbelieving Scottish supporters saw their team, including such renowned forwards as Delaney and Walker, being given a lesson in skill; and the lead might well have been far more than a single goal. However, in the second half, with the roar mounting by the minute, Walker created a chance for O'Donnell of Preston to equalize, and in the final quarter of an hour two goals by McPhail of Rangers gave Scotland victory. Though Matthews had now begun to expose the full range of his talents, the decision of the England selectors had been odd to say the least. Following a Probables v. Possibles trial at Burnley, and a win for the second team, such regulars as Bastin, Drake and Brook had lost their places. Uncharacteristically, Carter had wasted openings that might have put England three goals clear.

It was the first match in which the England team wore shirt numbers, and Beattie had plenty of time to observe the '7' on the disappearing back of Matthews that was to become all too familiar to three generations of full-backs. The press was fulsome in its praise. 'Showing only half his tricks, Matthews could always beat the nervous Beattie,' Carruthers said in the *Mail*. 'Matthews, when he got the ball, could amble – he never runs – past Beattie as much as he wished. He did not get it often, otherwise England might have won', reported Adjutant of the *Daily Mirror*. 'The pity was that Matthews, who during the first half seemed to have the result in his destiny, hardly received a good pass in the second half from either Carter or Britton,' Archie Ledbrooke reported in *Daily Dispatch*.

The match was another demonstration of the emotional lift which the Scots inherit every time they meet their southern foe. As *Athletic News* observed: 'The match with England is the strong wine of the Scottish season. Old players have said how they saved their pennies to witness the enemy from over the border and to glory in his downfall. Today's Scottish youth is fired with the same hope. I do not think it possible for English footballers to regard these matches in the same way.' Yet it was a day that had established the genius of Matthews. Peter Buxton of The *Sentinel*, who saw almost the whole of Stanley's career in two phases with Stoke, remains in awe of his hero to this day. 'The way he played in those pre-war years was quite unbelievable,'

Buxton says. 'The skill was breath-taking. No one man could hope to take the ball off him once out of ten. I saw him first when I was eight or nine, and soon you couldn't attract the attention of the bobbies sitting on benchs in front of the crowd, even if there were drunks causing a disturbance, because they were resentful of their attention on Stan being disrupted. He was an unusual man. He walked everywhere. He lived nearby, and I'd see him, even after he was married, stepping out the half-hour walk to the ground, to and from training each day, and always alone.'

Buxton was offered a tentative trial when he was seventeen by Major Buckley, the manager of Wolves, but he suspected that his father, a head teacher in Stoke, did not favour it, and he rejected the offer. During the war, Buxton served in the Navy and was on the Murmansk run, protecting Russian convoys, and then escorting trans-Atlantic troop ships, including the *Queen Elizabeth* and *Queen Mary*. 'We could do 27 knots, even in a gale. It was, I think, the first ship with computerized firing, and we could let off 25 five-inch rounds per minute. We were providing smoke-screens for the North African landings at Algiers when the back half of the ship was blasted and I lost my best friend. After repairs, we went to Sicily with the Eighth Army for the landings at Salerno and Anzio. Later we were off the South of France, but that was a bit of a joke, and we spent the time playing water polo off the beach.'

Against Wales in the autumn, Stanley was in scintillating form in a 2–1 victory, now partnered by Willie Hall of Tottenham. Carruthers reported in the *Mail*: 'It was Matthews' match. He scored the equalizing goal in the first half, and once more he appeared as the outstanding outside-right: brilliant, resourceful, and the maker of openings. I was sorry for Hughes, the Wales full-back, who was bewildered by the sway to the left and back to the right.' 'Matthews has come to stay,' Charles Buchan said in the *Chronicle*. 'Throughout the first half he had the crowd laughing and cheering when they were not gasping in amazement,' the *Daily Mirror* reported. Archie Ledbrooke wrote in the *Dispatch*: 'The inclusion of Matthews not only provided the side with greater artistry but, surprisingly enough, gave the forward line extra thrust. His display . . . was always accomplished with a minimum of effort and waste of time.'

There had arrived in the England team this autumn, in the opening match against Ireland, the considerable figure of Stanley Cullis, the Wolverhampton Wanderers centre-half, and he was now involved, in December, in one of Stanley's more unusually memorable international matches. Playing against Czechoslovakia at Tottenham, Stanley had to play at inside-right for much of the match and scored three goals, including the winning goal in a 5–4 victory, all with his left foot. Stanley Cullis, born in the Midlands, had grown up in Ellesmere Port in

Cheshire, where his father had moved to continue working with a steel company. Cullis grew up side by side with Joe Mercer – he an immigrant, Joe part of the indigenous population: literally the wrong side of the railway line, as Joe was always laughingly reminding him. They played schoolboy football together, but Cullis never 'represented Cheshire as a boy, let alone England. His career as a centre-half developed by sheer application and intelligence. He was regarded by schoolmates as serious and, later, by some journalists, unfairly, as boring. 'We can't all be Spike Milligan,' Cullis would say reproachfully, with that flat but endearing Brum accent which carries the trace of a lisp. Centre-forwards, however, never found him soft; in the 5–1 victory over Ireland he had replaced the massive Alf Young, and would remain consistently England's centre-half until he gave way to Neil Franklin just before the end of the war. He was as thorough and wilful, as a captain, as he would later be as manager of Wolves for sixteen years; and in both roles a strict disciplinarian. Though Wolves would be a renowned hard side, he never had one player sent off in the First Division. He was the kind of man who, given the choice of an £8 international fee or a medal, tended to take the medal. When, controversially, he accepted £15,000 from the *News of the World* – a newspaper he had hitherto refused to have in the house – for writing his memoirs after being sacked by Wolves, it was solely, and against his wife's objections, to help pay his son's school fees.

There was no team manager in those pre-war days, so the captain had to try and sort out the tactics [Cullis says]. Stan would never offer suggestions, just sit there very quietly. I remember Raich (Carter) once saying before a game: '*Please*, talk to Stan, he never gives me the ball back!', and I said to him, 'Never mind, just give it to him, and get into the penalty area.' I'd suggest to Stan that he come inside occasionally, which he didn't normally do, and which I felt could be more dangerous. It was remarkable how he would be kicked from pillar to post and never seemed to resent it, just concentrate on destroying his man. I remember playing with him against the Scottish League, and overhearing beforehand the Scots talking about how their new left-back 'would stop Matthews'. I mentioned it to Stan before the game, and he went out and ran the fellow dizzy. He really could make people fall over. Once, with this left-back sitting on the ground, Stan put his foot on the ball and waited for him to get up, and beat him again. Let's face it, a lot of people went to football for nothing more than to watch Stan. He was such an accurate crosser of the ball, with both feet. Whenever he played for England, I felt he put fear in the opposition. I didn't notice any deterioration in him after the war, but it's a reasonable assumption that he played his best just beforehand.

The Czechoslovaks were a fine side, with several of those players who had appeared in the World Cup Final of 1934, when they lost to Italy. Early in the match, Mills, the Chelsea centre-forward, was injured, and moved to the wing, Hall switching to centre-forward and Matthews coming inside. England led 3–2 at half-time on a heavy pitch that was cutting up badly. In the second half, the Czechoslovaks fought back and, with a few minutes to go, the match was level at 4–4: two of England's goals having come from Matthews. Stan Halsey reported in the *Daily Express* the next morning:

It was a bit of a farce, with the light disappearing in the closing stages. Around this point, Matthews, dribbling at goal by instinct, put in the shot which won the game. Planicka, the goalkeeper, had it covered, but Kostalek (the right-back), deflected it in. The moment he (Matthews) took over at inside-forward when injury hit the England team, he was transformed.

The interpassing of the Czechoslovak team had caused England many problems. Puc had equalized an early goal by Crayston of Arsenal; Morton, the West Ham outside-left and Matthews made it 3–1, only for Nejedly to narrow the gap with a brilliant goal before half-time. Matthews made it 4–2, then Zeman and Nejedly levelled the match. It was, Halsey wrote, the best Continental team yet seen. Hapgood, injured and watching from the stands, said that science was at a premium that day.

Two months later, in February 1938, there developed a dispute between Matthews and Stoke which led to his requesting a transfer. After five years as a professional he was legitimately entitled under League regulations to a bonus of £650. The club had offered him, through Bob McGrory, the manager, only £500. Mather had by now departed to manage Newcastle. Stanley held out for the full amount in the summer of 1937, and this had resulted in his being unable to go on tour with England to Norway, Sweden and Finland, and losing three months' wages. Against this background of unrest there had also developed a rumour, which had quickly spread around the close-knit community of the Potteries, that bad feeling had developed between Stanley and one or two of the other players. What was more certainly the situation was that McGrory, a former Stoke player, was to a degree envious of the publicity and acclaim which was being heaped on his young player.

SM: It was quite untrue that there was any feeling in the dressing-room. We were a very happy team. I am a peaceful man who doesn't like trouble of any kind. Even when the rumours simmered down, it left a nasty taste. And towards the end of January, I decided it might be better if I tried to start a new life with another club. Without a word to anyone else, I approached the directors, and was asked to see the Board to discuss the reasons for my request. After, an hour's discussion, they refused. The next morning my request was in all the newspapers, and I couldn't move in the streets without getting involved in arguments that didn't always concern the issue.

The revelation that the local hero was unhappy with the club caused unprecedented reverberations throughout the Potteries. Besides the dismay among tens of thousands that a uniquely fascinating and entertaining player might be lost to spectators on a Saturday, pottery manufacturers complained that the issue was affecting production. Five prominent industrialists called a meeting at the town hall in Stoke, presided over by Ashley Myott, chairman of the Wages and Conditions Committee of the British Manufacturers Federation. The King's Hall was packed with three thousand people, with an estimated two thousand locked outside. The meeting decided that a deputation should speak, separately, with both the club directors and with Matthews. Outside the hall, hoardings covered with posters proclaimed 'Matthews Must Not Go'.

SM: I was amazed to see what a transfer request could do to people. I wondered if it was really all worth it for the sake of that extra £150 bonus. I had opened a sports shop in the town, although it didn't really make that much. We supplied the club with some gear, and had one elderly sales assistant. It was a small place, up on the first floor above a drapery. It was quite a difficult situation for the directors, because there was the risk on the one hand, at that stage of the season, that we could still be relegated, while on the other they knew that Newcastle were willing to pay something like £20,000 for me to move to St James' Park. Tom Mather had moved there, being succeeded by McGrory twelve months before. When McGrory was a player, he'd lived in the same digs as Bobby Liddle, who was our outside-right. I'd taken Liddle's position, and I know McGrory resented me.

Stanley had discussed the situation with his father, who had sympathized; but had said that, considering Stanley was personally responsible for almost half the people who turned out to watch Stoke every other week, he didn't think they would let him go. His father warned him: 'You will walk out, if you go, into a packet of trouble.'
Stanley could have appealed to the Professional Footballers' Association for an adjudication, but was reluctant to do so, even though the dispute swirled out of control around him. Journalists streamed

down from London for interviews, and it was rumoured that Everton, Manchester City, Bolton and Aston Villa were competing with Newcastle for his signature. 'It was all rather embarrassing,' Jack, his elder brother, says. 'Demanding money, even when it was your due, was considered to be improper in those days. There would never have been any bother but for McGrory, if he'd been straight. I think McGrory wanted him to leave, that he hadn't liked him from the beginning. McGrory wanted eleven men working together, and was suspicious of stars.'

Never mind that Stanley was legitimately worth twenty times his £8 weekly wage from Stoke, he needed the balance of his bonus to help pay for the small semi-detached house which he and Betty had bought at Trent Vale. Following a week of further debate, public and private, the position was resolved, McGrory having had a personal talk with Stanley's father. Stanley re-signed; the club agreed to pay the full benefit at the end of the following season. This precedent for such a young player resulted in similar benefits subsequently being paid throughout the League.

England's next match, against Scotland at Wembley, was as undistinguished as the last one, against Czechoslovakia, had been memorable. 'The worst international I have seen for years; almost ever,' Henry Rose said in the *Daily Express*. Matthews and Bastin on the wings received no service, so that Matthews got little change out of Beattie. Preston North End, due to appear in the Cup Final a few weeks later against Huddersfield, provided four of the Scottish Team. The only goal came from a misdirected clearance by Hapgood, back in the side after injury, that was instantly exploited by Walker. It was with little confidence that the England party headed for Berlin, and another meeting with the now all-confident Germans.

Sir Stanley Rous, in *Football Worlds*, has said how much the European dictators of the Thirties saw success in sport as a political weapon, and that it was not long before Germany under Hitler was reflecting this attitude. *Strength Through Joy* was part of the philosophy, of impressing the world with Aryan supremacy. The Berlin Olympic Games of 1936 had been staged with this very much in mind. Hitler had exhibited a public tantrum when Germany was beaten by Norway at football in the preliminary stages of the Olympic Games, Otto Nerz, the coach, being dismissed the following year.

The return match in Berlin in 1938 certainly embroiled me in politics [Rous wrote]. When we arrived we were told that the Germans would stand to attention for our national anthem, and we were asked to return the compliment by giving the Nazi salute during the playing of theirs. Together with Charles Wreford-Brown, the FA official in charge of the team, I had an interview with the British Ambassador, Sir Neville Henderson, and asked what we should do. 'When I go to see Herr Hitler, I give him the Nazi salute because that is the normal courtesy expected,' Henderson said. 'It carries no hint of approval of anything Hitler or his regime may do. If I do it, why should you or your team not do it?' So I put that view to the players, leaving the choice to them, pointing out that the decision would determine whether the game was held in a friendly or hostile atmosphere. All agreed they had no objection . . . however there was heavy criticism in some of the press. Ivan Sharpe, himself a leading former player, was the man who best expressed my own view: 'Abroad there is generally a ceremony of greeting from teams to onlookers, so I can never understand the fuss . . . there was no appeasement about it. After all, we were friendly enough to be playing them at football.'

The England team were yet to start flying to foreign matches, so it was a long trip via Harwich and The Hook to Berlin.

SM: We arrived in Berlin two days before the match, and I would have liked to get a glimpse of this dictator who was dominating European politics. I went off on a sightseeing expedition with Bert Sproston (the Leeds right-back), and it almost happened. We were having tea at a small café when suddenly people rushed to the door. Women waved their handkerchiefs, and children stopped playing. I couldn't see anything except a procession of motorbikes and a couple of large black limousines. We had no idea who was passing, but a German who was standing next to us at the door said that the Führer had just gone by. He seemed overawed, and I could see that the Germans regarded Hitler as a god. I had not believed before this that such fanaticism was possible. Yet I have to say that throughout our visit we never encountered any hostility, everyone went out of their way to be hospitable, though they did go on a bit about the way that Hitler was working for the peace of Europe.

We realized that there was more at stake than merely a football match. We were photographed everywhere we went, were taken to the theatre, all with an air of great formality. The huge Olympic Stadium was one of the finest that I'd played in, and undoubtedly they had prepared at length for this match. Their team, which was in fact a combination of the best players in Germany and Austria (following the Anschluss) had been taken for two weeks' special training in the Black Forest. We must have seemed a pale group of footballers when we met the German team on the eve of the match. When I looked at Muenzenberg, the German left-back, who had played so effectively against me three years earlier, he seemed much older, and this gave me some confidence for the next day. When we arrived at the stadium for the match we found that the English dressing-room was situated at the top of the huge stand, and we had to climb hundreds of steps to reach it. Maybe the Germans wanted to unsettle us by this, but we took it in our stride.

There was one unpublicized personal crisis within this match. Only an hour before the kick-off, Hans Jacob, Germany's goalkeeper, learned that his eldest daughter, aged four, was seriously ill. He requested permission immediately to travel back south, but Sepp Herberger, who had succeeded Nerz as team-manager, and was the man who sixteen years later would take Germany to victory in the World Cup, stated that it was too late to change the team. 'Clearly, I didn't want to play,' Jacob says. 'I feel I misjudged three shots when England scored that maybe I would normally have held, but my mind was not in Berlin.' Tragically, his daughter died soon afterwards.

Bent on revenge, England won 6–3, having duly given the Nazi salute before the start. Every forward scored, including Matthews, with Bastin, the left-winger, scoring the first from a cross by Matthews, Robinson getting two, Broome and Goulden the others.

We felt sure to win beforehand [Jacob says]. We had improved a lot since the 2–0 defeat by Norway in the Olympic Games, when Hitler had been watching for the first time and when we were all nervous. Herberger was a much more practical coach then Nerz, who was theoretical. We had had release from our employers – we were all amateurs – on the orders of Hitler, in order to train together beforehand. There were plans for close marking by Muenzenberg on Matthews, but this time Muenzenberg could do nothing at all. Matthews was the best player on the field. We were on no financial reward, just 4.50 Deutchmarks expenses a day. We really did expect we would do better, because we had the best players from Austria included in our team, though on reflection this was not a good idea. Hahnemann, the Austrian centre-forward, was the best, but he could not make much impact on the English defence.

Part of England's success came from the tenacity of Willingham, the Huddersfield right-half, a little terrier of a player, who kept a tight grip on Szepan, Germany's creative inside-left, and England were 4–2 up at half-time. A mark of German thoroughness was that as the players walked off the field at half-time, a dozen youngsters ran forward with blankets for the English team to wrap around them on the long climb back to the dressing-room. In the second-half, Goulden, the West Ham inside-left, scored a wonderful goal, taking a knee-high volley from the edge of the penalty area. The perfect grass in the new stadium allowed the ball to run true, and favoured the skill of this outstanding England team.

There was no thought in their minds at this moment of the imminent rape of Czechoslovkia and Sudetenland. The report of the German magazine *Fussball* was ungrudging in its praise for the English players:

One hasn't seen wingers in Germany of the calibre of Matthews and Bastin for years, nor the kind of flank attack they were capable of delivering relentlessly. Matthews even surpassed Bastin with his unbelievable speed and drive for goal. Technically Bastin, too, was supreme, but Matthews excelled. His almost always successful duel with Muenzenberg was surely among the most unforgettable impressions of this remarkable game. From the inside trio, it would be Goulden who, with his rare but fabulous shots at goal, will remain in the memory. His superb passes made us realize how much England must have missed him against (recently) Scotland. The excellent wingers gradually became the overpowering personalities on the field. For heaven's sake, Muenzenberg is no spring chicken, he would like to think of himself as an old fox. Yet against this Matthews he was at his wit's end. Before Muenzenberg knows what has happened, the Englishman has gone past him, gained two or three metres, and is just about to make a pass: Goulden shoots, Jacob punches, Bastin volleys into the far corner. A marvellous first goal.

They don't quite play as they do at home. No (physical) attacks on the goalkeeper. But they fight! Our boys just don't seem to get to the ball, unless Muenzenberg puts it away for a corner. And now follows an example of masterly play. Matthews takes the corner with exhilarating accuracy far across to Bastin, the Londoner places the ball on Robinson's forehead. The following header we won't forget for a long time, going through the gap between Jacob's vainly grasping hand and the crossbar: 2–1. A fellow like Matthews risks everything and can do everything. He beats Jacob with a steel-like spring for another goal, and 4–1 at half-time would have been most depressing, even if deserved. So a second German goal just before half-time was greeted with applause. Muenzenberg had England's outstanding player lined up against him, and he wasn't up to him. Yet what other German defender would have dreamt of keeping Matthews quiet? These are the world champions after all; they buried the allegation of mechanized football. They were perfect.

England were not, of course, participating in the third World Cup of 1938, which was about to be won for the second time running by Italy. Yet, in the *Daily Express*, Henry Rose would write:

We may this year win the Davis Cup and the Wightman Cup, but the snappiest blow for British prestige was struck by the England football eleven. Matthews turned Muenzenberg dizzy. The final goal, Goulden's volley from Matthews' centre, was the goal that footballers dream about. Yet, under broiling sun, I couldn't beforehand see an England victory.

In the absence of Hitler, who had never attended another match after the Olympic defeat by Norway, Hess, Ribbentrop, Goering and Goebbels watched stone-faced from the main tribune. *The Times*, which the following day carried five pages of sport, said that it was the best English team ever to visit the Continent. Rous would recall later:

I was amused at the contrast between Sir Neville Henderson, sitting there wearing a shooting hat with a hawk's feather and an old pullover, and Hermann Goering beside him, glistening with medals and military magnificence. Henderson had a large pair of binoculars slung round his neck, and each time we scored would proffer them to the unsmiling Goering, saying: 'What wonderful goals! You really ought to get a closer look.'

No one could analyse the magic of Matthews. From Berlin the team moved on to Switzerland and France, ironically losing 2–1 in Zurich, but winning 4–2 in Paris. At the Grand Dolder Hotel, up in the hills above Zurich, Ivan Sharpe, himself a former international, asked Matthews how he did it; took him out on the lawns, and requested a demonstration. 'Honestly, I can't do it in cold blood,' Stanley told him. 'It just comes out of me under pressure.'

Before the FA party left Berlin, it was arranged for the Germans to visit London in 1940. In the event, they would come with bombs rather than footballs. On the field, Muenzenberg would never be the same man again. The heartbroken Jacob gained two more caps, against Ireland and Hungary the following year. He should have played in the World Cup, but withdrew because of his daughter's death; Germany were beaten 4–2 by Switzerland.

Public reaction was not harsh after our defeat [Jacob says]. It was realized that England was so much better. They had so much technique. I don't care for the game the way it is today, there's too much physical challenge. Herberger was an outstanding coach, but in the big matches so much depends on luck. In the 1954 World Cup Final, the Hungarians had a goal disallowed by Ellis, the English referee. I agreed, of course! Helmut Schoen was also good, he learned so much from Herberger. I shared a room with him for his first match as an inside-forward against Sweden in 1937. He was a bundle of nerves.

There was a controversy surrounding Stanley's first representative match of the 1938–39 season, in which the Football League outplayed the Scottish League 3–1 at Wolverhampton. Stanley dazzled his Scottish opponents, yet was afterwards accused by some of the newspapers of having starved Willie Hall, his inside-forward partner, out of the next England team. Hall was indeed dropped for the match against Wales. There was no suggestion of this on the part of Hall, and he was included again when the team was announced to play against Ireland in November at Old Trafford. In between these matches, they had played together for an England side against the Rest of Europe, which England had won 3–0, Matthews outwitting an Italian full-back, Rava, and creating the opening goal for Hall. His brother Jack relates that Stanley was stunned by the accusations after the League match, and went out, for the game against Ireland, with the deliberate intention of helping Hall to have the best game he had ever played. He did this to such effect that Hall scored five goals in a 7–0 victory, with Stanley himself dribbling through the entire Irish defence from the half-way line, including going round the goalkeeper, to score the final goal.

SM: It was certainly a happy match, because I was dismayed when I had read the previous criticisms. Willie was a good friend, and there was no intention to render him a disservice. Whatever mistake I had made at Wolverhampton I intended to put right, and it was nice of him that he wanted to share a room with me for the game at Old Trafford. It was a comfort to know that I had supplied four of the passes that contributed to his goals. The understanding he developed with me was uncanny. He knew when to go on the outside, when to go forward, when to stand still. I felt sorry for Billy Cook, the Irish and Everton left-back. Willie and I drove him to distraction.

This autumn had seen the first appearance of a young Tommy Lawton in the national team. Before Old Trafford, he had played against Wales, Europe and Norway; and he now scored, with Matthews, the other two of the seven goals. Lawton was nineteen, a phenomenal games player who might also have become a Test cricketer. Born in Bolton, he had signed for Burnley, the club having found a house for his family. He was a stone's throw from the cricket ground, and trained as frequently with a small ball as a big one. He had quickly made a name for himself in League cricket, having been coached in the Burnley nets by Manny Martindale, the West Indian fast bowler. On his debut in 1936 he had hit the legendary Learie Constantine, playing for Nelson, out of the ground on his first delivery, and made 30 not out. The following August he hit 87 not out, in a total of 115, in 64 minutes, and still has the ball which was presented to him.

If you hit 50 or took five wickets in League cricket, you could go round with a box, and on this occasion at Colne he collected £30, which for a sixteen-year-old was a small fortune. He had done a butcher's delivery round at Bolton before he signed for Burnley; from where, after only eighteen months – such was his talent with the large ball – he was transferred to Everton for £6,500, aged only eighteen.

Everton took a chance, and I was grateful for all they did for me [says Tommy, now living in retirement just outside Nottingham]. You read so much rubbish today about a player being too young, but if you don't play him, how do you know? My first representative game was at eighteen, against the Irish League in Belfast. We won 8–0, I got four, and Stan made *all* four for me. As we put our shirts on, he simply said to me, 'Give it square to my feet, I'll make the openings for you.' The first pass I gave him, I put it through down the wing, and he said, 'Remember, to my feet.' I never did it again, and he did the rest.

Everton put the polish on me, and that's why within twelve months I was in the England side. Ray Bennion was their coach, a former Wales and Manchester United wing-half, and he helped me a lot. Dixie Dean was my hero, and I learned so much from him in timing and positioning. He was only five feet ten inches. I was two inches taller, and at Goodison I practised endlessly. I never went for a ball in the air I couldn't get, I'd feint and make the goalkeeper go the wrong way, and then say 'thank you'. With the Liverpool Cricket Club, however, I really couldn't get used to the 'Yes, dear boy' kind of manner, and I drifted out of cricket. But at Goodison we *all* came back for training in the afternoon, and won the championship in '39.

How on earth can you describe Stanley? Was there ever such a master of the football, was there ever such a Peter Pan of sport, was there ever such a modest player? Many people have said Matthews was slow, but don't be misled by shuffling Stan. Watch him when he was showing a ball to an opponent, as if he was counting the panels, then watch that burst of speed that takes him clear. Other people accused him of being a bad team man, the sort who holds up a forward line, allowing the defence to get into position. What nonsense! Matthews was a perfectionist, and when he got the ball he refused to pass it just for the sake of passing it . . . if no one moved, Stan would hold the ball until colleagues were in position. No one could hold it like him. He had uncanny control, and still looked happy when there were three or four men around him.

Stanley, quite independently, echoes Lawton's view. 'Hold things up? Not really,' he reflects. 'When you're shut down, you can't just *go* randomly, you've got to wait for colleagues to get in position. If I take the full-back with me, I'm holding down one man *and* I have the ball. The public idea is that I was always on the wing, yet I moved around a lot to make space for myself. You should never allow yourself totally to get tied down. Even by 1937, I found I was being marked more and more. When I was accused of starving Willie Hall, against the Scottish League, I'd been forced to drop further and further back to get away from their full-back, who was really pressing me.'

The performance at Old Trafford by the England team, and by Matthews, was beyond the experience of everyone watching it. The newspapers overflowed with tributes. Youthful Walter Winterbottom, then the Manchester United reserve centre-half, was present and recalls that Matthews was 'a sensation'. Charles Buchan, in *A Lifetime in Football*, wrote:

> There are days when he's inclined to overdo the spectacular side of his play. The crowds love the way he leaves an opponent on one foot, but he often delays the final pass until the goalmouth is covered. . . . There was another day, however, when his wizardry brought goals . . . at Old Trafford. Stanley made most of the openings . . . he was given a terrific ovation as he left the field. I shall never forget the sportsmanship of Billy Cook, Ireland's left-back. Though he must have been hopelessly beaten scores of times, he never once brought down his tantalizing opponent, and as they left the field Cook put his arm round Matthews' shoulder. I didn't know what he said, but the memory of that grand gesture always remains with me.

Midway through the second half, Cook had good-humouredly said to Stan that if he brought the ball near him once more he would wring his neck. *The Times* wrote the next day:

> It is by the same means, an expert economy an adroitness of movement, that he is enabled to elude the danger he seems to court. The fact that the man who goes in to tackle him is, to all intents and purposes, beaten before he has properly started his work has, not unnaturally, a demoralizing effect on the defence as a whole. He made the Irish defence look vague and purposeless; and there was Hall to take advantage of the openings given him. . . . Matthews beat four men to score the last goal from an impossible angle.

Archie Leadbrooke, Frank Carruthers and Henry Rose vied with each other in their acclaim. Rose: 'If Bryn Jones is worth £14,000, and

Bert Sproston £10,000, what is the worth of Stanley Matthews? The solution was toyed with while we were trying to keep track of the score. Some said £20,000, some £30,000, and others went as far as £50,000. I am not disposed to quarrel with any of the suggestions. It was a long time since I heard cheering every time a player received the ball.' Carruthers: 'It is doubtful whether there was ever an era of the game richer in talent than was revealed by the England team at Old Trafford. It may be suggested that a defence which concedes seven goals is woefully weak, but the Irish halves and backs were overwhelmed. Matthews has been proclaimed as the greatest outside-right of all time. I have never seen a wing man perform with the majesty of the Stoke player. To his opponents, and Cook in particular, he must have appeared as a shadow, moving in every direction but the one to be expected.' Leadbrooke: 'The Stoke "white wizard" was the complete machine. His footwork when he dribbled was uncannily beautiful, his body swerve demoralizing. Those things we have seen before, but we have not usually seen him passing with such accuracy. . . . For myself, other wingers can stop trying for the rest of the season from now on. I'm not interested.' The teams that day were:

ENGLAND: Woodley (*Chelsea*); Morris (*Wolves*), Hapgood (*Arsenal*, capt.); Willingham (*Huddersfield*), Cullis (*Wolves*), Mercer (*Everton*); Matthews (*Stoke*), Hall (*Spurs*), Lawton (*Everton*), Stephenson (*Leeds*), Smith (*Millwall*).
N. IRELAND: Twomey (*Leeds*); Hayes (*Huddersfield*), Cook (*Everton*, capt.); Brolly (*Millwall*), McMillen (*Chesterfield*), Brown (*Leeds*); Cochrane (*Leeds*), Stevenson (*Everton*), Baird (*Huddersfield*), Doherty (*Manchester City*), Brown (*Birmingham*).

Jack Matthews, who had travelled from Stoke to watch his brother, recollects that the following day Stanley was too embarrassed, on hearing what the papers had said, to read them. 'When he dribbled through to score that last goal, he just turned and walked away,' Jack says. Ronnie, aged fourteen, who had travelled with a coach-load of players from Port Vale, stayed out late drinking, and received a reprimand from father when he got home.

That other all-time great, Billy Meredith, was at the match, his hitherto unchallenged reputation now under fire. In an interview the following day, he said with magnanimity:

Not till the match against Ireland had the fans talked about him being the best ever. Well, I agree with them. If he's not the best, there certainly never was better. And I saw them all. At the moment, Stanley stands alone in British football. There is nothing to touch him. There have been a lot of good wingers, all different types, but Stan has never been bettered as a ball juggler. My style was pretty much the same as Matthews'. How I liked defenders to come at me! It was too easy. While saying that, Stan's job might have been harder (in my time) than it is today, and he would certainly have had more competition for his national caps, but I still think that twenty-five years ago he would have been just as big an attraction as he is today.

From 1895 until 1914, Meredith played in 48 internationals. In 1898–9, he scored 36 goals in 33 league matches for Manchester City, gained two FA Cup winners' medals, scoring the winning goal in the final against Bolton in 1904.

Ivan Sharpe, writing in *Soccer Top Ten*, reckoned that Meredith in his day trod a rougher road at the hands of defenders; and recalled that Meredith had said that wing-forwards needed more individuality than any other position except goal. The same build as Matthews, at five foot eight and a half inches, Meredith was never a roamer, but a touch-line expert. Matthews, replying at one time to the accusation that he had not the scoring abilities of Alex Jackson, Cliff Bastin or Joe Hulme, or that he was not sufficiently robust in challenging for the ball, said:

My reply to the first allegation is that I always try and play pure football, to confuse the defence and to make openings for colleagues in a better scoring position. To the second, I would say that if my career depended on how well I could get 'stuck in', I would have retired from football many years ago. To dribble successfully, the most essential factor is supreme confidence to beat an opponent. If I even entertain the possibility that I am going to lose the ball when I am tackled, I would be a failure. I *know* I am going to beat the half-back or full-back, or both, standing in front of me. Eddie Hapgood once said I dribbled for the sake of dribbling, that I am not content to beat a man once. This is not true. I dribble to get on top of the defence, hoping to destroy their confidence. Once, when I was sitting in the Stoke dressing-room, aged sixteen, Meredith was there and said: 'You show promise of becoming a good'un. Don't lose your head, and remember to place your centre to the far post.'

The match against Ireland had seen the debut at left-half for the national team of Joe Mercer, who was to be a regular until 1946. His father had been a centre-half, but had died young, in 1937. Joe had played a couple of times for Everton's reserves before he was seventeen, living a tough life in Ellesmere Port, where part of his payment for a junior team had been a bag of vegetables on a Friday. With a sick husband, his mother, Ethel Daisy, had brought up five children on £1 a week.

Anyone less like a daisy you've never seen [Joe recalls affectionately]. She was tough and hard, with the most lovely long black hair. She took in washing for extra money, and I used to collect and deliver the baskets. At twelve, I did a paper round, and my first job was seventeen and six [87p] a week as a ledger clerk in the wagon repair shop of Shell-Mex, walking three and a half miles to get there at seven-thirty in the morning. You can imagine what it was like to sign on for Everton for £5 a week. Yet my mother had always made sure I had a pair of football boots for Christmas. I saw a lot of Stan Cullis as a boy. We used to refer to the Cullis family, with their funny language, as the 'wooflers'. It was murder when we played Stan's school.

So Mercer was a member of the England team that travelled north for the last of the pre-war encounters with the Scots. And after the Scots had been beaten 2–1 for England's first victory at Hampden in twelve years, Mercer recalls sitting in the bath afterwards: 'I didn't know whether to laugh or cry with happiness.' He had been, together with Matthews, the man of the match, but he was omitted from the touring party announced for the forthcoming trip to Italy, Yugoslavia and Romania on account of a scheduled trip by Everton to Germany. There was a public outcry, and he was included at the last moment.

John Macadam, reporting in the *Daily Express*, wrote: 'Mercer was magnificent all through, even in the first half, when it looked as if Scotland were going to have a runaway win.' Scotland had scored first through Dougal of Preston, and it was not until twenty minutes from time that Beasley, the Huddersfield outside-left, who was playing his first international, put England level. So heavy were the conditions that both teams had changed their kit at half-time. There were only two minutes to go when Goulden put Matthews away on the right. Matthews beat McNab, the West Bromwich left-half, and then full-back Cummings of Aston Villa; and from a seemingly impossible angle, from the corner flag, according to Carruthers of the *Mail*, put over a centre which hung in the air for Lawton to snatch the winning goal with one of those incomparable headers. Now the Scots spectators would go home and start talking about the greatest winger they had ever seen. It was, in the words of Frank Coles of the *Daily Telegraph*, 'a display comparable with the old masters, and every Scotsman I spoke to after the match agreed.'

Some might have said Matthews was not the equal of that supreme Scottish winger, Alan Morton, of Queens Park Rangers; though Billy Walker, the Aston Villa and England winger whose own reputation had been as high as Morton's said that he placed Matthews on a par with Morton. The Italians, who had the previous year retained their World Cup, were about to discover that Matthews was no longer the less than confident youngster who had faced them five years previously at Highbury.

The FA summer tour of 1939 took place against the background of the mounting anxiety which gripped Europe, and it was close to being cancelled, following consultation with the British government. In the event, the match in Milan took place without political incident: overwhelming hospitality greeted the players from the moment they crossed the border with Switzerland and took up residence for two days in Stresa.

As the players had set off from Dover to Calais, and thence by the Orient Express, the good natured Macadam of the *Express*, always one of the most sensitive and humorous of writers filed to his paper: 'The most political utterance I have heard so far came from Len Goulden, who said that he thought it would be a nice trip. The crowd at Milan station was such that a two-minute walk to the hotel took us a half-hour. When we had taken our rooms at the Piazza Duca d'Aosta, the crowd assembled outside to demand that the players come to the window.' Going to inspect the new San Siro stadium, Macadam inquired what the fences were for. Protection, he was told. 'Protecting whom? Maybe it's an old Italian custom to keep off the autograph hunters.' he suggested, tongue in cheek, to his readers. Meanwhile, Mussolini was in Turin addressing a crowd of fifty thousand Fascist fanatics, to whom he gave the reassurance that 'nothing in Europe is worth fighting for. We will march with Germany to give Europe peace with justice.' So much for dictators.

There had been not a hint of military intimidation during the stay in Stresa or Milan. The team was showered with flowers on arrival at Stresa station, was taken on a trip on Lake Como, and at almost every station on the way to Milan the train was halted for yet another reception, with thousands of Italians chanting 'Viva Inglesi'. A large crowd of English supporters arrived in Milan from Malta, many of them Maltese. And the day before the game the sunshine gave way to pouring rain. It was still raining heavily as the team arrived at the San Siro, and they discovered that wire netting was being erected to prevent bottles and other objects being thrown on to the pitch. The carabinieri had fixed bayonets. It evidently was not the English who invented the football hooligan.

SM: What followed in 1940 was not consistent with the marvellous attitude of the Italians towards us on that trip; and during the war, when I was in the RAF, I could not bring myself to believe the Italians wanted to fight us. When we left the hotel for the match we had a job to get through the crowd to board the bus. Italy might have been the world champions, but England were still regarded as the tops, and everybody went out of their way to show their appreciation of us. Of course, we already knew that many of the Continental teams had all the skills, that all they needed was an ability to shoot. The Italians were about to show us they had something of everything, and for the middle twenty minutes they almost overran us.

Compared with our team against Scotland, George Male had replaced Morris of Wolves at right-back, the half-back line was the same, and the only other change was Broome of Villa coming in on the left-wing in place of Beasley of Huddersfield. We didn't begin too badly for the first five or ten minutes, though I found their left-back Rava something of a handful. The other forwards, especially Tommy Lawton, were playing well enough, and the crowd of 70,000 showed its appreciation of our game. On one of the few times I managed to slip Rava, I was able to get in close to goal and centre for Tommy to head us in front. We felt we'd now get on top, but we were in for a surprise. Steadily the Italians began to outplay us, abandoned defence and tore into us from all sides. Within five minutes they were level, Bievat, their left-winger, running through the right-hand side of our defence and drilling a shot past Woodley. We never recovered from the brilliance of that goal, and if it hadn't been for a sterling performance by Joe Mercer, who held our defence together, we might well have gone under. We suffered the worst twenty minutes in an international match that I'd yet experienced. In fact, we'd just pulled out of this bad patch when Italy took the lead with what can only be called a disgraceful goal. Piola, their centre-forward, who was a fine player, undoubtedly handled the ball with the same kind of subtlety that Maradona used against England in the World Cup of 1986. As Piola was going for a ball in the air together with Male, he slipped, I thought, but punched at the ball with his right hand. Not only that, but with his follow-through he caught George in the face and gave him a black eye.

The foul was so obvious that we didn't even bother to protest. But it failed to catch the eye of Dr Bauwens, the referee from Germany, and we couldn't believe it when he turned and indicated a goal. Our resentment against this maybe helped pull us together, and what with that and encouragement from Hapgood (the captain) we fought back. Both Willingham and Mercer came up in support of the forwards, and so did that marvellous centre-half, Stan Cullis, so that in the last bit of the game we were attacking with eight men.

Even Italians in the main tribune acknowledged that the second goal of theirs should have been disallowed; and Stanley Rous was obliged politely to refuse the request of the Italian Crown Prince to accompany him down to the field to inform Dr Bauwens that the goal was illegal. Fortunately for England's pride, with five minutes to go Matthews ghosted his way clear once again; from his centre Goulden had a shot blocked, and Hall was able to equalize as the ball ran free.

'Italy played with great assurance,' *The Times* reported through Reuters agency. 'Serrantoni and Meazza, their inside-forwards, played deep during the early part of the match to help their defence, which robbed their attack, but they were transformed in the second.' Macadam, with his usual succinct style, said: 'The politicians got their draw only because Dr Bauwens didn't see Piola fist the ball into the net. Yet this was one of the best games ever played. I doubt whether we of this generation shall ever see its like again.' Macadam related that when he had complained to French and Germans attending the match that the Italians had been too dirty in their play, he had been told: 'That's nothing to what they do to each other every Sunday! The Italians have just played one of the cleanest games ever seen on the continent.' Meazza, the Italian captain, was said to be currently the world's highest paid player, with a weekly salary of £35, though the national average wage of the Italian professional at that time was approximately the same as in England.

SM: From Milan we travelled via Venice to Belgrade, where we arrived by train at 6.30 in the morning, and were astonished to see yet another tremendous crowd gathered at the main station. We were told some of them had been there since before dawn, and the friendliness and welcome of the Yugoslavs was as warm as anything we'd experienced in Stresa or Milan. Although there was a food shortage, wherever we went nothing was spared by our hosts. Banquets had huge menus; the Yugoslavs considered the visit of our team to be an occasion of immense importance.

Stanley and the rest of the players encountered a courier of unusual friendliness, full of stories and an intimate knowledge of the Yugoslav capital. However, the extent of his information did the England team one disservice, because he assured them that they would win comfortably. In his opinion, the Slavs were slow and ineffective. He could not have been more wrong.

There was concern before the match about Matthews' fitness. He had badly jarred a hip in Milan, but after a test the day before he told Tom Whittaker, the trainer, that he felt he was fit. It was to prove a misjudgement; on the first occasion that he attempted to sprint clear of Dubac, the Yugoslav left-back, his leg did not respond 'and felt as heavy as a wooden leg. I was virtually a passenger from then on, not in any great pain, but unable to extend the full-back.'

Macadam had filed: 'From Venice onwards, the countryside gets progressively Balkaner and Balkaner ... the crowds at our hotel were chanting endlessly 'Low-ton' or 'Matt-oose' half the night. There is speculation that because of disagreement within the team among the nine Serbs and two Croats, the Croats, goalkeeper Glazu and left-back Matosic, may withdraw.' The domestic racial conflict which has always undermined this wonderfully talented football nation was already at work; and the pattern would be seen repeatedly during World Cup tournaments of the next fifty years. The Croats did indeed withdraw.

This did not prevent Yugoslavia going in front after fifteen minutes, and the acclaim for this goal by Glisovic lasted for almost five minutes: a tremendous tonic to the home team. However, England held out until half-time, and four minutes into the second half they drew level. Broome and Lawton combined from the half-way line, switched positions, and Broome scored with a fine shot from near the penalty spot. A seventy yard run by Perlic, cutting in from the left past Male, ended with a drive past Woodley that put Yugoslavia ahead again. Broome might once more have equalized when clear inside the penalty area, only to be pulled down by the ankles from behind in a rugby tackle by Poseja. The French referee ignored this blatant foul; and on a hard, bumpy pitch, and with Hapgood now limping in addition to Matthews, following a clash with the centre-forward Petrovic, England could not save the day. Yugoslavia, to give them their due, had played superbly.

It was an experience about which Stanley retains few overall impressions. 'I remember little about the city of Belgrade, appreciated at the time as little as I appreciated London in all those years when I was travelling down from Stoke to play against London clubs. You never really *saw* the real London. There was so much to see, yet in those days it was just another working day for us.' There were, too, the social differences of that time which would exclude from professional players much of the society whirl of the capital. The barriers which would be bridged in George Best's day were still, in the thirties, prohibitive.

From Belgrade, an already weary party headed off by boat down the Danube for Romania, and the final match in Bucharest. Most of them were up at four in the morning to see the famous Iron Gates gorge, though they were disappointed to discover the poetic licence which turned a muddy brown river blue. When they arrived at Turnu-Severin in Romania, yet another huge crowd was awaiting them: two bands on the river bank, one of Boy Scouts, the other an ornately dressed military band. Both played 'God Save The King' – one rather faster than the other, recalled Hapgood in his autobiography *Football*

Ambassador. 'When the race had come to a galloping halt,' Hapgood relates, 'they started all over again, and we left them trying to play each other into the river.' The party was feted right across Romania to the capital: where they encountered, at King Carol's summer residence, a venerable gardener speaking fluent Cockney. Flowers and flags were everywhere, more bands puffed out 'John Peel', and as many other British tunes as they could muster. The hospitality, however, was to stop short of the pitch. The Romanians proved to be not only able but dirty, as Stan Cullis remembers:

> They kicked us from pillar to post. I think the referee must have had eye trouble, because it seemed he saw nothing. Once, Vic Woodley and I were kicked into the back of the net and still the referee did nothing. When I complained to Stanley Rous at half-time, he said firmly, 'your job is to keep the players calm, not to be a knight in shining armour.' If you misbehaved in those days, it could finish your career, and the players recognized this. One of the Romanians took off the sole of Joe Mercer's boot, and I saw Joe threatening him, so I had to tell him 'If you do anything, *I'll* send you off, never mind the referee. We're going to finish with eleven men, and win.'

Cullis was, at twenty-two, one of the youngest in the team. He had been in the Wolves team at eighteen and had captained the side at nineteen.

Considering the trouble I had in communicating with the *Daily Telegraph*, from the only phone at the hotel reception desk, on my first visit to Romania in 1960, it is interesting to learn from Stanley that, in 1939, the hotel where the players stayed had bedside telephones, and tiles in their private bathrooms. Cullis had his way, on the pitch, and England won by two goals to nil; and then began the three-day journey home. 'There was no crowd at Dover to greet us,' Stanley recalls with a smile. 'In those days, I doubt if there would have been even had we come home with the World Cup.'

4. WARTIME

I HAD Stanley Matthews trapped against the corner flag at Stoke. His back was practically touching the post and I was within a yard of him. I thought: "Got you! This time I've really got you."

Ten times, probably, he had beaten me in that game. He would bring the ball squarely towards me so that I would never know whether he would go inside or outside with it. He would lean so far that it would be obvious he had to go that way – but his balance is so perfect he would then sway and go the other way.

However, I had been working to a plan, pushing him up the wing all the time, and now I knew that he could not trick me. I was rather fit and fast at the time. So I moved in. And broke my thumb on the post.

What he did, how he got away, I will never know. Johnny Carey, the versatile Manchester United player, used to say, "Playing Stan is like playing a ghost." It was an apt description.

Stanley must have caused more tactical talks and planning conferences in opposing camps than any six men together in the history of the game. When he was honoured at the National Sporting Club for his silver jubilee as a footballer in 1957, I told our host Charles Forte: "Mr Forte, this has been a magnificent dinner, but don't think for one moment that it compensates for the miles and miles we have had to run after this fellow." *

JOE MERCER, *The Great Ones*

*F*RANK Swift, that indomitable goalkeeper of Manchester City and England who sadly perished along with eight players and seven other journalists when Manchester United's plane crashed at Munich in 1958 – Frank was then working for the *News of the World* – considered that the finest team with whom he ever played was that which beat Scotland 8–0 at Maine Road, Manchester on 4 October 1943. In his autobiography, *Football From The Goalmouth*, he wrote; 'I have yet to see such perfection in movement, unselfishness or team spirit as England showed that afternoon: or the courage to equal that of the Scots, beaten though they were but never humbled.' The opinion is echoed by Tommy Lawton; though, in his style, he is somewhat dismissive of the Scots and says that it was a one-horse race. For the record, the teams on that day were:

ENGLAND: Swift (*Manchester City*); Scott (*Arsenal*), Hardwick (*Middlesbrough*); Britton (*Everton*), Cullis (*Wolves*, capt.), Mercer (*Everton*); Matthews (*Stoke*), Carter (*Sunderland*), Lawton (*Everton*), Hagan (*Sheffield United*), D. Compton (*Arsenal*).
SCOTLAND: Crozier (*Brentford*); Carabie (*Third Lenark*), Miller (*Hearts*); Little (*Rangers*), Young (*Rangers*, capt.), Campbell (*Morton*); Waddell (*Rangers*), Gillick (*Everton*), Linwood (*St Mirren*), Walker (*Hearts*), Deacon (*St Mirren*).

It was sheer delight, Swift wrote, to be able to watch the England machine swing into action: the brilliance of the half-back line, Britton, Cullis and Mercer, the shooting of Lawton, the methodical destruction of the Scottish offence at inside-forward by Carter and Hagan, the wizardry of Matthews. 'It was Stanley's match in particular,' Swift said. 'At times he seemed to bamboozle the whole Scottish rearguard on his own. When he scored the eighth and final goal, entirely on his own, the crowd cheered for minutes on end. Even some of the Scottish players clapped.' Lawton says that he has never seen the equal of Matthews on that day.

With a certain kind of perversity, the war-time matches from 1940 to 1946 were deemed by the Football Association to be 'unofficial', and not deserving of the award of a cap. Stanley played in thirty such matches, and for him, as for many other players – and indeed for many civilians such as my father, whose prospects as an actor were effectively ended by war-time service as radar operator with the RAF – the war marred what should have been the prime of his career. Or rather, should it be said, the prime of normal men. When the war ended Stanley would be thirty-one. He would continue playing League football for almost another twenty years; international football, remarkably, for a further eleven years.

Yet to suggest that this war-time football was of no account would be a severe injustice to all those who, for the benefit of morale among both the forces and the civilian population, continued to play regular international matches of the highest possible standard. My colleague Brian James, formerly one of Fleet Street's more accomplished football correspondents during many years with the *Daily Mail*, emphasized this in his well researched *England v. Scotland*, a history of football's oldest international fixture:

> Those years took great bites out of the career span of some of the greatest players these islands ever produced [James wrote]. The mere fact of the concurrent world conflict should not deprive them of their credit, for it did not disguise the evidence of their talent. By their victory in 1939, England had given notice that a great team was emerging. The record during the next seven years – sixteen games played, eleven won, two drawn and only three lost, with a goal record of 53 scored to 21 conceded – shows that England had been no one-match marvel. Nor will it do for Scots to complain that this was phoney football.

James goes on to quote players of the time in substantiation of his claim. Bill Shankly, that doughty wing-half of Preston and Scotland, who would subsequently become one of Britain's most successful – and most quoted – team managers, said: 'You cannot even *argue* about this. This was a great England team. They had wonderful players in the side, and just as many waiting to get a game. If I had been picking a team from the best players in the country at the time they beat us 8–0, I would have picked that same side . . . it was hard for all of us (in war-time) but it was no harder for the Scots. I can't think of any players that were not available for Scotland because of the war.' Joe Mercer recalls: 'I wasn't as good a player before or after as I was during this time.' It would be necessary, too, as James points out, to claim that Hampden with 130,000 fans or Wembley with 75,000 were not the true setting and a true audience for 'full' international matches.

It was decided, as a matter of policy by the War Office, that the most significant contribution to the war effort by leading players would be to provide entertainment, which they could give to large numbers of troops and to the civilian population, by continuing to do what they did best. So Stanley and many of his contemporaries were drafted into Army or RAF units, usually as physical education instructors. Nevertheless, it was often only with extreme difficulty that they would get duty relief in order to be able to travel, by an erratic war-time railway service, to arrive in time for the kick-off in these matches. There was no public resentment of their privilege, only gratitude.

'I was able to work a great deal on my fitness during the war,' Stanley says. 'I'd be out on the beach at six in the morning before going on parade at seven, doing an hour's exercises and running. My body was used to it, and it continued to be my main form of training after the war, with the Stoke and the Blackpool teams.' In one sense, the war had a specific influence on Stanley's career, because his RAF posting was to Blackpool, to where he would be transferred from Stoke. It was rather different for his brother Jack. As the British Expeditionary Force was withdrawing successfully from the Dunkirk beaches in 1940, Jack, working in his barber's shop and being beyond mandatory call-up age, thought to himself: 'Bugger this, I'm going to join them.' So he closed his shop, and the next day walked down to the recruiting office.

The first two war-time matches were both against Wales in November 1939, Stanley playing in one of them. After some doubts, a match was arranged against Scotland at Newcastle in aid of war-time charities, which England won 2–1, and the success of this fixture determined that matches would continue to be played when circumstances permitted. Wales were played again the following April, and then Scotland at Hampden in May. By now the Blitz had begun, and there was official alarm at the risk implicit in assembling a huge crowd that might be imperilled by bombing. Whether or not the general anxiety affected the quality of play cannot be known, but a tame match ended in a 1–1 draw. Stanley missed the next encounter, a 3–2 victory for Scotland at Newcastle in February 1941; but he shared in a 3–1 victory for England at Hampden three months later. The match at Newcastle had witnessed the arrival on the scene of Wilf Mannion from Middlesbrough. Mannion would grace England teams for the next nine years: a wonderfully balanced, compact little inside-forward with an instinct for openings that were often unseen to all but himself. Some years later, I would be taken as a schoolboy to Stamford Bridge by a friend to see him for the first time, rather as one is taken by an uncle to see Canterbury Cathedral or the Tower of London. It was an act of homage, the recognition of an institution, without experience of which you could not be said properly to understand the game. Wilf, like all great players, did things on his own terms, seemingly without effort, controlling the ball almost without thinking. He played the game with the feather-like touch of someone playing the flute. He was the destroyer of Scotland both at Hampden and again at Wembley in October, when England won 2–0, both times partnering Matthews. At Wembley, the victim of Matthews' mesmerizing footwork was once again Beattie.

The regular captain was Cullis: who was happy to endure the many hardships of travelling around the country, often without adequate food or sleep, when he paused to consider where he might have otherwise have been:

I used to tell the players how lucky we were to be able to be doing what we did [Cullis says]. Off the pitch, we were just like the rest of the population, wondering what the next week, the next day, would bring. I remember queueing with my wife to get into a match, at Windsor Park in Belfast, with everyone else and someone saying, 'I'm *sure* that's Stan Cullis.' We were only paid thirty shillings (£1.50) for a match: even the gate men were getting more than we were, but there were two million of our fellows fighting for their lives, and for ours, and I wasn't going to ask for more. On one occasion Tommy Lawton was waving a pound-note in one hand and a ten-shilling note in the other and saying, 'there's 70,000 here, and this is all we're getting for turning out today.'

Someone from the FA heard him, and he was dropped for the next two matches. Claiming expenses was always a bit of a laugh. I remember on one occasion Denis Compton putting down 'miscellaneous', and I said to him, 'You don't even know how to spell it.' Trying to claim a taxi was really something special. And the FA treasurer knew the bus and tube fares down to the nearest penny and would say 'too much!' We were nearly always out of pocket on the trip. Denis was hopelessly disorganized. One time, he even asked me if I could put one or two studs in his boots. A nightmare to have on the team, but a charming fellow. This typified his game: you never knew what he was going to do next.

The first match of 1942 was played against Scotland at Wembley in inches of snow, but a crowd of 65,000 still turned up to see England win by three goals. Cullis at centre-half was said to have given the Scottish attack no chance, while Mannion and Hagan schemed England's control: the first goal came from a brilliant run by Hagan, the second and third by Lawton, laid on respectively by Compton and Matthews. At Hampden in April, the Scots achieved one of their rare victories: they won 5–4 in spite of a hat-trick by Lawton, and owed much to the brilliance of Waddell on their right wing. Scotland's wing-halves on that notable day were Shankly and Busby, the latter on the books jointly of Liverpool and Hibernian at that time. Neither side could score in the third meeting of the year, Matthews on this occasion being restrained by one of the better performances of Beattie, and by Busby.

The thrashing of October, 1943, at Maine Road was preceded by a 4–0 victory by England at Hampden. On this occasion, as in October, Matthews was partnered by Carter rather than Mannion. Matthews had a field day, and Carter scored twice in the first half. Strangely, when England beat Wales 8–3 at Wembley, immediately prior to scoring eight against Scotland a month later, the press accused some members of the England team of deliberately starving Matthews out of the match. Matthews himself was unaware of any such policy; and it is an indication of the extent to which he seldom discussed beforehand the tactics of other players that he was now unaware of a deliberate ruse by Cullis, his captain. Cullis was conscious that Wales had a calculated plan, devised around Hughes and Burgess, their defenders on the left side, to keep Matthews out of the game. To counter this, Cullis decided that England should play to the left much of the time, and exploit the space that was being given to Carter, Marsh and Hagan by Wales's concentration on Matthews. The scoreline speaks for itself.

Burgess, a sensitive and commanding left-half for both Wales and Spurs, finds his admiration undiminished to this day. 'Stan always gave me trouble,' he recalls. 'There weren't many who could hold him. He had such balance and body swerve and he was pretty nippy. The only way to counter him was to hit him hard, which wasn't me. There was only one way he could play, which was to take people on. Yet he read the game so well, he'd let the ball go if he was pinned down. If you were playing with him, you wanted him to have the ball so you could have a rest!'

England's victory at Maine Road was, and still is, the biggest margin ever recorded in the history of the fixture. When Matthews scored the eighth goal it was the first time he had scored in an international match for five years. The others came from Lawton (four), Hagan (two) and Carter. Scotland would not suffer another such reverse until 1961 when, in Winterbottom's second last match in charge against them, they lost 9–3 at Wembley.

A frequent opponent with Scotland, though not on this occasion, was Matt Busby, an eloquent wing-half who won a Cup-Winners' medal with Manchester City and subsequently moved to Liverpool. Busby was an artist, a player who would give his directors heart attacks by dribbling on the edge of the penalty area. He confirms the magnetism of Stanley. 'These were exceptional England teams, never mind the war-time, because there was so much ability among the players.' Busby recalls in his eighty-first year. 'Stan was always a truly great player, with skill that few if any have had, and he could turn it on in a way that made opponents tremble and captivated the public.'

England were as unmerciful against Scotland the following February, when they hit six to Scotland's two; thanks to a blue-print performance by Matthews in the second half, Scotland having held their rivals to a goal each at half-time. In 1944 England would win three times. A 3–2 victory at Hampden in April was described by Lawton as the toughest match in which he'd ever played. In three matches England scored fifteen goals, the Scots reeling from the onslaught of a forward line including Matthews, Carter, Lawton and Hagan or Goulden. Leslie Compton, Denis's older brother, made his first appearance at full-back. The luckless Tommy Walker, pride of Scotland, was powerless to respond to this continuing onslaught; Lawton scored six of the fifteen goals against Scotland that year. Tough the 3–2 match may have been, but afterwards, such was the spirit in which the game was played in those days, all was handshakes. There were no vendettas.

Maybe, as Lawton suggests, the stern tussle was for the benefit of Field-Marshal Montgomery, who was guest of honour. At a luncheon before the match, Monty had said: 'Those who fight overseas and those who work on the home front are members of one and the same team. One cannot do without the other. There are two things to be done – to fight the Germans and keep the mass of people at home from worrying.' It was less than two months before the Allied forces would launch the D-Day invasion of Normandy, and Montgomery, for all his off-duty bonhomie, must have had tactics other than football on his mind.

Of the second 6–2 victory that year against Scotland, at Wembley in October, Roy Peskett wrote in the *Sunday Graphic*:

Tommy Lawton beat Scotland. England's dynamic centre-forward, giving the greatest display of his life, pulled back a match which looked well won by Scotland only thirty-four minutes from time. They say the occasion finds the man. Now it found Lawton. With the England forwards held in clam-like fashion by the sturdy Scots defence, it looked as if the match would run out with the Scots holding their well-deserved one-goal lead. Then Lawton went to work. In the eleventh minute of the second half he fastened on to a long pass from Frank Soo (of Stoke), eeled his way past Stephen, beat Baxter in his stride, and with 93,000 throats roaring him home, smashed the ball past the Scottish keeper. The England team stood still and clapped Lawton back to the middle. Even some of the Scots patted him in the back as he made his triumphant way to the centre spot. It was more than a goal . . . it was victory. Four minutes later Lawton scored again, and from then on it was a rout. England scored four more goals, one by Lawton and the others made by him.

The match was remarkable for the appearance, at the last moment, of a relatively unknown young player, Bobby Thyne of Darlington. When the Scottish party arrived in London, Bill Shankly was limping with a knee injury, and after consultation the next morning with the Chelsea club doctor at Stamford Bridge, it was decided he was unfit. Sergeant Thyne, normally a centre-half, had travelled with the team merely to gain experience of a big match, and was still convalescing after being wounded in the Normandy landings. His relative naïvity at this level no doubt contributed to Scotland's downfall.

One of England's now emerging young players, who would become one of the most famous of all, was Tom Finney, but the war disrupted his career more than most.

I only gained two war-time caps, and they were both in Switzerland, against the Swiss, in 1945 [Tom recalls]. I was flown back from Naples specially for the matches. Stanley Rous met me at Croydon Airport. Because Switzerland was a neutral country, I couldn't fly there still wearing my uniform, so Rous had to take me off to Moss Bros, armed with the necessary clothing coupons, to buy me a civilian suit. The matches in Berne and Zurich were in the summer, and it was very hot, but this didn't bother me because I'd been serving in Egypt.

As ever, an understatement from this most modest of men. When he joined up with the Army, Tom had played for a while in regional football in the war-time league, with Shankly, Beattie and the rest at Preston, taking the Cup and League in his first year; winning a Cup Final replay against Arsenal 2–1 at Blackburn, after drawing 1–1 at Wembley. He had got the better of Hapgood. Playing against Matthews, for the FA against the RAF in 1941, Finney had been one of only two players on the pitch who were not internationals, the other being the Preston goalkeeper Jack Fairbrother. The FA won 4–3. Finney was on embarkation leave, and Rous assured him that he would arrange for his posting to be deferred. The intervention came to nothing; Finney landed in Egypt in December 1942, with the Royal Armoured Corps. He played football regularly for the next two years just outside Cairo, but when the push into Italy began, Finney was transferred as a driver to the 9th Queen's Royal Lancers, and was weaving a tank in and out of shell fire in his inimitable style in the battle for Rimini. You will not easily get him to talk about it: it was something that had to be done.

Stanley's brother Jack, meanwhile, was holed up in a dug-out somewhere in North Africa – 'I honestly couldn't tell you where, I've no idea, it was where the R.A.F. took me' – waiting patiently for the war to end and hoping he would be alive to see it. On the day in 1945 when England met Wales, Jack was on guard duty, and listening on a crackling short-wave radio to the commentary from London. It came as a shock when the commentator said: 'Stanley Matthews will not be playing on account of a family bereavement.' It was the first Jack knew of his father's death. He had known for several months that his father had been ailing with cancer of the stomach; the illness had been suddenly diagnosed that year, and his father was advised that he had only a short time to live. Whereupon, always a man of some style, he had announced: 'Right, let's have a bottle of champagne, I've never tasted the stuff, so it's about time I did.'

Ronnie recalls that his father, in one of many moments of advice, had said to him: 'If you're *going* to drink, make sure you always go to the best bars!' At the outbreak of war Ronnie had been playing with the third team at Blackpool, together with a young wing-half named Mortensen. 'I was on the groundstaff, together with Morty, Harry Johnston and others,' Ronnie says. 'I played a bit of non-League football, but I would never have been good enough to make a living at it.' Ronnie as an infant had been pushed around in his pram by Stanley, the way Stanley had been by Jack. This was usually on Thursday afternoons, when their father, on his half-day, went out with their mother. On these afternoons, Ronnie would be fed with custard. 'It was the only thing Stanley could make,' he recalls.

Young Mortensen was in the England team which defeated Scotland 3–2 at Villa Park in February 1945, scoring two of the goals, including the winner. Also making his first appearance that day, in place of Cullis or the Arsenal amateur, Bernard Joy, was Neil Franklin. Frank Butler wrote in the *Express* that Scotland were no nearer to answering the Matthews-Carter combination, after a second victory in two months, 6–1 at Hampden. All the England forwards scored, Matthews included, with two for Lawton. Bobby Brown, later to become one of Scotland's many post-war managers, was in goal for Scotland.

In spite of the occasional visits of foreign international sides to England before the war, foreign football was still a curiosity, never more so than with a visit in November 1945 of Moscow Dynamo.

SM: They provided surprises on and off the field almost every day. After their opening match at Stamford Bridge, when they held Chelsea to a 3–3 draw, it was clear they played football that would be a test for any of our League sides – in spite of doubts widely expressed beforehand about their ability to match the alleged quality of an English First Division. The Russians complained about having to play their first match in mid-week, which they regarded as something of an insult. They may have changed their minds when 85,000 spectators packed into Stamford Bridge to see them. The crowd broke through on to the pitch, and the police decided it would be safer to let them remain along the touch-lines. The Chelsea team were a bit taken aback when the Russian players presented them all with flowers before the kick-off, which is a normal gesture in Russia but was an oddity over here. The Dynamos soon revealed what accomplished players they were, with inter-passing of exceptional skill. None of them dribbled, but kept the ball moving from man to man at high speed.

Though controlling the play in the first half-hour, the Russians failed to score. Chelsea led through Goulden and Williams, but the Russians drew level. Lawton, by now transferred to Chelsea, headed a third, but four minutes from the end Bobrov again equalized, to appreciative applause from the crowd.

SM: The next Saturday I went down to see the Russians play at Cardiff. They'd complained about that, too, not wanting to leave London, or play a Third Division team, and they proved their point when they ran ten goals past the Welsh side. Beskov, their centre-forward, scored four goals, I think. The Russians' ball control was marvellous, and I hoped I would get a chance to play against them. When I heard that they were next to play Arsenal, Neil [Franklin] and I asked Bob McGrory, our manager, to offer our services to George Allison, the Arsenal manager, who was having difficulty getting a strong side together. Because Bernard Joy was flying home from Germany, Neil was not needed, but I was given a place in a makeshift Arsenal team which included Bacuzzi and Ronnie Rooke of Fulham, myself and Mortensen from Blackpool. On the day, there was one of the thickest London fogs you've ever seen, and the match was one of the most farcical on record. From the centre circle you couldn't see either of the goals. The Dynamos were said to have won 4–3, but I could hardly see more than a few yards in front of me. The fog got worse in the second half, and there was a lot of jeering from the crowd, who couldn't see a thing. In their last match, the Russians were held 2–2 by Rangers in Glasgow. In four matches, more than 260,000 people had paid to see one of the finest teams yet to visit Britain.

By the time of the next encounter with Scotland, the Victory International of 1946, the war was over . . . and Matthews was about to experience the fluctuating and fickle mood of the re-established FA selection committee. For six years during the war, under the more or less single-handed guidance of Rous, the England team had operated almost as a club side, with the consistent selection of the same players; a policy, which the selectors, in their ignorance and through the vested interest exercised on behalf of their own clubs, would promptly abandon. As Rous said to James: 'I tried to use the war-time experience to get one-man control to operate for England. The FA wouldn't have it. I wrote memoranda on this time and again when the FA was starting to reorganize itself, but the selectors came back despite that. Walter Winterbottom knew what ought to have been done, he was just never able to recapture that system that worked so well in the war. They wouldn't let him.'

Duly asserting itself, the selection committee in its wisdom fielded an experimental team, dropping Carter and replaced him with Shackleton, then still with Bradford; and England lost by the only goal, their first defeat by Scotland in ten matches. Matthews was selected but forced out by injury, being replaced by Elliott of West Bromwich. Delaney of Manchester United, playing at centre-forward, scored the goal from a free-kick just outside the penalty area awarded for obstruction on Shackleton, that conjurer of the ball who would inexplicably play only five peace-time matches for England following his transfer soon afterwards to Sunderland.

5. *RIVALS*

'*I*T is argued now that Matthews would have failed in modern football because of his limited specialization, because he never tackled an opposition forward or assisted in any sense in his own side's defensive pattern, because he would have been smacked hard to the ground by today's much faster, lighter, more tenacious defenders. We are never going to know the truth of this. I question it, not just because I dislike having my boyhood heroes squashed like trodden-on Plasticine, but because I think people confuse Matthews' unique talent with all the lesser examples of the genre. Matthews did not invent dribbling with a football; he raised it to its highest degree. Lots of other players did the same kind of thing at a lower level before him and throughout his career. Until George Best's arrival, dribbling had been dead for nearly a decade for every player except Matthews and Bryan Douglas of Blackburn Rovers, for any purpose except brief hiding of the ball from the opposition. It is now being restored to the game, accepted grudgingly by managers again as a player's last resort against the sophistication of the retreating, blocking defensive technique. Running with a football, deliberately showing it to the opposition to force a tackle so that the defender can be eliminated, is such a knife-edge matter that a player hardly dares to fail. It needs extreme talent. It went out of favour, taking with it the reputation of the man who was best at it, because it lacked performers of sufficient quality. It always had, of course; but now defences were nimbler and could snuff out the second-grade ball players at first stride. It is endlessly beguiling to consider who was the greatest player in this position or that, and to wallow in that marvellous game which alone made those school revision periods bearable, of picking the team called the All Time Greats. I would have the 35-year-old Matthews on my right wing and Best at inside-right, and invite the opposition to find the ball. *

ARTHUR HOPCRAFT, *The Football Man*

SELECTED against Belgium in the Victory International at Wembley in January 1946, Stanley overtook Eddie Hapgood's record of 43 international appearances for England, and his target now was to surpass the 51 appearances for Wales by Billy Meredith. He nearly had to cry off against Belgium, suffering from influenza following night duty with the RAF during a bitterly cold spell, his watch having involved turning out of bed repeatedly at all hours of the night. Hot milk and whisky kept the germs at bay, and after sweating out a couple of uncomfortable nights in bed at the team's hotel, Stanley declared himself fit. In the dressing-room, fortunately for him, the England side were handed for the first time special track suits, and this helped him to keep warm while the teams limbered up on the snowbound pitch before presentation to the new Prime Minister, Clement Attlee. Stanley played, hardly surprisingly, without distinction in a 2–0 victory.

Two months later, on 9 March, he was involved in the tragic match at Burnden Park, Bolton, when 33 spectators were crushed to death and five hundred were injured as a result of hundreds of gate-crashers gaining entrance.

SM: It was for the cup-tie against Stoke, Bolton having gained a two-goal lead in the previous match, the Cup being on home and away basis that season. Over seventy thousand supporters were jammed into the ground, Bolton hoping to clinch the tie. Early on, thousands spilled off the terraces on to the area behind the goal, which at first was not worrying, because that had happened before with a near record crowd for a big game. Then they started to come on to the pitch and the referee called a halt to the game. After discussions with the police, the players were taken back to the dressing-room and it was there that we first heard people had been killed in the crush, though at first we had no idea how many. We were in the dressing-room half an hour, when we were told that, on the advice of the Chief Constable of Bolton, the game was to continue. We got back on the pitch and some spectators shouted out that it was a crime to carry on, but we were professionals, doing as we were told. We played to the finish, concentrating on the match, and Stoke were beaten. I motored back to my home in Blackpool, and it was not until I read the papers at breakfast the following morning that I realized how awful the disaster had been. I felt sick.

For several days Stanley was so distressed that he could not train. Jack, his brother, recalls that two days later he went over to Blackpool to visit him. 'Stan may have seemed hard on the outside, but inside he was extremely soft, and the disaster had really hit him,' Jack says. 'He had written out a cheque for the Disaster Fund which had been launched, I think it was for £30, which was about two weeks' wages, and he asked whether I thought it was enough. At times he could be very emotional, but the outsider would never know because he covered it up with armour.'

Bad luck throughout the 1946–47 season, and the rising challenge of Finney, seven years his junior, together with the oscillation of the selectors, impeded Stanley's progress towards Meredith's record. Torn knee ligaments kept him out of the Victory International against Scotland, though he was fit to go on tour that summer for matches against France and Switzerland. 'I was chosen for the first two internationals of the autumn against Northern Ireland in Belfast and Eire in Dublin two days later. I particularly wanted to play in the Dublin game, because it was the first appearance of an England eleven there since 1912. But a repetition of the knee injury forced me out of the side, and this was a lucky break for Tom Finney, who had been included in the reserves.'

Finney played in both matches, and scored in both, with Bobby Langton of Blackburn on the left wing. To give the selectors their due, a front line of Finney, Carter, Lawton, Mannion and Langton played unchanged in the first four matches of the season, the others being against Wales and an 8–2 win against the amateurs of Holland. Ever since Finney's first appearance in the same match as Stanley, back in the early days of the war for the FA against the RAF, some of the critics had been saying that Finney was the obvious eventual replacement for Matthews; and after those opening four games of 1946, the football correspondents were suggesting that Finney was there to stay. Tom recalls:

We beat the Irish 7–2 at Windsor Park in my first international, with Wilf [Mannion] getting three, but it was a pretty awesome occasion for me, because I was only five weeks out of the forces. George Hardwick, the captain, Carter, Lawton and others were very helpful towards me, there was a fine team spirit, and I was able to settle in quickly. I'd been given special leave to be demobbed from Italy, because I was in the building trade, and received what was called a 'B Release' because they were short of builders back home, and I was soon back to my work as a plumber, training with Preston on Tuesdays and Thursdays.

Undoubtedly, although never one to react to public comment, whether acclaim or criticism, Stanley was unnerved by headlines which accompanied Finney's first appearances: 'The King Is Dead,·Long Live The King' and so on. Finney scored the only goal in Dublin, where history was made, with a crowd of 32,000 Republicans standing bareheaded while the band played 'God Save The King'. The football writers were being given fuel for their promotion of a rivalry which was meat and drink to the back pages. Finney scored again in the rout of Holland. Asked a few years later how he had viewed what was seen by some as potentially the end of his international career, Stanley said:

There's no need for me to say anything about Tom Finney. His name is known far and wide. He lives only a few miles away from me, and there is no animosity between us. When the England team was announced against Wales, my name was missing, even though I was fit again, and I was more than a little hurt when people who once professed to be my friends turned around and began to say that I was out for good. At first I was a bit bewildered. I felt lonely and disheartened. I began to believe it myself. More than ever I missed my father. If I could have gone to him he would have put my mind at ease with his sound common sense. Yet to my surprise, and to the confusion of those who had predicted that I was out for good, I was recalled to play against Scotland at Wembley in April the next year.

It was not an auspicious match in which to make a return. McLaren, the Preston inside-right, put Scotland ahead after fifteen minutes, a lead they retained at half-time. The competitive Scottish halfback line of Macaulay (Brentford), Woodburn (Rangers), and Forbes (Sheffield United) subdued Mannion, Lawton and Carter. Carter equalized in the second half and should in fact have won the match for England when clean through towards the end with only Miller, the Celtic goalkeeper, to beat. A whistle in the crowd made Carter suppose that the French referee had pulled him up for off-side; Carter looked round with his foot on the ball, realized his error, and went on, only to drive the ball straight into Miller's hands. A less than impressive performance by Stanley resulted in Finney being recalled for the meeting with France at Highbury a few weeks later, Finney again scoring in a three-goal victory. However, Stanley was selected for a Great Britain team to play the Rest of Europe at Hampden the week after that, a match arranged to celebrate the return of the Football Association to the ranks of FIFA. Stanley's name was subsequently among those selected for the summer tour of Switzerland and Portugal; as was Finney's.

SM: There was no personal rivalry. *Really*. For England matches, I'd catch the train to Preston, and Tom and I would arrange to meet on the train to London. Usually he'd be there waiting for me, would keep a seat and wave from the window. I remember discussing with him the fact that we were supposed to be rivals. I admired him, because he could play on either wing or at centre-forward. Indeed any forward position. He was a very deceptive player. And such a nice man, no swank about him. He and Wilf and I spent a lot of time together when we were with the England team, going for walks together. Often I shared a room with Tom. I never thought about whether I'd played better than him, or vice versa, when we were in the team together. He was so good that I felt if the critics compared me with him that I couldn't be that bad. I was never concerned that because he was a goal-scoring winger he was better than I was, because my aim and my satisfaction was providing goals. I'd always rather do that than score. I didn't enjoy scoring goals. There was no pleasure for me, say, in getting a hat-trick. I never thought because I scored a goal in my first international that I'd played well. And anyway, I changed my style during those early years. Tommy Lawton was a great player, but if he got three goals I didn't feel he'd had a better match than I had, because in all these things it's the final pass that counts. Someone has to create the opening, and that was my satisfaction. If I stayed upfield, where maybe I'd have more chance of scoring goals, then I felt I was losing touch with the team.

Tom lost his mother when he was four, his father being left with six young children under ten to bring up, Tom being the fourth. His father was a clerk, and took on extra work as a waiter in the evenings to supplement his wages, while Madge, the elder daughter, kept the house ticking over.

You don't forget those days [Tom says], though the neighbours pitched in and helped. My early playing days were pretty casual, twenty a side, playing till it was dark, that was what we lived for as kids. Bill Tuson, who later became Preston's chief education officer, was my games master at Deepdale Secondary Modern, and he was a great encouragement. Once or twice a year my father would take me to see Preston. My idol was Alex James, I'd see these big defenders sliding all over the place in pursuit of this little man, and I was very upset when he was transferred from Preston to Arsenal. The choice when I was fifteen was £2.50 as an apprentice professional, or six bob a week [30p] as an apprentice plumber, but my father, wisely enough, believed I should learn a trade, and so I just trained with Preston as an amateur two nights a week and began in plumbing.

I was playing in a junior league from fourteen to sixteen, and signed on for Preston when I was seventeen, continuing with the plumbing. Preston Boys reached the final of the English Schools Trophy, against West Ham, who had Ernie Gregory in goal. I was reserve. Then I played in the Lancashire Under-18 League, in which one professional was allowed, but I couldn't get into the side, I was always reserve, until someone was injured and I got a place in a match at Old Trafford at outside-right. I must have played OK, because the chairman Jim Taylor decided that I should continue playing in that position. At first I didn't enjoy it, but then began to find it an advantage, being able to collect the ball with my left foot when facing my own half and then being able to go inside or outside.

When I first gained a place in the England side it was a great honour, but an honour never unanimously applauded by the press or the public. The Matthews-Finney controversy had begun, the newspapers lapped it up, the correspondence columns were devoted to the issue. There was a weight on my shoulders all the time I kept a 'living legend' out of the England side. 'What right has Finney to be selected in place of Matthews?' one newspaper asked. What really got my back up was the suggestion that I was trying to copy the Matthews style. That was never so, I never tried to be anything but myself.

Tom was as diligent off the field as he was on it, and in due course set up his own business with his elder brother, Joe, who was an electrician: 'Finney Brothers, Ltd'. All his spare time was spent at the workshop, and within a few years they had expanded to the point where eventually the company was employing eighty people, thanks in part to the growing popularity of central heating. 'In those early days, on ten or twelve pounds a week, you had to look at what would happen when you finished as a player. When I stopped in 1960, my football wage was £20 in the season, £17 in the summer. There was a big difference between then and now, when after ten years at the top you can be made for life and don't need to be brainy.'

Following Stanley's return against Scotland in 1947, he mostly held his place in the national team for the next two seasons, he and Finney often playing together with Finney on the left flank, but in the three seasons from 1949 to 1952 Stanley made only three appearances, against 33 by Finney. Walter Winterbottom, who was England team manager and director of coaching from 1946 to 1962, recalls:

I thought at one time Stanley was going to stop playing because of injuries, on top of which we'd begun a policy of trying to bring players through from the Youth and Under–23 teams. When you look at the statistics from an analysis of games, it sometimes can be difficult to believe the facts. Finney tended to have more 'assists' with goals than Matthews, a higher effectiveness, but Matthews gave the entertainment. Stanley tended to have either great games or ordinary ones, but I think it was unfair to compare the two of them after the war because of the difference in their ages. Stanley was the matador, goading and provoking the opposition. In the years before the war he was without parallel, he was the Maradona of his time. His play had a vendetta quality, in the technical sense, and his crosses were devastating. It was extraordinary how he could get the ball to float. Yet wingers were isolated figures within a team, and could only dictate the play if they were given the ball. Great players like Puskas, Di Stefano, Sivori and Cruyff achieved their effectiveness because they played in the middle of the field. Cruyff, for instance, was everything: player, captain, coach, leader, scorer. Stanley was so quiet off the field that sometimes he almost didn't exist, yet he was always an entertainer, and one should remember that in his day, on muddy pitches, the weight of a fourteen-ounce leather ball when wet could be almost doubled. What Stanley could do with it in those circumstances was extraordinary.

Winterbottom's comments reveal, I think, a degree of ambivalence towards the genius of Matthews; something that is often apparent among team managers confronted with a player of extreme talent and individuality. They tend to feel that they cannot *control* the player. Although the selection committee would have the final say, Winterbottom had the opportunity to argue for those players he preferred, and there is an unavoidable inference that the obvious versatility of Finney, his more immediately apparent all-round effectiveness, was for Winterbottom more appealing.

Like Stanley, I never compared the two of us [Tom says]. Maybe I was *involved* more. If there was a fifty-fifty ball, I would tackle, the same with heading. Stan was essentially an individual player, though I never understood why he wasn't more of a goal-scorer. He got past defenders so often, seemingly into scoring positions, but preferred to find a colleague. He had the most perfect balance, and could take the ball so close to his man. The only defenders who ever had any success against him were those who stood right up on him and *made* him go outside. On odd occasions, we'd talk about full-backs we'd played against, but he would never enquire of me how I did what I did. Once he got a full-back square on, however, the full-back had no chance. We got on very well together, though Stan was a bit of a loner. With the England team he'd train on his own, his way. Walter was happy with that, Stan had his own routine. He was so fit, who could argue with him? He'd concentrate on short sprints. Don't forget, he was seven years older than I was, but he didn't need much to keep him fit. What seemed, at the time, to have settled the controversy was the match in Lisbon [against Portugal in 1947]. On the summer tour that year I was not selected in the first match against Switzerland, which we lost by the only goal, with Langton on the left wing. I'd played the 'B' match, a goal-less draw. Then we went on to Portugal, and Langton was unfit. Walter told me I was playing outside-left, yet I'd never previously played there. We won 10–0, Lawton and Mortensen got four each, Stan and me one each, and the public said that 'this was the answer'.

The position I liked least of all, however, was outside-left, which may surprise people, though I never complained, because it was an honour to play anywhere, and I must have played some thirty times in that position for England.

Such was Finney's versatility that at one time or another he played in every forward position for both Preston and England. As a young player at Deepdale, he had begun as an inside-left, and later in times of club crisis showed himself to be a wonderfully fluid centre-forward, rather in the manner of Ronnie Allen for West Bromwich and England, or, later, Johnny Byrne for West Ham and England. There was even an occasion, briefly, against Scotland in 1951 at Wembley, with Mannion carried off injured, when he moved to inside-right as partner to Matthews; and with the instinct of great players they combined as though having done so for years. It happened again in 1956, against Yugoslavia, when Haynes was injured. Tommy Taylor came on as substitute and Finney switched places with Brooks to play alongside Matthews, once again successfully.

In that match Finney had been selected at centre-forward, and, following the 3–0 victory, Winterbottom asked Finney what he thought of playing at inside-right alongside Matthews. Finney said he had enjoyed it. For some reason the selectors thought better; and, in the next match against Denmark, Finney was back on the left wing, with Brooks, a large bustling inside-forward from Tottenham who played in a formation, fashionable at that time, of double spearhead with the centre-forward, nominally at inside-right alongside Matthews, but providing little service.

Like Matthews, Finney could be mesmeric. He was one of those few distinctive players who made any match worth the journey irrespective of the quality of performance of the other twenty-one. He had such lightness, in the days when I first saw him playing for Preston at Stamford Bridge, that he seemed hardly to touch the ground. His balance and control were so co-ordinated that, among other players,

Below: Ada, a loving and indulgent mother, once wrapped young Stanley's foot in a tea cosy when, aged six, he had a poisoned toe, so that he could go outside and still kick a ball with the other foot.

Above: Jack Matthews, the Fighting Barber of Hanley, with Mr Blackburn, one of his most enthusiastic supporters.

Below: Sparring with Jim Washington, another local boxer, at the 'gymnasium' at Hanley: Mr Blackburn leaning on the gate.

At Wellington Road School (third row, right). 'I was very happy throughout my time at school.'

Stanley, playing as an attacking centre-half, captains Hanley Schools against Chesterfield Schools, aged 12.

In plus-fours, the contemporary wear of
an important man, Stanley sets off to
meet the Stoke City directors and discuss
his transfer request.

Ground staff attempt to de-frost the
Victoria Ground pitch with braziers
before a cup-tie. Roy Brown, handling
the barrow, subsequently signed as a
forward with Stoke City.

Above: Returning from England's 1939 summer tour of Italy, Yugoslavia and Rumania, Stanley enjoys a holiday at Llandudno with Betty and six-month-old Jean.

Centre right: Jean, aged four, tries out her birthday tricycle, accompanied by father, near his boarding-house war-time billet in Blackpool.

Top right: Stanley junior takes a ride – on the garden grass tennis court that will shape his future career.

Right: The family has a day at the races at Ayr – a favourite pastime of Stanley senior.

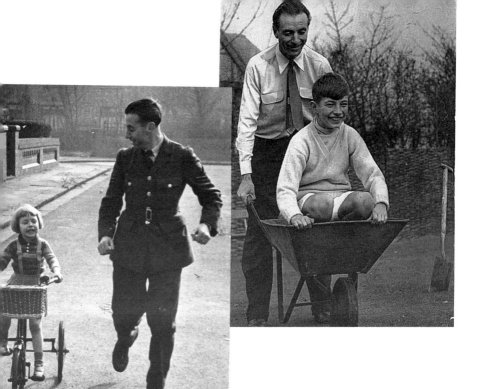

Top: Off to Paris with the RAF XI a month after Liberation. From left: Frank Soo, Wally Barnes, Jimmy Jewell, George Hardwick, (unidentified), (unidentified), Maurice Edelston (partly hidden), Raich Carter, Matt Busby, S M, Joe Mercer, Bernard Joy, Frank Swift, Jimmy Mullen.

Bottom: Putting in some hard preparation at Brighton for the encounter with Scotland at Wembley in 1947. From left: S M, Jimmy Mullen, Frank Swift, Raich Carter, Tommy Lawton, Billy Wright. Result: 1–1.

Top right: Mortensen (white shirt) beats goalkeeper Crompton (hidden) to put Blackpool 2–1 in front in the memorable FA Cup Final of 1948. Cockburn (6) and Chilton (5) arrive too late, but Manchester United turned the tables to win 4–2.

Centre right: King George VI is introduced to the Blackpool team by Harry Johnston (partly hidden). Other players from left: Mortenson, S M, Munro, Crosland (shaking hands), Dick, Rickett.

Bottom right: The Blackpool goal under pressure. From left: Pearson, Johnston, Robinson (with ball) Shimwell, Crosland, Hayward, Delaney.

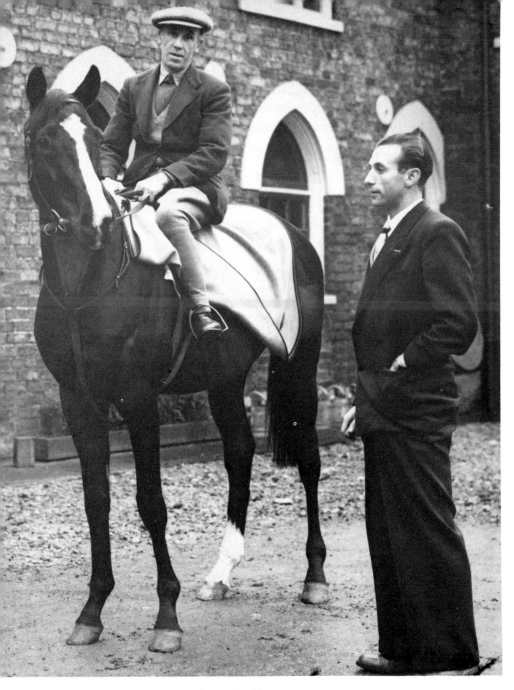

Stanley meets his new racehorse, Parbleu,
at the Beverley, Yorkshire, stables, with
head lad Llew Jones in the saddle.
Parbleu always won when Stanley was
absent . . . including when his owner was
losing in the World Cup in Brazil six
months later.

he was as the smoke of a bonfire drifting among trees, untouchable. Throughout football, among his contemporaries, it was as easy to find those who would put their shirt on Finney, when playing for the match of their life, as it was to find loyalists for Matthews.

Joe Mercer played with both and knew them intimately. 'Stan wanted the ball always to his feet,' Joe says. 'If you knocked it over the top of the defence, he didn't want it. Tom would accept the ball anywhere. When Stan said, "give me the ball and then go," that was the end of the move. You left it to him, and there'll never be another like him. But week in, week out, give me Tom. On his day he was unplayable, even when the opposition threw two or three people at him. With Tom, you'd get the ball back off him. But Matthews was the best player I ever saw, and I think he was the bigger match-winner, he rose to the occasion and was great when it really mattered.'

Bill Perry, a South African winger who was a colleague of Matthews in two FA Cup finals for Blackpool, has mixed feelings. 'If Stan was playing, you felt you had a goal start on anyone,' he says, at the small printing works which he owns half-way between Preston and Blackpool. 'But against certain teams, Stan wouldn't pull his weight. Against certain full-backs, such as McMichael of Newcastle, he found it difficult. Yet, against other clubs, you felt sorry for the full-back. It was not a question of whether Stan would get past, but would the full-back ever halt him? In our team, as soon as Stan got the ball, we just ran up the field, because we *knew* it would come across. He so rarely if ever lost the ball to put your team under pressure.'

Jimmy McIlroy, a thoughtful, sensitive Irish inside-forward whose velvet touch helped Burnley to win the League title in 1960 and who later would join Matthews when he returned to Stoke, thinks that, as a manager, he would always give Finney the preference: because he scored goals. This was, too, the view of Shankly, who was passionate in his devotion to Finney's cause, having played behind him as an admiring wing-half. Yet McIlroy, like almost all of those who give a points decision to Finney on a comparison of relative value to a team, finds himself compelled to eulogize about the qualities of the other man. 'Finney was the most complete player I ever saw, but Matthews was the greatest winger,' says McIlroy, now a journalist with his local Burnley paper. 'The greatest pass in football is the ball back from the line. When I was working for the *Lancashire Evening Telegraph*, I used to go on alternate weeks to watch Preston or Bolton, and often sat beside Finney. We'd see, say, Peter Taylor playing for Crystal Palace, and he'd beat the full-back, go to the line, and pull the ball back for a goal by his centre-forward. The press box, and the crowd, would stand in acclaim, and Tom would merely say, "if I didn't do that half a dozen times a game, I'd get told off." Every Saturday from the age of fifteen to fifty, Stan would do that to his full-back. The full-back knew he was going to go past, was determined to stop him, yet Stan would beat him almost every time.'

Finney's own opinion of Matthews is that his individuality was so great that there was no point in any other winger, however talented, attempting to emulate him: that Matthews' genius depended firstly on his ball control drawing two or three defenders out of position, and than on his centres being so tellingly accurate. The winger who runs down the line and sends across high, hopeful centres is playing into the hands of the defence, Finney says.

Stanley's daughter Jean, who was a fine tennis player and then coach, and now runs her own cosmetics business near Whitstable on the Kent coast, has an interesting view on her father's style: 'Part of his aim, I think, was to get the full-back to lose his temper. That, I suspect, was part of the reason for his sportsmanship, never himself to get rattled, but to show a psychological superiority. If he could get his opponent to lose his temper, he knew he was half-way there, and I found the same kind of attitude creeping into my own game of tennis.'

Peter Buxton, who has retired from *The Sentinel*, recalls the day that Stoke were playing Sheffield United, and Stanley had endlessly tormented Alex Forbes, that fiery Scot. Finally, Forbes took a wild kick at Stanley's knee. Stanley merely swayed out of the way like a hare evading a coursing whippet. 'That kick could have put Stan out of the game, and the crowd would have buried Forbes if he'd connected,' Buxton recounts. 'People still talk about it, yet if you mention it to Stan he will only say, "that was long ago, Alex and I are friends".' There are many such anecdotes.

'I may be prejudiced, but whenever Stoke played against Preston, home or away, Stan always seemed to overshadow Tom, as though he were deliberately putting on a show,' Buxton says. 'People say that Stanley wouldn't be able to do today what he did then, but that is to suggest that the teams in those days didn't tackle, whereas they probably tackled far harder than they do now.'

Billy Wright, who was England's captain for ten years, played behind and against both Matthews and Finney, and who himself came into the England team when Finney was reaching his peak, nonetheless says: 'At the highest level, I think Stan was the cleverer of the two. He was the more magical kind, he would do things no one else could do. But Tom would do it *every* match; whether it was muddy or tough, you knew he'd deliver. I've seen Tom get kicked to bits in Montevideo and resist, but there were times when I've seen Stan kicked out of a game.'

The tendency, I have found during discussions with dozens of players of three generations, is that those players whose own game was based on integration had an identification with Finney, while those whose job was to put the ball in the net, centre-forwards especially, had a higher esteem for Stanley. 'He always knew that *I* knew where he could find me,' Tommy Lawton says, in retirement at home just outside Nottingham, where he still writes the occasional comment for the Nottingham evening paper. 'When Stan got the ball, it was very rare that he lost it. I knew I just had to go to the far post – only to the near post for balls on the ground, if Stan had cut in. He really didn't know how good he was, it was something that didn't bother him.'

Nat Lofthouse, an opponent in the Bolton team which lost the Cup Final of 1953 to Blackpool, is England's fourth highest post-war goal-scorer with 30 goals – the same as Finney – in 33 matches. He scored 19 goals when Finney was on one or other wing, and seven when Matthews was on the right. He recollects:

I was the luckiest man in England to have the opportunity to play with both of them. Tom was more of a team man, and you could ask him to fill a role that was foreign to him. He would cut in, draw people, slip the ball, always varying it. Stan wanted the ball to his feet, and took the view that if he had to run for it, he'd wasted energy. Yet Stan nearly always went to the line, and this meant that you were never off-side, and he tried to make it as easy as possible for his colleagues. Stan set a standard and never fell below it. He might not have the ball for much of the match: then he'd touch it twice, and you'd won.

George Birks thinks that, in the immediate post-war years, Stanley reached a peak in applying his skills; and that the centre-forwards of that period, Lawton, Milburn, Lofthouse and, with both Blackpool and England, Mortensen, were the best at exploiting the opportunities he created: more so than some of the centre-forwards before the war. 'His *own* physique was superior before the war,' Birks says. 'We had a defender at Stoke, whose name I can't recall, who had been a Powderhall sprinter, and yet Stan could beat him over short distances. One of the things that fascinated me in later years would be the way, when he was hemmed in by two or three defenders near the corner flag, that suddenly the ball would climb vertically out from this group, and fall at a colleague's feet. You couldn't see Stan or see how it was done, and yet I saw it happen dozens of times.'

One of Stanley's most loyal colleagues, unsurprisingly, is Mortensen. When they came together at the end of the war it was as though they were made for each other; Mortensen with the fearlessness, speed and accuracy to hurl himself headlong on to Matthews' penetrating, lingering passes. 'He had everything,' Morty says, glad to have a chat about the old days over a cup of tea at his neat home presided over by his over-attendant wife. 'Fitness, balance, confidence, pace over ten yards, body swerve, instantaneous ball control, two-footed, marvellous temperament, right down to changing studs during the course of a match. How many corner kicks did you ever see him waste in the course of a season. Not three, I'll wager. And his confidence! He'd take players on when you thought he had no chance.'

The diplomatic view, of course, is that put forward by Harry Johnston, the Blackpool captain who played behind both men for England. Sadly, Johnston died in middle age, but in his biography, *The Rocky Road to Wembley*, he wrote, with a permissible degree of subjectivity: 'The Hungarians, the Uruguayans, the Italians – none of these teams has anybody to come within striking distance of Finney or Matthews. For the sake of English football it should not be Matthews *or* Finney but Matthews *and* Finney. I cannot agree with those who say they would select one or the other.'

Bob Ferrier, a perceptive journalist who wrote with sensitivity and affectionate observation for several newspapers and whose ability was utilized for some years, when it was still a worthwhile paper, by the *Daily Mirror*, has written:

The Matthews-Finney controversy is highly inconclusive. Perhaps the most significant thing about their long, overlapping relationship in the England team is that each man has a tremendous respect and feeling for the talents of the other. . . . Matthews has been able to dominate a team and a game more than any other player, partly because of an elusiveness which is a product of the highest imaginable ball skill. On uncountable occasions, Matthews has been ringed by four or five defenders, and by feinting, swerving, fluttering his feet, sometimes without even touching the ball, he has them running around and over-balancing until one laughs out loud with sheer wonder and delight, until the onlooker as much as the defender is exhausted with the ecstacy of it all. These are moments of a different quality from any produced by Finney. Ball skill for Finney has been a means to an end.

It is perhaps indicative that in setting out to compare the two men in his *Soccer Partnership*, and having drawn attention to the statistical superiority of Finney's thirty goals in 76 international matches against Matthews' three goals in 34 (post-war), Ferrier still finds himself obliged, like so many mesmerized defenders, to dwell more upon the extraordinary qualities of Matthews. Fate helps shape reputations. Would we regard Matthews and Finney respectively in a different way had those two Cup Finals, Matthews' triumph of 1953 and Finney's comparative disaster of 1954, had opposite results? I think not.

6. BAULKED

'*MATTHEWS* I have watched scores of times, and could go on watching him till the end of time. Countless other thousands, too, will remember with gratitude the immeasurable entertainment he has provided over recent years. He, perhaps, has been the greatest dribbler, the most superb ball manipulator, in the whole history of the game, and we must never forget his witchcraft, for we shall probably never see its like again. He has been the wrecker of defences by drawing opponents on to himself, drawing them in as close as an expert bullfighter draws the bull. And by much the same method, and expert economy, he eludes the danger he seems to court, having created fatal gaps in the defence elsewhere for others to turn to account. There has always seemed a conspiracy between the ball and Matthews' feet to meet at some given point of time. And having made contact, it has been a joy and a fascination to watch him probe defences, then bewilder, then exploit. He has been, and is, the sensitive antennae of every forward line he has graced at outside-right. It is in working within limitations that the true master reveals himself, and the limitation, the very condition of art, is style. Matthews has fulfilled every demand of the connoisseur to make many an afternoon a wondrous thing by his unsurpassed magic. *

GEOFFREY GREEN, *Great Moments in Sport*

T*HE* peace-time England team which set out again for unknown horizons in 1946 was very much, to repeat Male, a group of professionals playing as amateurs: both in the spirit in which they played the game, and the continuing naïvity of selection and instinctive spontaneity of tactics. Male, of course, was no longer part of the scene, having been succeeded by his Highbury colleague, Laurie Scott; while at left-back the reign of Hapgood had given way, on the first occasion back in 1943, to George Hardwick of Middlesbrough. As captain and player, Hardwick was the personification of the old professional school.

In 1935, at the age of fourteen and a half, George had joined the firm of Dorman Long as an apprentice draughtsman at the grand salary of eight shillings and ninepence (44p) a week, playing for a school eleven on Saturday morning and South Bank East End Juniors in the afternoon, together with Harold Shepherdson, who in later years would become the England trainer. At seventeen, Hardwick signed for Middlesbrough, having played in their reserves, with confidence, in a team that contained five senior internationals, such was then the size and competitiveness of professional staffs. He had been born at Saltburn in North Yorkshire, then moved to nearby Linsdale where his father, an electrician, found work in the ironstone mines. There were three thousand inhabitants in Linsdale, and it was not uncommon in those days to have a crowd of two thousand five hundred watching the school team on a Saturday morning. Unemployment in the mid–1930s in the northeast was running at 65 per cent; mothers knitted the players' stockings.

Much was expected of the young professional. At a medical inspection by the club doctor, Hardwick recalls a boy being reprimanded for having no tie, being told to get one and reminded: 'You are part of an honourable profession, and don't forget it.' If a youngster arrived at training not having shaved, he would be reported to the manager. If he misbehaved on an away trip, he was out of the team for the next match.

I made my first-team debut six weeks after signing professional, and at that time I was the youngest player to appear for the club in the First Division [George recalls]. I had a run of sixteen matches, one against Stan. Wilf Mannion was two years older than me, and I remember, the first time we were together in the international squad, Wilf saying, 'this is the easy weekend, we're with the good players.'

If you called for the ball in the England side, you could expect to get it. In that first match against Stan at Stoke, I'd never seen the ground so heavy, your feet disappeared, yet even on that surface he was so quick. Nobody had advised me anything about him beforehand, but even if they had I think I'd have been too frightened to listen. Yet later, when I became England captain, I found I could control the senior players, such as Mannion and Carter – they'd listen. Stan was always so tense in the coach on the way to the stadium, he'd never join in any singing with the rest. We used to pull his leg about not scoring goals, but he'd have his thrill before the ball was in the net. I think he was quite shrewd, he would only play thirty games or so each season in later years, and this preserved his physique. I only played against him once at Ayresome Park [Middlesbrough's ground].

There was always some difficulty in those early post-war years between Walter and some of the established players. Walter expected discipline. Once, we were training at Southport before going over to play Ireland, and Walter had us practising the wall-pass, and Raich was saying, 'I was doing this when I was ten, what's the effing point?' Raich didn't take kindly to being told how to play the game.

Winterbottom had been appointed in the summer of 1946, and though he had the first-hand experience of a reasonably competent professional player, his studious, slightly earnest manner as manager, well-intentioned and friendly in the extreme though it was, tended to put some of the players, especially those with far greater ability than he, on edge.

International matches, were, let's face it, still a bit of a jolly in those days, a matter of 'Let's have a go, lads' [Winterbottom says]. Hitherto, trainers had been people who looked after the baggage and saw you went to bed on time. My role was restricted by the fact that I was discouraged, both by the selectors and the managers of individual clubs, from playing people out of their normal position, even though it might have suited our team and in some instances the player himself.

Chairmen and managers would ring me up and say that I was disrupting their side. When I wanted to play Bobby Charlton inside rather than on the wing, Matt Busby objected and said he was best on the wing. Yet that [inside] was where Bobby ultimately played for both Manchester United and for England. When we picked Billy Wright at inside-left against Austria in 1951, specifically to counteract the threat from Austria's most creative player, Ocwirk, the Wolves chairman publicly protested that we were disrupting his team.

Winterbottom discovered to his dismay that many managers and coaches were unfamiliar with the laws of the game, and at a seminar shortly after Rous had published a referee's chart, only five of the managers attending the course had read it, taking the view that 'that was referees' business'.

Another principle which Winterbottom attempted to introduce, if and when his selection committee was agreeable, was the use of two or more players from the same club team. Stoke, as recalled, had on one occasion before the war provided three forwards, and there had been those seven members of the Arsenal team included in 1934. In the post-war period there was no club colleague at Stoke with whom Stanley could be linked in the England side. That situation was soon to change.

Having missed the opening four matches of the 1946-7 season – as described in the previous chapter – Stanley once more found himself in disagreement with Stoke around the time of his recall to the England side against Scotland the following year. As before, disagreement arose between him and Bob McGrory, the Stoke manager. The rift had opened during his period of injury in the autumn, which led to absence from the England side. A pulled thigh muscle had resulted in Stanley's withdrawal from his club team for some weeks, during which time Stoke enjoyed a successful run, including the 5–2 defeat of Chelsea in front of 68,000 spectators in London. Stanley's replacement, George Mountford, received much praise; and the following Saturday, now fit again, Stanley expected to return for the away match against Arsenal. McGrory suggested that he should instead have a run with the reserves. Stanley declined; he was not defying the manager, for the suggestion was not an instruction.

SM: I don't know why, but somehow McGrory wasn't happy with me, even before the war. Envious? Maybe he was, because he'd been a player with Stoke, and I'd replaced his pal Bobby Liddle. There was always that feeling, an undercurrent between us. In 1947 Mountford, who had been on the groundstaff and came from Kidderminster, had played well in my absence, yet I honestly couldn't take seriously McGrory's suggestion that I was not worth my place in the first team when fit. He and I had words, and I told him to leave me out of the reserve side. The next morning the story was in the newspapers, and to make matters worse there was a suggestion in one of them that the players had sent a deputation to McGrory requesting that I should not be brought back. That was hurtful. For the next few days life was a turmoil, though I tried to continue attending to my own affairs, training at the Blackpool ground each morning and supervising the hotel which we now had in Blackpool. Yet I was in a perilous position. Football was my livelihood, and once I began to slip, I intended to go out of the game. But I had no reason to believe that I'd already started to decline, and that was why I thought it was ill-advised to agree to play in the reserves. I was delighted, I must say, when Neil Franklin, the club captain, let me know by letter that he had called a meeting of the players, in order to deny that they had any grievance against me. They had agreed that Franklin should communicate this to the directors.

Franklin, who was himself to become the centre of a transfer controversy with Bogota in Colombia, says:

It is rubbish to say that Stan was not popular. He was a man admired and loved by us all. Every footballer recognized his genius, and no player would be silly enough to be jealous of a genius in his side. Matthews, or course, is the reserved reticent type, but that does not mean he is unpopular. Quite the reverse. I didn't blame him for disagreeing with the suggestion that he should play in the reserves. As soon as I heard about the rumours [the request to leave him out of the first team], I felt it essential as captain to ask the players if I could deny the story, which I did.

Following a meeting with the directors, it was agreed that Stanley should take another week's rest, should continue to train at Blackpool, and there were handshakes all round. A press release announced that differences had been resolved. But not for long. Troubles rose to the surface again by Easter. With the usual crowded holiday programme of games on Friday, Saturday and Monday, and in view of the fact that he was due to play the following Saturday against Scotland, Stanley asked to be rested for the Good Friday game at Grimsby. McGrory agreed, but he expected Matthews to be at Stoke the following day to play against Huddersfield. Stanley said he would be there.

Stoke won comfortably at Grimsby, and Stanley was prepared to co-operate if McGrory wanted to keep a winning side. 'At 10.30, the manager said he wanted me to play, and to be at the ground at the usual time,' Stanley recalls. 'Yet when I arrived an hour before the match I was told I was not needed. That was fair enough, but McGrory could have told me straight-forwardly in the morning. We beat Huddersfield, and I was told an unchanged team would be fielded against Grimsby at Stoke on Easter Monday. Sound enough policy.'

Stanley played against Scotland the next weekend as scheduled, and his name was included among six forwards named the following Wednesday for Stoke's match that Saturday at home to Brentford. Stanley played on the wing, and Mountford moved to inside-right. Yet after the match, Stanley discovered that he had only been included because another player was injured; and the evidence was there in the original selection, without his name, printed in the match programme. The directors denied that he was to have been left out, but it was clear to Stanley that there was a declining degree of mutual confidence between him and the club. So he requested a meeting with the directors once more; this was fixed for 23 April.

Following a lengthy discussion with the board, and Stanley's explanation of his wish to leave so as to avoid continual travelling to Stoke, which made even a home fixture an away game, the directors, after initially refusing, agreed to his transfer to Blackpool. It was a condition that no statement should be made, that he should remain until the end of the season, and that negotiations with Blackpool would open in July. Secrecy within football is as secure as water in a sieve; within twenty-four hours the news was round the country. Reporters were waiting for Stanley when he caught the boat for Belfast, two days later, to play with the Football League against the Irish. Accusations of bad sportsmanship and an ultimatum to the Stoke directors were rife.

SM: The breaking of the news, not by me, again made my private life miserable with all the publicity, but it did have the effect of accelerating my transfer to Blackpool. Negotiations were held up because Stoke asked for far more than the £11,500 they would eventually receive. The Blackpool chairman, Colonel Parkinson, insisted that, as I made the request to go to Blackpool, he was not prepared to pay a record fee. I was sad to be leaving, but I knew that in his heart McGrory wanted to get rid of me. Besides, business is business, you can't necessarily stay all your life in one place, and I was now thirty-two. Blackpool were taking a chance, even at a fee of £11,500, because of my age. Many people thought that I was almost finished, on the way out, though Blackpool didn't ask for a medical, they just said, 'we'd like you.' I signed the forms in Glasgow, just before midnight, following Great Britain's match against the Rest of Europe. One of the embarrassments was when Blackpool went to play Stoke shortly afterwards, and we beat them. The Stoke full-back, Kennedy, was getting a bit rough with me, and was sent off. I was grateful that Sir Francis Joseph, the president of Stoke, had taken me aside and wished me the best of luck with my new club, a generous gesture.

Peter Buxton was present for the Blackpool match when there was, predictably, a huge crowd. Buxton requested a couple of tickets from McGrory and received the reply: 'Sorry, bighead's got them all.' There was undoubtedly resentment on the part of the manager; wholly without justification in Buxton's opinion. Disillusionment with the club was not confined to their former outside-right. The rift had also developed with the Supporters Club, as a result of which George Birks and several colleagues co-ordinated to build a social club, provocatively, right opposite the main entrance to the football ground.

Joe Smith, Blackpool's wily old manager, had one or two conversations with Stanley before the transfer; as you might suppose, considering they both lived in Blackpool. 'You're thirty-two. Do you think you can make it for another couple of years?' Joe had asked him. The moderate question had received a modest answer. Stanley said he thought so; and had proceeded to substantiate his personal optimism during the match in Glasgow. The Europe team contained two of the outstanding Swedish forwards, Gren and Nordahl, who would the next year win the Olympic Games in London, while the captain at right-half was Johnny Carey of Manchester United and Eire. *The Times* reported: 'Only in the first half-hour did Europe live with England. Matthews, supplied by Mannion, lost Steffen, the Swiss full-back, and the rest of the defence from the beginning. What remains to be said that has not been said a thousand times before?'

SM: We went off on a beam that day, and you could tell from the start that we were heading for an easy victory. Wilf scored after twenty minutes, and there should have been more, but Praest, the Danish left-winger, beat Hardwick to make an opening for Nordahl to equalize. Mannion put us in front again, and Billy Steel beat three defenders and knocked in the third from at least thirty yards. I'm sure this goal will have bumped up the £15,500 fee which Derby had to pay to Morton for his signature following the match. Tommy Lawton scored two in the second half, one from my cross, and the sixth in a 6–1 win was an unlucky own goal by Parola, an excellent centre-half from Italy. It may not have been a serious match, but the crowd of 134,000 had really enjoyed themselves.

Five days later, the England party flew to Switzerland for the start of the summer tour, and Stanley's first match for his country as a Blackpool player after seventeen years on the books at Stoke. As mentioned earlier, Stanley played in a match which England lost by the only goal in Zurich, with Langton on the left-wing; and from there the party moved to Lisbon.

SM: Our headquarters at the resort of Estoril, eight miles out of Lisbon, were luxurious. The gardens there were some of the finest I'd ever seen, a mass of colour and perfume running from the sea-front up to the casino. With the sea and the blue sky and the palatial white buildings, it truly was a millionaire's playground. There were some odd local customs that puzzled us. You had to wear, in those days, a singlet as well as bathing trunks to go swimming, and we had the police coming up to us on the beach to explain our error. It was also forbidden to use a cigarette lighter on the street without a licence, apparently in deference to the government-controlled match-making industry. And there were on-the-spot fines for jay-walking. We were taken to a bull fight, though it isn't something I care for. The bulls are not killed, the way they are in Spain, which is better, and you had to admire the horsemanship and the skill of the matadors. Before the match we drove out to see the wonderful new national stadium. I'd played there for the RAF, yet every time you go there it is as impressive as ever – a semi-circle of white marble costing, in those days, almost half a million pounds, with seating for 70,000 and a pitch as perfect as Wembley's used to be, with turf that had been brought from Cumberland.

As already related, Langton was unfit, so Finney was included on the left wing. An argument about the ball delayed the kick-off, the Portuguese wishing to use the smaller Size Four. Winterbottom insisted on a full-size ball. The first time it went out of play after the match started, the Portuguese adroitly switched back to a Size Four: but the ball had had to be retrieved from their own net. Lawton headed England in front in little more than ten seconds. The ball change would not protect the Portuguese from a thrashing, as England proceeded to give a sumptuous display.

SM: Within seven minutes we were two up when Morty scored a typical goal with a raking shot. Four minutes later, Lawton put one in from almost twenty-five yards, and Finney scored the fourth following a twisting dribble that began in his own half. The crowd applauded, but were beginning to jeer their goalkeeper, Azevedo. The team manager tried to switch goalkeepers, sending out Capela. Walter tried to protest, but the referee allowed the change. Then they switched their right-back, but nothing could hold us up now. Lawton scored his third and we led 5–0 at half-time. My full-back, Feliciano, had given up by now. Morty got another, and even I scored, so that we reached double figures. The Portugal team were so ashamed that they failed to attend a banquet that night and were later suspended by their association. I was glad when the FA requested the Portuguese to lift the suspension.

The revelation of the match had been Mortensen. Roy Peskett reported in the *Mail:* 'The introduction of Mortensen gave a lightning thrust to the attack, and he justifiably shared eight of the goals with Lawton.' Mortensen himself considers that this may have been his best match with Matthews, but that his own peak performance came the following year in Italy. Although the British national newspapers nearly all sent correspondents to Lisbon, the coverage in the middle of the cricket season was slight. After all, who were the Portuguese? The mentality at home was as insular as ever. Lawton, who played fifteen consecutive matches immediately after the war, believes that this team was better than that which scored so freely in 1938–39. 'After the war, Stan, for instance, was twice as good a player,' Tommy says. 'He knew when to go, when not to. Before the war, he could be impetuous, but now he had experience. *I* was a better player after the war. What a forward line we had! There was such understanding, a line without selfishness. If you were in space, you'd get the ball. We had such great players that they didn't give you the ball, even if in trouble themselves, if you were pinned down.'

Stanley's assurance to Joe Smith was being vindicated; never more so than in England's opening match of the following season, when they went to Brussels and whipped the Belgians 5–2. Stanley, though not scoring, had a hand in all five goals by Lawton and Finney, who scored two each, and Mortensen. The match is remembered, not with pain but almost pride, by the Belgian left-back, Joe Pannaye. It has been the experience of so many left-backs to discover that to be roasted by Matthews was in a strange way often an enhancement of their reputation. Certainly their names became better known on account of an afternoon's embarrassment; and Pannaye, like many other left-backs, has dined out on his experience of September 1947 for the past 42 years:

Every other day I meet someone who I haven't seen for a while, and they ask if I remember that afternoon against Matthews at the Heysel Stadium [Pennaye says]. It's no surprise, of course, for Matthews was a brilliant player and I was a bit ridiculous against him. I'd played in England when we lost 2–0 the year before, and had had a reasonable game then. Yet you couldn't, as a defender, resist his dribble: the feint inside, the sudden switch outside. It's used by many players now, but it was unusual at the time. If I'd had a third chance, maybe I would have known better. Matthews also had a marvellous way of crossing the ball, such an accuracy for finding Lawton or Mortensen, to create an opening for them to shoot. He was the best player I've even seen. A ghost. I never played against Pelé or Cruyff, but in my time it was an unwelcome task to play against Matthews. That day he gave a brilliant performance. His first three dribbles were fantastic. I asked some of those close to me to help, but they too could do nothing. When he beat me, he'd beat another. The next day was the fiftieth anniversary of the Belgian FA, and everyone was happy that we should lose to such a side as this. I never met Matthews again afterwards, but have had many opportunities to talk about this phenomenon. It was remarkable that he played so long. He was exceptional in many ways, both as an athlete and as a professional, someone who did so much for the sport.

Billy Wright, who played at wing-half for the first sixty or so of his 105 caps, has a vivid memory of that match:

Belgium were on the way up as a soccer nation at that time, and 70,000 people ignored the heavy rain and wind to be there. With such bad conditions, you would never have expected such a classic exhibition, and to stand behind Stan on that bleak afternoon was a pleasure for which I would willingly have surrendered all my previous caps. He did amazing things with the ball on such a slippery surface, and I felt sorry for Pannaye, the young Belgian left-back. As Matthews sent him the wrong way with a shrug of his shoulders time after time, the misery on the Belgian's face became more and more noticeable. On several occasions Stan was even too quick for his English colleagues. To Pannaye's credit, he never once stooped to anything unfair in his attempt to halt his opponent. It was an exhibition of artistry I would never see again.

Winterbottom recounts that when Matthews made the fourth goal, an extraordinary moment, not only the crowd of 70,000 but both teams and the whole of the VIP box stood and applauded him back to the half-way line. The result of the match had until that moment been uncertain. In the first half-minute Matthews had beaten Pannaye and crossed for Lawton to head a first goal. Fifteen minutes later another centre, in the middle of a cloudburst, found Lawton, whose header sent Mortensen through for a second goal. Five minutes later Matthews, when fouled, took the free-kick and enabled Finney to head the third. However, Belgium hit back to score twice, and with the crowd roaring for their team, England were now wilting under some pressure. Ivan Sharpe describes what happened next:

Matthews came to the rescue. He received the ball on the half-way line, tricked one opponent and moved ahead. He tricked another opponent, evaded a third tackle, then a fourth. Now he was running along the goal-line from the corner flag, and the goalkeeper, seeing the invader at the door, started to advance towards him. No sooner had he left his goal than Matthews – I use a golfing term, as that is how it struck me – seized his niblick and scooped the ball over the advancing goalkeeper's head. It fell in front of the empty goal, and Finney scored.

George Hardwick, who remembers that moment as one of the

highlights of his professional career, says: 'I'm sure Stan did it just to show us. And having done it he walked back to the half-way line quite unconcerned, with his head down.' Both teams had just witnessed something beyond their comprehension, yet to this day Stanley remains disarmingly casual about it. 'It was greasy that day,' he says, with a far-away, matter-of-fact gaze. 'And that was beautiful, because it helps a forward.' He says it with that lack of assumption, as though anyone could have done what he did, had they been so minded. Afterwards, Harold Palmer of the *Evening Standard* came down to the dressing-room to ask why, seemingly, Stanley had held on to the ball so much over the last ten minutes. 'I said to Harold that if they didn't know in the press box, then certainly I didn't.'

Genius carries no briefing, and a month later Stanley was dazzling the Welsh in Cardiff. The same forward line was at work: Matthews, Mortensen, Lawton, Mannion and Finney. The myth persists that the greatest post-war England forward line was Matthews, Carter, Lawton, Mannion and Finney; yet in fact that formation never took the field, for in the seven opening matches, which were the only times Carter was present, either Finney or Matthews was on the right and Langton or Mullen on the left.

England beat Wales 3–0, and the luckless full-back on this occasion who faced Stanley was Wally Barnes of Arsenal, making his first international appearance. 'The newspapers were full of conjecture about whether Ronnie Burgess and I could hold the Blackpool wonder-wing of Mortensen and Matthews,' wrote Barnes in his autobiography, *Captain of Wales*. 'Matthews was a name that began to haunt me. I tried to recall all that I had heard and seen at first hand of the men who had been both colleague and opponent in Services matches. The result was not comforting. He was about to play his fifty-second international for England . . . and with this problem-picture in my mind, I reached our hotel in Porthcawl, where the first person I set eyes upon was Stanley. He greeted me in his usual friendly manner. We spent five minutes or so together while he signed autographs for friends of mine. It was the nearest I was to get to him during our stay in South Wales!'

The team which had overwhelmed Portugal and then Belgium now took Wales apart, and within twenty minutes the match was effectively over. After nine minutes, Finney half-volleyed a superb goal from an oblique angle, and five minutes later Matthews bemused Barnes to lay on the second goal for Mortensen. In the twentieth minute Mannion made a third for Lawton.

By now I had lost face with a large section of the crowd [Barnes wrote]. They considered I was giving Matthews too much room. 'Get into him!' was the cry that rang in my ears, but I took no notice, retreating from Matthews' snaky runs like a cagey mongoose. I refused to do the one thing that the crowd most wanted me to do, which was to *tackle* him. Stan was dangerous enough as it was; if I allowed myself to be drawn, I was sure that he would create havoc, and a Lisbon-like result would follow. . . . I resigned myself to attempting to delay and hinder Stan from crossing the ball accurately. This I think I achieved fairly successfully. . . . Reporters criticized me for standing back in a 'tackle-less trance'. All I can say in my defence is that I played Stan the way I thought best . . . and I retained my place for the next match against Scotland. Two or three weeks later, I applied the same method when Blackpool played at Highbury, and had the satisfaction of gaining credit from the critics for 'shutting him out of the game'.

Barnes, who was one of the gentlemen of the game, died a few years ago. He played for Arsenal against Newcastle in the first FA Cup Final which I saw at Wembley in 1952, and seriously twisted his knee in attempting to hold Newcastle's effervescent left-winger, Elliot: an injury which contributed to Arsenal's 1–0 defeat that day.

With that performance in Cardiff, Matthews overtook Billy Meredith's record; and he was now in the middle of his most sustained spell of post-war appearances, thirteen in fifteen matches. England drew against Ireland 2–2 in November, and in April won 2–0 against Scotland at Hampden. The Scotland left-back that day, from Hibernian, was known as 'Tiger' Shaw; but the combination of Matthews and Mortensen, which was proving almost irresistible for any defence, would draw Shaw's teeth. In Hardwick's opinion, Stanley murdered him. However, Franklin was regarded by neutral observers as the man of the match for the way in which he subdued Thornton, the Rangers centre-forward, a fellow Desert Rat with Finney. *The Times* reported:

England had only two wins at Hampden in the previous twenty years, in 1927 and 1939, but this victory fell short of what was expected. Scotland set out to stop England from playing. Shaken and battered, England produced only flashes of brilliance. It was totally against the run of play when, a minute before half-time, a long clearance from Swift in goal reached Lawton; a flick to Pearson – who was deputizing for Mannion at inside-left – and on to Finney, who beat Govan and Young with a twist and then Black in goal. Scott and Hardwick were in trouble against Delaney and Liddell, and needed Franklin to be playing the game of his life. Macaulay at left-half was helping to mark Matthews, who seemed to have no appetite. The second goal came as Lawton put through an accurate pass for Mortensen.

This may not have been one of Stanley's better matches, but by now he was being mercilessly judged at the highest standard: by everyone, including his mother. Jack recalls that his first wife used to go regularly to international matches with his mother, and if Stanley had lost the ball twice in the match, his mother would come home and say, 'Stan's had a bad game today.' Hardwick, who on that day among a hard-pressed defence was captaining England for the last time, recollects: 'Stan loved to beat the Scots, he saved himself for those matches, especially at Hampden Park. You could almost see the gleam in his eye. If ever we wanted a rest, we gave the ball to Stan. He would hold it, and give you a breather. He'd only ever lose the ball into touch, never put you in trouble: he was so sound on the ball and in his passing.'

Meanwhile, the investment of Joe Smith was paying dividends, Blackpool progressing steadily towards their first appearance at Wembley in the Cup. Smith, who loved life almost as much as he loved football, was as euphoric as someone who has just bought a Derby winner. He would puff on his cigar and tell his men that he didn't care if they lost by six goals so long as they went out and entertained him. They do not make managers like that any more.

The contrast between Smith and McGrory could not have been more marked. Smith gave Stanley the freedom, of mind and style, that left his genius unfetted. 'Get a goal up before half-time if you can, Joe would say, so that I can enjoy my cigar,' Stanley relates. 'Mind you, he could be a mean old so-and-so over tickets. I'd have to wheedle with him just for another four in the paddock for a few friends: say to him, "We won last time, Joe, so how about it?" and he'd say "Oh, all right, here you are." He'd give me £2.50 in lieu of a pair of boots, which I got for myself from my deal with the Co-op, who marked a boot with my name. Joe would send cigars to the foreman at the factory. I developed one of the first lightweight boots; they were so soft, without toe caps, you could fold them up and put them in your pocket. Oh, they were beautiful! I used to sit and look at them, and feel the pleasure that they gave me. Yet when we played at Wolverhampton, you used to need webbed feet out there. It seemed they watered the pitch all winter. And the ball.'

Stanley continued to live, as he always would, his almost monastic existence, to which his family had become accustomed. His daughter Jean recalls his rigid self-discipline:

Often I went with him, as a youngster, to the beach at seven in the morning, because I enjoyed it, and liked being there with him. Every day his diet was the same: carrot juice at lunch-time and steak with a salad for dinner. Every Monday, he would go without any food at all, because he said that fasting one day a week made him feel so much better. Yet on Mondays you tended to keep out of his way, because he would be a bit short-tempered; and it was the same on Friday, the day before a match. The pattern of his life was as regular as can be. To the Turkish baths on Monday, which he enjoyed. He loved routine. When I started tennis, he gave it a try, he wanted to keep fit in the summer. We would play a family foursome. The fact that there were different wages between summer and winter left him free to go on independent tours in the summer, when he was not on a contract.

I was aware that he was something of a loner, but that was because he was both shy and anxious not to have a fuss, not wanting fame. If we went as a family to the cinema, we would arrive late and leave early, before the lights went up, so as to avoid publicity. And he had us all trained not to say anything on the telephone if strangers called. He didn't much like going to functions, he was happiest being at home. He was always playing something: cards, table tennis, whatever. He was such a sportsman on the football field, yet at home he could be so competitive, even with his children. 'I can't play social tennis,' he would say. Yet sportsmanship was taken for granted, that was how you were *expected* to be. He never reacted badly to failure, though on a Saturday night he rarely slept, whether they won or lost. He'd come in after a match and play solo with Jimmy Vallance, my uncle. He liked to win, but if the team lost, he didn't let it linger. Tomorrow was another day. His concession to his fame was exploiting the magnetism that he had for the crowd, and he would work on that during a match to utilize it.

Living close to nature, whether it was his preoccupation with a diet of carrot juice and salads, or being as free as a seagull on the beach, was part of the secret of Stanley's remarkable durability. 'The attraction was to be up at six and to know that I was settled in my rhythm for the day, out there before I went training. I'd have the place to myself, apart from one or two people out walking their dogs. I'd be back on the beach three afternoons a week after training, and walk from the South Shore to St Anne's (some six miles). One afternoon a week I'd go to Lytham for a seawater bath and a massage. Training on the beach was always on hard sand. I always loved that, it was a wonderful exhilaration in the open air.'

Stan Mortensen was profiting from the arrival of this rare winger, and never underestimated his own good fortune. It is fair to say that, for all Mortensen's own talent, his career blossomed through the development of his partnership with Stanley. Morty was a South Shields boy from Northumberland, and was brought to Blackpool by his father. He was seventeen when the war broke out, joined the RAF as a wireless operator/air gunner, and was stationed at Lossiemouth. During a train-ing flight, his Lancaster bomber crashed in fir trees, killing the pilot and bomb-aimer. The navigator lost a leg, and Morty, wriggling out through a hole in the top of the fuselage, had nothing more than a cut head. He was in hospital at Gleneagles for three weeks; but a short time after that was back in his football boots for a Scottish Select XI against the British Army at Aberdeen, scoring all four in a 5–4 defeat. He had the war-time distinction of representing, at different times, England, Scotland and Wales in the makeshift teams that were scram-bled together.

After the crash and my head injury, I couldn't take Morse Code any more [Morty says], so that was the end of me as a wireless operator, and I was grounded and sent to Chigwell. I played with Stan quite a bit during the war with different teams, and he was a great help. At Blackpool, we tried to work out one or two things during the week, small signs and so on to give an indication of what we were doing. I shared a room with him for years. We talked all the time, Stan would persuade me endlessly to go on repeating my old jokes. He used to pull my leg about the fact that I was nearly always last to arrive in the dressing-room, because the house of my wife's parents was only forty yards from the Blackpool ground, and I wouldn't leave until twenty minutes before the kick-off. 'Never fear, Morty's here,' Stan would jest, as I raced in to pull on my boots at the last minute.

We worked exactly the same together with England. I knew where to put the ball; and once he had it, I'd head off for left of the penalty spot, and then veer back towards the near post. That way, the near post was often left unprotected, and we worked at this. Stan had so many virtues: perfect fitness, superb balance, total confidence in his own ability, tremendous pace over twelve yards, a beautiful body swerve, mastery of the ball, complete two-footedness, an ideal tempera-ment and self-control. In short, the ideal poker player.

Such admiration took root everywhere. '*Alex James?*' Jimmy Seed, the manager of Charlton, would exclaim. 'James had the same powers as Matthews? Don't you believe it. James was never in the same league as Matthews is today. This winger has a pair of feet which are the greatest entertainment that football has ever known. They mesmerize the crowd so that it can't look at anything else. James never had the skill that Matthews showed in the international against Ireland [before the war]. The only way you could deal with him is never to let him get his foot on the ball. Once he gets possession, he is away and you're done.'

When Blackpool met Birmingham during 1947–48 the Birmingham left-back was Jack Badham. Blackpool won 2–1, and John Macadam wrote: 'Badham was mesmerized, hoodwinked, and pulverized with science all afternoon, yet never put a boot wrong against the master.' Such an attitude, an acceptance of their execution without resort to wanton fouling, was characteristic of the game in those days. I am conscious of the risk, in relating a professional career lasting 33 years, of sounding repetitive in the description of Stanley's mastery of one defender after another. Yet this is an aspect of his career which makes it so extraordinary. It was not that he had occasional masterful matches, perhaps two or three times a season, such as John Barnes or Chris Waddle has at the present time. Stanley destroyed defences week after week; and his bad matches, even his poorer matches, were the exception. It was a poor performance, not a good one, that was news.

When we played Spurs in the semi-final, the all-important equalizing goal was made possible because we exploited a move which we had not previously tried in that game [Mortensen has related]. Stan moved in slightly towards the inside-right position, and got the ball. Spurs expected him to dribble, as he had done so often during the second half. After a brief pause, Stan changed intention. The pause was important, because it enabled me to rush forward, directly ahead of him. While I was still moving, he gave me the through pass, which I was able to take without the need to bring it under control. The defence had held off, waiting for Stan to start his dribble, so that I was not put off-side. We did the same against the Italians in Turin a few weeks later, and again it led to a goal.

Before the final, Stanley was to be honoured with the award of the first Footballer of the Year trophy from the newly-formed Footballer Writers' Association: a bronze statuette which has come to be regarded as the most respected of English football awards. Members had voted for Mortensen in second position and Frank Swift as number three. In those days the dinner in London took place the night before the final, though in recent years, as a concession to the wish of managers anxious that their players should be properly rested, the statuette is presented on Thursday night.

Johnny Aston, the Manchester United full-back who would succeed Hardwick in the England team the following autumn, was the man due to face Matthews at Wembley. As a boy, Johnny played with Ravensbury School and then Clayton Methodist Chapel team, but never made it to the Manchester Boys XI. Apprenticed as an engineer with the English Steel Corporation, he then spent five years in the Marines, and his war-time football had been as an inside-forward. Demobilized in January, 1946, he did not think he would make the grade in professional football. Instead, he looked for a job in engineering. He is now retired and helping part-time in the retail business of his son John, who followed in his footsteps at Old Trafford and would appear in the winning European Cup side in 1968.

I'd written to Matt Busby from my troop-ship in the Middle East [says Johnny], and I posted the letter in Aden. When I arrived back, Matt asked me to go to his office, and suggested I join in training to see how I shaped. I lacked confidence, and wanted to play in the third team. After one match, I was promoted to the reserves, and after two matches found myself in the League side.

Stan had not played a lot in Manchester by 1948, though I knew he was something special. Yet I never worried about him, or any other player, once I had grown in confidence. If you stood close in on him, players tended not to give him the ball, but once he had it he was fantastic, and difficult to handle. You had to intercept before he got it. In that final, by then he was thirty-three, he did very little, and I think in our personal clashes I came out first. There's a newsreel flash of the Wembley game, which shows me on my hands and knees, but I think that was the only time he beat me! I enjoyed the occasion, it was a challenge. Stan wasn't averse to giving you a push: if he got a yard past you, you couldn't get back at him. I preferred playing against Matthews rather than Finney. Tom was more competitive, a grafter. Against Tom, you'd have to be up fighting for any ball in the air. Yet Stan was the better entertainer, and sometimes he played to the gallery a wee bit. Not that he went on the field with that intention. Busby's advice on Matthews for the final was to try to contain him, but I wanted him to have the ball so that I could really get into the game. Matt wanted Charlie Mitten, our outside-left, to come back and tackle, the way they do these days. I resented that, I thought it was an insult, and told him to bugger off.

In all his time as a professional, including his three seasons as an England full-back, Aston never earned more than £1,000 in one season.

It is indicative of the approach to football during this period, more than a criticism of Joe Smith, that Blackpool had no pre-match plan for their first ever Cup Final, other than to play football at all costs: no special provision for dealing with United's dangerous wingers, Delaney and Mitten, no plan about how to close down Rowley, the opposing centre-forward. The only scheme, if it can be called that, was Smith's decision to play Mortensen at centre-forward, instead of in his normal position as partner to Stanley, on the expectation that Mortensen would exploit the lack of speed of Chilton, United's centre-half. This indeed happened, but the link with Matthews was broken; and none can judge whether Smith's tactics-by-selection were correct. Certainly they would be criticized, before and afterwards. In the semi-final against Spurs, there had been only three minutes to go when Mortensen equalized; and then, in extra time, he scored twice more to put Blackpool in the Final.

SM: We were a team without nerves, and that applied even to Johnny Crosland, an accountant and part-time professional, who had been brought in at the last minute in place of Ronnie Suart at left-back, Suart being unfit. Johnny had won the DSO in the Fleet Air Arm, so a Wembley crowd wasn't going to unnerve *him*, even though he'd never played at left-back, his six League appearances having been at centre-half. Everyone sympathized with Jimmy McIntosh, our regular centre-forward, who made way for Mortensen, but this made an opening for Alec Munro. He'd been outside-right when I was transferred from Stoke, and now he came in at inside-forward.

Manchester United were appearing in the final without having played a single tie on their own ground. Old Trafford was still under repair and alteration, after being damaged by German bombs, and United shared the Maine Road ground with Manchester City. As City had been drawn three times at home, United had been forced to play elsewhere against Liverpool (3–0 at Goodison Park) and Charlton Athletic (2–0 at Huddersfield). Preston were beaten 4–1 at Maine Road; and Derby, including Carter and Steel, 3–1 in the semi-final at Hillsborough. Their Cup run had an aggregate of eighteen goals against six in five cup-ties, all on 'away' pitches. Blackpool had been equally prolific, disposing of Leeds (4–0 at home), Chester (4–0 at home), Colchester (5–0 at home), Fulham (2–0 away), and Spurs (3–1 after extra time in the semi-final at Villa Park): an easier run, with an aggregate of eighteen to one. On a sunny day, the teams lined up as follows:

MANCHESTER UNITED: Crompton; Carey, Aston; Anderson, Chilton, Cockburn; Delaney, Morris, Rowley, Pearson, Mitten.
BLACKPOOL: Robinson; Shimwell, Crosland; Johnston, Hayward, Kelly; Matthews, Munro, Mortensen, Dick, Rickett.

The cards appeared to favour Blackpool, and it continued to look that way, when, after presentation to the King, Blackpool set the pace and took the lead after a quarter of an hour. Taking a long through pass down the middle, Mortensen swept past the tall and ponderous Chilton. Mortensen seemed clear, when a lunging tackle from behind by the centre-half brought him down. The referee, C. J. Barrick of Northampton, pointed to the penalty spot. It had been a crude foul against a player usually deadly in such a position; yet photographs would later show that, although Mortensen fell inside the area, the trip had been committed in the 'D' just outside. Shimwell drove the penalty past Crompton; but Manchester, undeterred, began to play some fine football built around their fluid inside-forward trio of Morris, Rowley and Pearson. After half an hour, following a string of corners, they were level as Hayward and Robinson confused each other on a lob from Delaney, and Rowley was able to glide between them and score.

Within five minutes Blackpool were ahead again. A cunning free-kick by Matthews found Kelly, whose pass sent Mortensen away to beat Crompton with a cross shot. The score was still 2–1 at half-time; and as the second half began, Blackpool began to establish a clear command of the match. With only twenty minutes remaining, the Cup seemed theirs. Now came the turning-point.

Hugh Kelly, Blackpool's 24-year-old left-half, clashed with Morris to the right of the penalty area. While Blackpool's defence hesitated, not sure which way the kick had been given, Morris quickly placed the ball on the head of Rowley, and Manchester had equalized again. Kelly was mortified, for he considered he had not fouled Morris in any way, merely stumbling and putting out a hand as Morris cut across him. But the damage was done, and now Blackpool's poise was gone.

Yet still the Cup could have been theirs. With twelve minutes to go, Chilton, in trouble the whole afternoon against Mortensen, lost the ball once more and Mortensen was away, racing through an open defence. His shot was going for the corner of the net, only for Crompton to pull off the save of the match at full length. Within moments, at the other end, Pearson had struck to put Manchester in front for the first time and now Blackpool were groggy. When Anderson, Manchester's right-half, drove past Robinson from thirty yards, the match had turned a somersault.

SM: None of us had any grudge against the referee, but Morris's free-kick was the turning point. The referee was in a good position and thought Morris had been pulled off the ball. Kelly at the time thought the free-kick was in his favour. We didn't complain, and we might still have won if Morty had scored when he broke clear with the score still 2–2. We were not disgraced, and it had been, in the opinion of many people, then and ever since, one of the best of all Cup Finals. Both managers, Matt Busby and Joe Smith, and both teams had only one intention, and that was to play good football.

I think the decision to switch Morty was justified, though frankly the players in the team never really thought about it. In those days, when the manager announced what the team was, nobody questioned it, even in their mind. You just accepted it, and got on with the job.

109

Oddly, perhaps, for someone regarded throughout his career as such a sportsman, it was Stanley's opinion that a Blackpool player should have knocked the ball away at the moment of Morris's free-kick, before he had time to take it. That, at least, was his opinion expressed some time after the match; now, however, having seen the lengths to which such gamesmanship is carried nowadays, he is less sure that such a ploy would have been legitimate. The final analysis on the day was that Manchester's victory had been a just reward for one of football's other fine sportsmen, their captain Carey. There is almost no player in the modern game to compare with Carey's versatility, though maybe Bryan Robson, his successor forty years on, comes close. Carey's positional sense and passing were supreme, and he played for Manchester United, in this period of intense competition among great players, in nine different positions; and, as an international for Ireland, North and Republic, as was still possible prior to 1950, in seven.

Carey, a benign figure as player and later as manager, and much in the mould of Busby, has the warmest recollections of the 1948 final. 'It was a marvellous match,' he says, 'because both teams on the day played nearly at their best. The turning point was certainly the free kick. Stanley had a fine match. He was a truly astonishing player, because his speed off the mark was the fastest you ever saw, I never met anyone like him, he was there one moment and gone the next.'

Jack was there at Wembley with the rest of the Matthews family. 'We all went up, as you'd expect, and I'm sure Blackpool would have won but for the free-kick,' Jacks says. 'They were too gentlemanly about it, they should have stood in front of the ball. But that's fate. On the other hand, looking back all these years later, I think maybe it was best that Stan lost his first two Cup Finals, otherwise there would never have been that historic climax, would there?'

Putting disappointment behind him, Stanley set off a week or two later with the England party to play Italy in Turin. They were travelling by four-engined propeller aircraft – a journey that would take almost twice as long as in the days of jet travel – via Zurich, where they changed to two smaller Dakotas, one each for players and press. Raymond Glendenning, the BBC commentator, needed oxygen going over the Alps, while Vernon Morgan of Reuters, fortifying himself with neat schnapps from a bottle, fell flat on his face on arrival in Milan, in front of ten thousand waiting spectators. As in 1939, on arrival the team rested first at Stresa, lying on the edge of Lake Maggiore; and as in 1939 the weather soon turned wet, which the English, with that strange conviction that it seldom rains anywhere but England, therefore regarded as a good omen.

SM: During the flight, my mind turned back to those earlier matches against Italy at Highbury and Milan. We knew that the Italians would be as difficult to beat as ever, and we'd been told that they were on a bonus of a hundred pounds each to win. We were getting nothing more than twenty pounds – win, lose or draw. We should also have been going to play Czechoslovakia in Prague, but the match was cancelled after the country fell to the Communist coup, and the FA was unable to arrange an alternative against Spain in Madrid because, we understood, of currency exchange problems. For the first time since the war, we were going to be without George Hardwick as captain at left-back, because he was unfit, and his place was taken by Howe of Derby. There'd been a worry about Frank Swift being fit, but he was cleared for the trip and, for the first time, a goalkeeper was named as captain. He'd been skipper of Manchester City for a couple of seasons.

The match would be memorable for two things in particular: a wonderful first goal scored by Mortensen, and the refereeing of Pedro Escartin of Spain. Twice, after Mortensen had scored, Escartin disallowed goals by Menti, the Italian outside-right, for being off-side. Geoffrey Green, celebrated correspondent of *The Times*, who was on his first overseas trip with England, recalls that both were fractional decisions, and that Escartin 'was a fearless and honest man to have had the courage, as a Latin, to refuse two goals to fellow Latins beneath their own blue Italian sky.' The rain had relented and it was now a scorching day, even at the late kick-off time of five in the afternoon.

Green, nowadays turning over the leaves of memory in his cottage by the Thames at Twickenham, says that there were 400,000 applications for tickets for the match, from all over Europe, when the ground capacity was only 70,000. 'In Stresa, it was as though we were the Beatles of another era, showered with flowers, surrounded by television cameras – absolute chaos at all times,' Green says. 'Charlie Buchan, working for the *Chronicle*, had a birthday, and so did I, but it was not a good day: because of the storm in the morning, all the telephone lines were down and we were unable to get through our preview stories for the morning of the match. There was a raging black market for tickets in the hotel, and some heavy betting.' The teams would line up as follows:

ITALY: Bacigalupo; Ballarin, Eliani; Annovazzi, Parola, Grezar; Menti, Loich, Gabetto, Mazzola (capt.), Carapellese.
ENGLAND: Swift (*Manchester City*, capt.); Scott (*Arsenal*), Howe (*Derby*); Wright (*Wolves*), Franklin (*Stoke*), Cockburn (*Manchester United*); Matthews (*Blackpool*), Mortensen (*Blackpool*), Lawton (*Notts County*), Mannion (*Middlesbrough*), Finney (*Preston*).

It was a year later that many of this great Italian team would perish in an aircrash, their plane hitting a hill on the outskirts of Turin while returning from a club match. Now they were in full flood as they almost overran the England defence, and it was thanks mainly to Swift in the opening quarter of an hour that England were able to hold on to a slender one-goal lead, as Billy Wright recalls:

Frank made one amazing save from Gabetto, their centre-forward. Gabetto was left beating the turf with his fists in frustration. We were in a bad way at this stage, and I remember Henry Cockburn shouting at Matthews, 'Get your bloody self in the game, we're chasing shadows.' Stanley as usual was wanting the ball to be played out to him, but Henry didn't care about that; though at half-time someone joked with Henry, 'You can't speak like that to Stan!' Wilf Mannion had fought the Italians in North Africa and was disparagingly saying to Tom Finney, 'I'm going to get this Italian waiter's feet [Annovazzi] red hot before I'm finished.'

Mannion was true to his word. Towards the end of the match, Vittorio Pozzo, a renowned coach who had guided Italy to World Cup victory before the war, was dashing up and down the touch-line squirting his players with a soda syphon, as they hung on for dear life in the attempt to prevent England extending a four-goal margin. What drama had surrounded that first goal. As Green recalled in *Great Moments in Sport:*

It remains the most spectacular bolt from the blue in my experience. It was scored by Mortensen a mere four minutes after the kick-off, and it was so astonishing, so unlikely, that it knocked all the breath and arrogance out of an Italian side which, at that time, was generally regarded as the most talented in all Europe. It set the tide running for an English victory which Walter Winterbottom still regards, dispassionately and objectively, as one of the best performances achieved by England in the international field. I can still see it, still hear the astonished, painful grunt of that 75,000 crowd, like some huge animal stopped in its tracks by a hunter's bullet. It happened in the bat of an eyelid. Wright came out of defence, brushing aside the pressure as he fed Matthews down the wing. A feint to the right, a swivel inwards to the left, and the maestro had left two defenders on the wrong foot. But instead of holding the ball close, Matthews released a long through pass some forty yards ahead with his left foot and beyond the Italian left-back. He had spotted his partner Mortensen moving ahead like the wind, along an inside-right course. In a few strides Mortensen was level with the pass, clear of the defence, still going like a train but perfectly balanced. In a flash, Parola saw the danger. Leaving the centre of defence, he too moved to his left, aiming either to tackle or shepherd the intruder away towards the touch-line. As Parola hit his man, Mortensen had reached a point some three or four yards short of where the penalty area joins the goal-line. Fractionally before he was sent sprawling, Mortensen released a piercing right-foot arrow, which miraculously bent into the top near corner of the Italian goal, a shot which perhaps not even the great Pelé himself would have thought feasible from such an angle and at such a speed.

Aston was sitting on England's bench, and says that the ball was thrown out to Wright by Swift. 'It went from our goal to theirs without them touching it and was the first time we'd been in the penalty area,' Aston says. In spite of this stunning setback, Italy's accomplished players responded with character, style and venom, and would surely have scored two or three times but for Swift. Gabetto had another shot which crashed against the cross-bar, bounced down, and was smothered on the line by Swift. Two close-range headers by Carapellese were also parried by Swift, and the soul of the Italian team was crushed, soon after those off-side decisions against Menti, when England scored again to go two up. Once more it was a counter-attack, of similar pattern. Franklin played the ball out of defence to Matthews, who sent two defenders the wrong way as he swayed towards them like a scavenging gull. Another long forward pass sent Mortensen clear of their defence. This time, instead of shooting, Mortensen pulled the ball back across the goalmouth, and Lawton was there to hit it from near the penalty spot, a knife of a shot past Bacigalupo's right hand. Lawton, in fact, was carrying an injury, and had not told Winterbottom; who, though thrilled with the result, was less than impressed by Lawton's attitude. For whatever reason, Lawton played only once more for England, at the start of the next season.

For the first fifteen minutes of the second half Italy rallied, but again Swift was their equal, turning away a couple of possible goals. England eased themselves into the final phase of the match that saw Finney sweeping in on passes from Mannion for two more goals, while Pozzo writhed in distress on the touch-line.

Afterwards, Green and Mortensen met in the bar: a rendezvous where their respective colleagues could usually expect to find them during the next few years. 'Will your report be in the paper?' Mortensen enquired with enthusiasm. 'I assume so,' Green replied, with that casual, old-school manner which endeared him to two generations of footballers. 'Did you intend that goal?' Green asked. 'You've got to have a bit of luck sometimes,' Mortensen answered, with an enigmatic grin. His was an incredible record: 23 goals in 25 international matches, and 21 in 35 FA Cup-ties. Finney recalls: 'We weren't given a cat in hell's chance before the match. That was probably the best we ever played. They were a great side, and they roasted us for half an hour.'

Following a draw against the then outstanding Danish side, in Copenhagen the next September, England moved on to Belfast where they thrashed the Irish 6–2. 'Denmark was my last game, I had a stinker,' Lawton reflects. 'Len Shackleton missed about four, and so did I. After the match, Winterbottom told me that Milburn would be picked the next time.' A small boy on the terraces behind one of the goals at Windsor Park was Jimmy McIlroy, aged fourteen, who remembers the game vividly:

The waves of English forwards kept coming towards me, and I was feeling sorry for our keeper, Tommy Breen of Linfield. England were unstoppable. I'd seen them two years before, when they won 7–2, and Carter, taking on the half-volley a ball headed down by Lawton, almost broke the net just above me. Lawton's heading was so impressive. He got so high and then seemed to hang there. The memories of Stanley are of those old cigarette-pack cards, and pictures of him in the newspapers crossing the ball with, in the background, two or three players whom he'd beaten sitting on the ground. That day in 1948, Stan scored the first goal, in off a post, and early in the second half Ireland were holding on 1–1. Then Stanley destroyed us, making three goals in ten minutes for Mortensen, who got two, and Milburn. Tom Finney was there, giving Carey a hard time, weaving his way past him.

Two months later and it was another six goals, this time against Switzerland at Highbury, the match postponed a day because of fog. Matthews and Hancocks, of Wolves, who was deputizing for Finney on the left, ran rings around the Swiss, according to *The Times*. Rowley scored on one of his six appearances for England; and Ramsey, 'who kicked beautifully', gained his first cap at right-back in place of Laurie Scott. The encounter with Scotland at Wembley in the spring was an anti-climax for England; and a triumph for Billy Steel of Derby, who scored the decisive goal, five minutes into the second half, which put Scotland 2–0 in front. Reilly of Hibernian and Milburn were late scorers in the 3–1 victory, in which Cowan, the Morton goalkeeper, had kept out England during the first half-hour. Steel had additionaly helped Cox, the Rangers left-back, to stifle Matthews.

In 1948–49, Blackpool had been knocked out of the Cup by Stoke, and towards the end of his second full season with the Lancashire club, now in his thirty-fourth year, Stanley was increasingly troubled by injuries. This caused him to miss the Scandinavian summer tour of

Sweden and Norway. Instead, Stanley spent the time trying to get fit, partially by his bizarre involvement in a tour of the vaudeville halls, playing head-tennis with his brother Ronnie. 'We were on stage twice nightly for about a quarter of an hour, and even in that time my ankle would swell up,' Stanley recalls. 'It was something I was talked into, and I didn't much enjoy it, but the reason I went was entirely because of the ankle. Some young full-back had whacked me in a charity match, he followed me everywhere, I suppose trying to make his name, and wouldn't lay off, even when I pointed out that we were only playing for charity.'

The head-tennis had come about through Stanley's friendship with Wee Georgie Wood, the midget comedian who used to appear at the South Pier, and with Charlie Chester, who spent two seasons at the Blackpool Opera House. Charlie stayed at Stanley's hotel and, after that was sold, at his house every time he appeared in Blackpool. They remained friends for thirty years, with Stanley's son, Stanley junior, staying with the Chesters at Finchley when his tennis career began to take off and he was playing in London. It was through Tom Moss, another comedian and a favourite in Lancashire, that Stanley was introduced to Arthur Millwood, an osteopath in Bury, who began treating him for the ankle injury and continued to nurse his limbs for the remainder of his career. Unquestionably, Millwood extended Stanley's playing life; being a vegetarian, he also had a strong influence on Stanley's diet, a further factor in maintaining such remarkable fitness.

'Stan was into bio-strath, and all that stuff, in a big way,' Charlie recalls, nowadays commuting to his weekly radio show for the BBC from his picturesque house in the Kent countryside. 'If you opened his cupboards, you could smell the malt; they were packed with phials of vitamins, B1 and B2. Stan and I have similar traits. I can sleep leaning up against the wall, and so can he. I could sleep before a Royal Command Performance [Chester appeared in four], and Stan could sleep on the coach on the way to a match. "I'm having a little practice," he would say, and it became a catch phrase.'

The venture into showbiz coincided with Stanley's brief sortie into horse-racing, with his ownership of Parbleu. The horse won him a few races, but never when he was able to watch it. 'After two years I sold it and got half my money back,' Stanley says. 'I used to go intermittently to all the northern courses: Pontefract, Doncaster, Haydock, Ayr. I was always interested in racing, though I wasn't a betting man.'

7. *SHOCK*

'*H*E moves about his house in much the same way as football crowds have seem him pad softly away from his wing, looking for a ball in an open space; a thin cat, sure of himself, but getting on a bit. Stanley Matthews never hurried himself on the football field, except in short spurts, and he is very much in repose off it... The figure you remember on cigarette-packet cards of the Thirties, and then in England's white shirt, with a clerk's hunch and his head plumb-line over the ball, is a mild surprise, close up. You half expect the freakish top-dressing of that spirit of youth which is claimed for him; but the face has all his years. It has absorbed experience, reacted to pain and effort. It is not innocent; it is acute to all around it, and it breaks up in frank and unreserved pleasure when friends touch a hair of the nostalgia which pokes through the skin of middle age. A player fixed big in the public eye ever since his teens, he has never yet taken football lightly. "It gets you here," he says, and the right fist taps his heart. The gesture has total conviction... He says he has enjoyed it all immensely, and we would be outraged if he said anything less. He gets up as daylight blooms, every morning all the year round, takes a cup of tea, and drives from his home to the beach; he breathes deep, he stretches, he sprints. After half an hour, or one-and-a-half, according to how soon his metabolism tells him he has done enough, he drives home, takes a cold shower and a breakfast of cereal, toast and honey... The way he has always played is the clue to his character: the intense concentration, so that he could walk right to the edge, as it were, before throwing all his speed, all his precision, into one sudden movement. He needed peak fitness for that. He was allowing no margin for error, and none for irrelevant matters like grumbling on the field and living it up off it.'

ARTHUR HOPCRAFT, *The Observer*

THE World Cup had been, until 1950, a closed book to the British home associations, but now they were back in the fold, with the prospect of competing for the first time in Brazil. FIFA had specified that the first two teams of the British championship would qualify for a place; but Scotland, with a certain perversity, decided that they would only go if they won. And finished second. However, the prelude to qualifying for the finals was disrupted, for England, by the controversy created over lucrative offers being made to Football League players by clubs in Colombia. The problem was that Colombia at that time was not a member of FIFA; and therefore players registered with its clubs would be ineligable to play in FIFA tournaments. The attraction of the money being offered by such clubs as Millionarios and Santa Fé was not merely spectacular in itself, but carried an inherent attraction against the background of institutional stinginess that still existed in Britain.

Tommy Lawton, as already recounted, was one of those who tended to voice publicly his disapproval of the relative pittance awarded to even the star performers in English football, who were personally drawing thousands of additional fans through the turnstiles. Lawton relates how his gross annual income in the post-war period, at the time he left Chelsea for Notts County, was a grand £531.50. This was comprised of a winter season wage for eight months at £8 per week of £226; a summer wage at £6 per week of £100; £8 per match for eight internationals plus 50p per day expenses; a League championship winning bonus of £25; £1 a point League bonus of £59; and £1 a victory Cup bonus of £7. Professionals such as he and Matthews were entitled to be disgruntled at this absurdly disproportionate reward for pulling packed houses of between 60,000 and 100,000. Not only that, there was a continual meanness regarding expenses of even the most lowly denomination, as recorded by Willie Watson, a double international at cricket and football for Yorkshire, Sunderland and England. Watson recounts in his autobiography *Double International*:

In between an FA tour of Italy and Holland and the departure for Rio, we had two training sessions in London, and I asked permission to bring my wife for the last weekend so that we could be together before I left. The FA agreed to this; and I remember putting in an expenses sheet covering a shilling [5p] booking charge on the first journey to London, and the excess fare for first class over third class

A lifetime of fitness earned on the beach.
'I loved the fresh air and the breeze of
the early morning, mostly running on the
hard sand uncovered by the tide, with
six miles to St Anne's and back in the
afternoon four times a week.'

Top left: The start of an unforgettable climax. With Bolton leading 3–1 with only 20 minutes to go in the 1953 FA Cup Final, Mortensen exploits Hanson's error to snatch Blackpool's second goal, following a cross by Matthews. From left: Banks, Mortensen, Hanson, Barrass, Ball (2), Hassall.

Bottom left: Perry, arms spread, scores the injury-time winning goal, from Matthews' pass (grounded, extreme left). Mortensen (foreground) and Taylor turn in triumph.

Top right: The young Queen presents his medal to a national hero. 'I was in the clouds, and nothing really registered till afterwards.'

Bottom right: Jubilant Blackpool, third time lucky. From left: Robinson, Garrett, Johnston (holding Cup), Shimwell (hidden), Fenton, Mudie, S M, Mortensen, Perry, Joe Smith (manager).

Matthews, aged 42, Duncan Edwards, 20, and Billy Wright, 33, train together for the 1957 fixture against Scotland. Ten months later Edwards died at Munich. 'So quick for a big man, and strong as a horse . . . what a future he would have had.'

A few days after inspiring England's victory over Brazil at Wembley in 1956, **Stanley** is coaching in Kenya, an association with Africa that was to last almost 30 years.

Matthews takes on Nilton Santos, the world's best left-back . . .

and leaves him floundering.

Marche, the French captain, shows no respect for a forty-year-old, at Stade Colombe in Paris. 'Oh Lord, he never left me wherever I went, one of the most effective markers I ever played against.'

Above: Five against one, a normal day. Stanley takes on the rest of Europe in his Testimonial Match, aged 50. From left: Popluhar (Czechoslovakia), Di Stefano (Spain), Masopust (6) (Czechoslovakia), Schnellinger (West Germany), Yashin (Soviet Union).

Below left: Has he, at last, done the sensible thing? 'I thought afterwards I'd made a mistake retiring. I still felt good, and about that time, with Alf Ramsey, the game was starting to be played backwards. I could have managed that.'

Below: Still foxing them – at an invitation indoor tournament in Scotland, aged 56. George Cohen (background) takes a breather.

The unchanging, bewitching shuffle, *right:* against Scotland in 1949, and *above:* against Eddie McCreadie of Chelsea on the way to promotion in 1963.

Below: The fans of half a century greet Sir Stanley at the unveiling of his statue in Hanley, some having travelled hundreds of miles. 'Why me, and not Reg Mitchell who saved Britain?' he asked Colin Melbourne, the sculptor.

Top: The mother who gave him sympathy
and understanding all her life shares his
receiving the Freedom of Stoke.

Bottom: Mila and Stanley together in
Canada . . . on golden pond.

which we were allowed for the second journey. I travelled first class because the train was full, and I didn't think it was right that I should stand all the way from Yorkshire to London prior to a most important training session. On my return from Rio, I received a cheque for £60 from the FA, being my fee for the trip – I didn't play in any of the three matches – and included in the letter was a note saying that I had overcharged sixteen shillings and threepence [81p] on expenses. I must say this annoyed me. I received sixty pounds for going to Rio and not kicking a ball, and at the same time I lost something like three hundred pounds by not playing cricket for Yorkshire. Yet here was the FA quibbling about sixteen shillings and threepence. I don't think I've ever been so hopping mad.

Stanley recalls: 'If you got away with charging for afternoon tea, you'd achieved something. We all tried it.'

The sense of unfairness was exaggerated by the fact that players were being transferred at this time for £20,000 or more, yet they received no percentage of this, and their salaries remained proportionally laughable. Suggestions that a percentage of transfer fees should be received by players were scornfully ignored by the League Management, which has spent a century failing to understand that they are in the entertainment business rather than being jobbing builders, which some of them have been. Several League players fell for the Colombian bait, led by the Stoke pair, Neil Franklin and George Mountford, who had departed with their wives and families to play for Santa Fé. They had left without informing either their club or the FA, and within a short time the disciplinary committee was obliged to suspend them. Stanley Rous had attempted to explain to Bogata officials the damage that would be done to Franklin's international prospects; but neither party would relent, and Franklin, who had deceived the FA when declining invitations to play against Portugal and Belgium in the spring of 1950, duly missed England's trip to the World Cup Finals. The suspension was lifted in 1951, but his international career had been ruined.

Others to follow the Stoke pair to Colombia were Higgins (Everton) and Flavell (Hearts). Paul (Swansea) and Hedley (Everton) flew to Bogota, but returned to England without playing or signing. Jock Dodds, a former colleague of Stanley's at Blackpool and now with Lincoln, was found to be an agent of Millionarios, and was expelled from the League. Charlie Mitten, who had played for Manchester United in the Cup Final two years previously, left to join Santa Fé, at the same time as a disillusioned Franklin returned home with his wife. Mitten was said to have been offered a down payment of £5,000, and an annual salary of £2,000. Aston and Cockburn of Manchester United, who would join the World Cup party in Rio after touring with the FA in Canada, also received offers but rejected them.

A subsequent offer, following the World Cup, was made to Stanley for six exhibition games at the end of the following season, together with Johnston, Mortensen and Shimwell, at £400 each. This would not have involved leaving their club; but they did not go, for even such an offer as that still infringed FIFA regulations.

SM: I never thought about playing abroad seriously. I had my football income and the Co-Op boots deal, I was writing regularly for the *Sunday Express*; and my home was in Blackpool. I didn't at the time think Neil was unwise to go, if he wanted to. It was big money. But I realized afterwards what a mistake it was. Not many players in the League were too impressed with the offers. We knew we were tied by a contract; and although that contract was unfair, nobody thought about the alternatives too much. What's more, those that went to Bogata soon got home-sick. Of course there was resentment about the size of our wages. Andy Beattie had said some of us should get together and go touring all over the world, that twenty players should break away from the Football League and get paid what we were really worth. Andy talked to many players, including me, but we all wondered where we would be able to play such matches? Normal stadiums would be unavailable because of FIFA regulations. And anyway, nobody had the nerve. Andy always thought that this was the future, but most of us just accepted the situation. When I started in football, it was a good wage compared with the average man. Of course, you would have liked more money. I had an offer, after the Cup Final of 1953, to join PSV of Eindhoven for £200 a week.

Sir Stanley Rous wrote in his autobiography:

From my own and the FA viewpoint there was no bar to movement within clubs affiliated to national football associations, although the League was naturally resistant to depredations from Europe as well as South America. Gigi Peronace, the smooth-talking Italian who fixed up so many deals, was a *bête noire* for them. But the FA made no objections to the trickle of players abroad to clubs within FIFA's orbit. John Charles, Denis Law, Gerry Hitchens, Eddie Firmani and Jimmy Greaves were free to make a name and money in Italian football after Franklin had pointed the way. Some, however, found the money too hardly earned and were soon home-sick for English football. When Greaves fell out with Milan, the club inhibited his return by setting an impossibly high transfer fee when Tottenham first enquired. I saw Gigi privately about his, suggesting it was in his interest to use his influence to get it reduced to reasonable levels, because otherwise the adverse publicity might prevent future transfers. Fortunately, Tottenham were able to settle, and our greatest goal-scorer of a generation came home.

For Stanley, the World Cup of 1950 was no more than a brief bow at the footlights during a period of comparative isolation from the international team. His last appearance for England had been against Scotland in April 1949. He was an absentee when England beat Scotland by the only goal at Hampden in 1950, the wingers being Finney and Langton. For the first time England had introduced the twin spearhead formation, with Bentley of Chelsea partnering Mortensen. Bentley scored the goal, but Clifford Webb of the *Daily Herald* observed that 'Mortensen is not snapping up chances with his old spring-trap quickness.' The FA revealed a degree of indecision when they selected Matthews for a tour of Canada but then announced that he could join the World Cup party travelling to Rio if he wished. There had been public pressure for him to be included in the World Cup squad, and Winterbottom had telephoned to ask if he was fully fit, and whether he would be prepared to break off from the Canadian tour to go to Brazil. Stanley and Jim Taylor, the Fulham centre-half, both did this.

The trip to Canada was to establish for Stanley an affinity with the North American people, and in later years he took up semi-permanent residence there.

SM: When we arrived in Quebec, I was asked about wages in English football, and Canadian journalists said that their ice hockey and baseball stars would not even put in an appearance for the kind of money we were receiving in England. I was offered a job as a coach out there for fifty pounds a week, and said I'd have to think about it, merely trying to be polite. The next day a story appeared that I was going to Canada. We went sight-seeing, we visited the Niagara Falls, and in front of a crowd of 32,000, the largest at that time in Canada, we defeated Manchester United in Toronto. After that match, Jim Taylor and I set off to join the World Cup party in Rio. Johnny Aston and Harry Cockburn of Manchester United met us on the way in New York, from where we travelled to join those who were already in Brazil: Williams (Wolves), Ditchburn (Spurs), Ramsey (Spurs), Scott (Arsenal), Eckersley (Blackburn), Wright (Wolves), Hughes (Liverpool), Dickinson (Portsmouth), Watson (Sunderland), Nicholson (Spurs), Milburn (Newcastle), Mortensen (Blackpool), Bentley (Chelsea), Mannion (Middlesbrough), Finney (Preston), Mullen (Wolves) and Baily (Spurs).

We travelled through Port of Spain, Trinidad, and the journey took fifteen hours. We arrived in Rio with three days to go before our first match. It wasn't a good hotel that the England team had. Most of the players were eating bananas, because the food didn't suit us. We were right on the main highway along the Copocabana beach, and although it was winter, it was still warm enough for an Englishman to swim, even if the Brazilians didn't fancy it. Anyway, the beach was put out of bounds to us. The day before England were due to play Chile, there was the opening match between Brazil and Mexico, and most of us went off to see this at the new Maracana Stadium. This had seating for 130,000, with another 25,000 places for standing behind the goals. Workmen were still hard at it getting the stadium ready almost up to the time of kick-off. Huge traffic jams built up, and we had to abandon our coach some way from the stadium and walk. You've never seen scenes quite like it. Fans were climbing fences to try and get in illegally, and when the Brazilian team ran out on to the pitch hundreds of fireworks were let off. When they scored their first goal, a cannon was fired. It was our first experience of seeing fans behave with such fervour.

It was a fascinating spectacle. Didi, their inside-left, had a brilliant left foot and took all their free-kicks. He hit the cross-bar with one, and it was the first time we'd seen the *bent* free-kick. They had particularly lightweight boots, and I bought a pair. I realized that with a pair of these I could be even quicker, if only by inches in a few yards. When I got home, I took this Brazilian boot to the Co-Op factory, and from this we designed an entirely new boot with kid leather and a thin sole. A pair of these would last me only four or five matches. When I was a boy, the main boots were *Villa* and *Hotspur:* thick, heavy things, with toe caps, that came over the ankles, and you had to spend days soaking them in the bath.

Brazil beat Mexico by four goals, but they left spaces in their defence and I had an idea that Stan Mortensen could create a bit of trouble for them. There seemed no reason, if Brazil were the chief danger, why England could not win the World Cup! Brazil, I admit, were rather special – the way they trapped the ball on the chest, the way they passed it around. But their skill made no difference to me, you can't change the way you play, no matter how much they might use short balls, even their full-backs.

Stanley is expressing the same logical loyalty to the English style and characteristics which, when upheld twenty years later by Ramsey as manager of a defeated England team at the World Cup in Mexico, caused scorn to be heaped upon him. The selection in Brazil was determined by Arthur Drewry, the only FA selector on the trip, and in consultation with Winterbottom he named the majority of the team which had recently won 4–1 against Belgium in Brussels; the only changes being Hughes for Jones at centre-half, Finney in place of Milburn on the right wing, and Mullen replacing Finney on the left. The team performed adequately, against Chile, in spite of its lack of acclimatization, winning 2–0, and assisted by the arrival of rain to reduce the temperature. Yet it was hardly cup-winning form. With the humidity, some of the team had difficulty with their breathing and needed oxygen in the dressing-room. Billy Wright recalls:

We'd had a break after playing in Brussels, and then a fortnight together before leaving London, arriving in Rio about ten days before the game against Chile. It was horrible. The hotel, the Luxor, was on the busy main road by the beach, and we had difficulty getting the meals that we wanted, though Winterbottom and Harold Shepherdson tried their best. The first breakfast of cold ham and fried eggs arriving sitting in black oil. Alf [Ramsey] was one of the first to be ill, and soon half the party was under the weather. There'd been, in my opinion, too many changes in the team, though the players were never brought into the discussion. Our best team was the one with both Matthews and Finney playing. If the forward line of 1946–48, Matthews, Mortensen, Lawton, Mannion and Finney, had been kept together for the World Cup, we would have been fine. What we lacked in Brazil was goals, apart from the two against Chile. We didn't create the goals, but with both of those two on the wing, the creation would have been better.

Rous agreed, as he made clear in his memoirs:

Matthews seemed to me to be the ideal man to undermine a team like theirs [the United States, England's next opponents], which was clearly long on spirit and short on skill. Special arrangements had had to be made for him to join the party, and it seemed sense to put him in for this game. That I thought also to be the view of team manager Walter Winterbottom, so I went to see Drewry to urge some changes, and especially Matthews' inclusion. Drewry was adamant, however, that we should not change the team that had beaten Chile 2–0. 'Never change a winning team' was his philosophy. But I felt that we were also regarding the USA as a push-over, when in fact they had a fair record in the World Cup, having once reached the semi-final, in 1930, which we were not to do for another sixteen years.

The match against America was to be played in Belo Horizonte, an hour's bumpy flight from Rio. The team were to be guests of a British mining firm, and when they finally arrived, after a hazardous bus trip from the airport, the conditions and the hospitality were a vast improvement on Rio. But not the pitch.

SM: The stadium had been built specially for the World Cup, but was nothing like the Maracana. It was far smaller, with a rough pitch, and the changing-rooms were so limited that we arrived for the match already changed. The United States team had already shown their ability against Spain, holding them to 1–1 at half-time before Spain scored a couple in the second half. Now the Americans were favourites with the crowd because they were underdogs. We ought to have scored two or three in the first half-hour, but instead found ourselves behind five minutes before half-time when Gaetjens, their centre-forward, bundled in a cross from the right wing.

The team of novice nationals and a sprinkling of foreigners was achieving the impossible. The Americans had a Belgian left-back, Maca, a Scottish wing-half, Eddie McIlvenny, who had been given a free transfer by Wrexham the previous year, and Gaetjens, who had been born in Haiti. Borghi, their goalkeeper, was a former baseball player who would be a central figure in this bizarre match.

With a supportive crowd of 20,000 crammed into the little ground, the United States were now brimming with confidence, and little would go right for the England team. Winterbottom's view of this disastrous match is philosophical:

Football wouldn't be the same without these results, but that does not make them any more palatable when you are the victim. And it has to be said that they usually happen on a bad or small ground. At Belo Horizonte, the grass was the South American kind, with tufts every six inches or so, like individual plants, and spaces in between, so that the ball tended to sit up, and our forwards repeatedly hit the ball on the rise. We so dominated the game it was impossible to believe that we could lose, and it was said that in all we hit the bar and posts eleven times. Jimmy Mullen had the most chances and, of course, there was the occasion towards the end when a header by Mortensen was almost certainly over the line before it was scooped out, but the referee would not allow it. This is not to make excuses. We missed our chances and paid the penalty. We had no proper preparation the way teams have today, and our players were not used to foreign, unfamiliar conditions the way League players are nowdays, with regular overseas competitions.

Some accounts of the goal by Gaetjens suggest that it came from a cross-shot by Bahr, the left-half, from outside the penalty area, the ball striking Gaetjens on the back of the head. The Americans claimed that it was a calculated dive by the centre-forward at a shot from Bahr which Williams had covered. Whatever, England were behind and seemingly unable to do anything about it; even when Winterbottom switched Finney to the middle in place of Bentley. Mortensen remembers: 'The Americans' defensive tactics were rugged, to say the least. Twice in the first half I was clean through on the edge of the area when I was dragged down. I'm not saying I would have scored, but I must have had a great chance. When the game finished, we were disgusted with ourselves. I'll never forget it. We threw it away. Tactics then weren't a part of the game. We were still playing *totally* attacking football. That was what the crowds at home expected. Walter was very thorough, and would tell us the characteristics of our opponents, but he would never attempt to manipulate our players. People wanted attacking football, and that's what they got.'

SM: Those who didn't play can count themselves lucky. Sitting watching, it was agonizing. We could have played for twenty-four hours and not scored. It was a bad ground, and the Americans fought and chased. Our rhythm eventually went. We felt we had let everyone down. Yet there wasn't the same awareness about the World Cup then. If we'd won, well, it would just have been a cup. In the next match against Spain, there was a lot of fouling. It was very dirty that day. They were usually like that. I played against them in Madrid in 1955, and that was bad, too.

England flew back to Rio knowing that they had to beat Spain to have any chance of continuing in the final two groups, the tournament then being staged throughout on a league system. A draw or defeat against Spain would mean a return home. Victory would then require a play-off against Spain. Four changes were made. Stanley was recalled, Eckersley of Blackburn replaced Aston at left-back, Baily of Spurs took over from Mannion, and Milburn replaced Bentley. Finney switched to the left wing in place of Mullen. An Italian referee permitted untold obstruction and shirt-pulling by the Spaniards, and Spain scored the only goal soon after half-time through Zarra, their centre-forward. England, the alleged masters of football, had failed to get through even to the final round of the World Cup.

It might have been different if luck had been with them after a quarter of an hour. Milburn headed past Ramallets, who had an outstanding match in goal for Spain, only for Galeati, an Italian referee, to give the goal off-side – though photographs reveal that a Spanish defender clearly put Milburn on-side. The returning England party left no one behind to study how other, and better, teams were playing. The

English journalists went with them, so that they too were none the wiser: the blind reporting to the blind. The outstanding teams of the final pool were Brazil, Sweden, Yugoslavia and Uruguay. It was only by coincidence that the final match of the league system would determine the destination of the Cup, Uruguay defeating Brazil and reducing Rio to a river of tears.

In Zizinho, Ademir and Jair, Brazil had a breathtaking trio of inside-forwards, the Uruguayans almost equally brilliant players in Andrade in defence, Ghiggia in attack, and Varela in midfield. The FA were not entirely without wisdom on their return home. A report was published by the Chairman of the selection committee which acknowledged that Brazil had trained together for four months in preparation for the competition, and that other competitive football had been suspended during this period; while Uruguay, 'it is understood', had been in preparation for two years. Forty years later, however, neither the FA nor the Football League have acted upon that observation in any serious way which might be of assistance to an England team manager.

8. REWARD

'*W*E all have little passions in life, and there is no limit to them. They range from spring in Green Park to Brighton Beach or drifted snow on a Yorkshire moor. They may include Gracie Fields and the memory of Garbo, the taste of fried onions and the call of a seagull and the vision of a country pub in sunshine. One of my passions is Stanley Matthews, the very name itself, and the spectacle of a man, standing still with a football stationary at his feet and a fluster of defenders scurrying into haphazard and hopeless positions to check him. This, as it has been these twenty years, is the most astonishing single sight in football. And this, no matter what else happens on the Wembley field, will make the Blackpool-Bolton Wanderers match today probably the most extraordinary Cup Final of them all. From 100,000 people, the partisans included, will come a wave of sympathy for Matthews in his third Cup Final in five years such as football or any other sport has never known. It will be almost tangible. Over the dog track, over the dirt track, over the touch-line, as it does across the footlights in the odd magical moments in the theatre, will flow and counterflow a flood of emotional compassion from the crowd to the players, and to Stanley Matthews. It may seem to you to be putting a football match and a football player on rather a high plane, but this match will offer the greatest unspoken tribute, on the sport's greatest occasion, to a man who has graced and dignified football for two decades. He is a legend in his own lifetime. Mr R.E. Cann, of Station Road, Swanage, Dorset, writes to me: "In this part of the country we never see First Division football. Even as an old player, it is difficult for me to imagine what Matthews does with the ball. Can you tell me?" Maybe the picture can do it better than I. Which way is he going? Bolton will have to find the answer to that if they hope to win the Cup. He has written that his greatest strength is confidence – confidence that he is always complete master of the ball and therefore complete master of his opponent. His ball control, speed, balance, personal physical fitness, all the outcome of original talent, practice, and the thing you cannot buy, experience, are merely parts of the pattern. His greatest asset, to me, is his perception of the balance of his opponent. Matthews will sway his body over the ball to make the full-back move. In that one fleeting moment, when the back is moving from one foot to the other, Matthews moves the ball quickly and follows it in a flounce of billowing shirt and shorts, clear, high, wide and handsome. *'*

BOB FERRIER, *Daily Mirror*

INTO the evolving Blackpool team had now come a little Scot, Jackie Mudie. He had arrived at Blackpool at the age of sixteen, just at the end of the war, and did not play in the first team until he was nineteen. There were, in his time, sometimes seven internationals in the reserves. When Matthews arrived from Stoke in 1947, Mudie was in the fourth or fifth team. He had been the youngest of six brothers in Dundee, and there, at the age of fourteen, he had seen Matthews and Mortensen playing for the RAF against the Army. He had been only just tall enough to see over the low wall surrounding the pitch.

My idol as a boy had been Jimmy Delaney [Jackie says]. He was with Celtic and then went to Manchester United. Up in Scotland, we had thought he was a better player than Stanley, and it wasn't until I arrived at Blackpool that I realized the truth. Ewan Fenton, who lived in the next street from us in Dundee, came to Blackpool, as did a number of Scots such as Farm, the goalkeeper, Kelly, Allan Brown. The club had a good Scots scout, Oliver Hamilton.

I always thought it was a privilege to be in the same club as Stan, and I probably got to know a lot more about him over the years than even Morty. Undoubtedly, there was a bit of envy and jealousy about him within the club, with players like Ernie Taylor, who joined us after the 1951 Cup Final, and maybe even with Morty. Stan never went to the pubs, never went in and out of the players' entrance but always through a side door. He didn't mix a lot, seldom went anywhere, always dashed off home. It didn't help that Joe Smith, the manager, would never have a go about anything at Stan or Morty, and in my time I complained about that. There were the usual groups you get off the field: the two Stanleys, Harry Johnston and Shimwell in one; Greatrix, Taylor and Garrett in another; and then the Scots with Farm, Kelly, Brown, Fenton and myself. Yet on the field we were always together as a team. I've had my rows with Stanley. I once didn't speak to him for six months, after he turned on me when I pulled his leg during a summer tour that he hadn't wanted to go on. He could be very short sometimes, but of course we made it up, and we're still as close as can be today.

Although continuing to be largely ignored by the England selectors, Stanley in the early Fifties was giving one dazzling display after another for Blackpool. In his first match in the autumn of 1950 following the disaster in Brazil, he took apart that fine left-back of Tottenham, Charlie Withers. This was the Spurs push-and-run team created by Arthur Rowe, which had just been promoted and would win the League title at the first attempt. Out came Spurs, full of bounce and confidence and, as Macadam wrote in the *Express*:

> You began to feel a little sorry for the frail-looking 35-year-old standing on Blackpool's right touch-line. Then Matthews got the ball. He took it straight to Withers and let him look at it. Then he took it away this way and then he took it past him that way. The direction of the sorrow began to shift: and began to shift violently when he bored and wove and feinted his way through a maze of such players as Burgess, and at the precise moment gave the ball to his captain and right-half, Johnston, who scored the first of two glorious goals from the same uncanny source. That was only the start of an exhibition of ball control, the subtlety of swerve and footwork that belongs as much in Covent Garden as it does on the soccer field.

And so it went on. A month later, at home to Burnley, he ran Harold Mather dizzy for ninety minutes, repeatedly leaving him lying on the turf. Back to London, and the destruction of Charlton, who tried both Revell and then Lock at left-back in the attempt to halt him but still lost 3–0, to the laughter and delight of their own crowd. And this for a player who was almost thirty-six. The same month, Blackpool were drawing 4–4 at Highbury, after which Mercer, Arsenal's captain, said: 'The old maestro gave one of the best displays I've ever seen from him and is still the best outside-right in the country.' Arsenal led 3–1, and then collapsed as Matthews took their defence apart. Arsenal used Roper, Smith, Mercer, Forbes and Leslie Compton in the attempt to pin down that two-way swerve: and failed. By the finish, it was almost a one-man exhibition. This was to be Blackpool's second best season in the League during Matthews' fourteen seasons with them, finishing in third place.

It was this season that Billy Wright, because of an injury to Shorthouse, was once switched by Cullis to left-back against Blackpool. 'Make him come inside, and we'll have no trouble,' Cullis told his captain. Wright did just that; Stanley went inside, made two goals for Mortensen, and afterwards Cullis complained: 'Never again, Billy.' Stanley had played in the opening international match of the season, a 4–1 victory over Ireland, and, after being left out against Wales and Yugoslavia, was recalled in April against Scotland at Wembley. This was the occasion when Mannion was injured after only eleven minutes, and Finney switched from the left wing to inside-right, a successful experiment upon which the selectors would turn their back. Though playing with only ten men for almost the whole match, England gave a sturdy performance of fighting spirit, and narrowly lost a fine duel by the odd goal in five. Stanley would not play again for another two and a half years and twenty matches.

Not only did Blackpool finish third in the League, but they skilfully played their way to a second Cup Final appearance in four seasons. On the way they disposed of Charlton, after a replay, Stockport, Mansfield, Fulham and, after a replay in the semi-final at Everton, Birmingham City by 2–1. According to the *Manchester Guardian*, Matthews at Everton was in his finest form:

His extraordinary control and speed of footwork defy the years and he remains the finest ball player of this generation. He gave Badham an awful time in the first-half and, indeed, the full-back spent a most trying afternoon in his efforts to check the Blackpool winger. . . . From this point (2–1 down) Birmingham improved. Little Berry made several spirited runs and Blackpool were fortunate during one furious bustle in the goalmouth, but their defence was sound against a thrustful but inaccurate attack. The game ended with Matthews again baffling the defence and making perfect openings, but three open goals were missed. The official attendance was 70,114.

If there was a final that Blackpool should have won, this was it: certainly on the form guide. 'Between the semi-final and the final, there were about eight League matches,' Mudie recalls. 'We won the majority of ours, and Newcastle, our opponents at Wembley, lost five or six. We were the unquestionable favourites, though we weren't over-confident. We didn't go away for special training before the final, but stayed at home, going down to St Anne's to practice on some lush grass in anticipation of Wembley, and having salt water baths at Lytham. Stan revels in the big event, but I think on this occasion he was more nervous beforehand than anyone else in the team. He under-performed like the rest of us.'

Newcastle had arrived at Wembley with victories over Bury, Bolton, Stoke, Bristol Rovers after a replay, and, after a semi-final replay at Huddersfield, Wolves. On the way they had conceded seven goals compared with Blackpool's four. In spite of considerable previous expenditure on players since the war, now only Fairbrother in goal, their right-half Harvey, Brennan at centre-half and their left-wing pair of Robledo and Mitchell had cost transfer fees. The other six were all locals. Blackpool had three internationals in Johnston, Matthews and Mortensen of England, Newcastle three in Brennan, (Scotland), Milburn (England), and Robledo (Chile). Newcastle, it has to be said, were among the most renowed of Cup fighters, and had three times won the trophy, with four losing finals between 1905 and 1911. If Matthews, the national hero, was thought to be the main threat to Newcastle, then Milburn, who was to become the greatest Tyneside hero in history, was the menace to Blackpool: fast, powerful and fearless and a regular centre-forward for England.

The man who would be up against Stanley at Wembley was Bobby Corbett, a quick, stern and competent left-back. It is one of my sadnesses that, in the preparation of this book and the many interviews conducted with colleagues and opponents of Stanley's, I missed the chance to talk with both Corbett and Jackie Milburn. I had planned to go to Newcastle in the autumn of 1988. Bobby was not on the telephone, and some weeks beforehand I had called Wor Jackie, as he was known by all, to arrange a meeting, unaware that Jackie was ill. 'Give me a call back in a month or so, I'm not too good at the moment,' Jackie had said, friendly as ever. Before I had done so, he and Bobby had died within days of each other, Tyneside turning out in their tens of thousands to mourn at Jackie's funeral procession. Twenty-five years after his retirement, the city's affection remained as deep as ever.

So I went instead to talk to Bobby's full-back partner, Bobby Cowell, one of the three men to gain winners' medals with Newcastle in their three glorious seasons, in five years, from 1951 to 1955. Back in 1943, Cowell had been playing for the Home Guard team of Trimdon Grange, a village between Durham and Hartlepool. He had joined the Home Guard 'because they gave you an overcoat and a pair of shoes'. One day he had a call from Stan Seymour, the Newcastle chairman, telling him to bring his boots for a game in the war-time reserves. He played two games and heard nothing more. Then a telegram arrived, saying to report at Durham Station for a first-team game against Bradford Park Avenue. Such was the prestige of any invitation from Newcastle that Cowell and his father turned up at the station an hour early. Shackleton was playing for Park Avenue, and Cowell's partner at left-back was a guest, Bill Nicholson of Spurs, who was stationed in the north-east. Nicholson would later lead Spurs to a Cup and League 'double' in 1961.

When the war finished, I was down Blackwall Colliery [Cowell says]. The shifts were two till ten, ten till six, six till two. I'd come off a shift, go home for a wash, and then down to St James's for training, and back home again on a couple of buses that took fifty minutes. I didn't even own a bike. Jackie was the only one in the first team with a car. Newcastle was a very generous club: they'd give you anything except money. I was down the pit until the end of '47. It was a hard life in those days, even if you were playing football. There was a two-pound bonus for a win in the early Fifties, and I remember when we were playing Blackburn away: Joe Harvey had come into the dressing-room beforehand and said 'I want that two pounds, my kids need some new shoes.' Early in the game Joe thumped Bobby Langton, their left-winger, a couple of times. The next time, Langton side-stepped him and Joe bellowed at Bobby Corbett, 'Thump him, Bobby, or I'll thump you.' Bobby caught him all right; and poor Langton had to go off. He'd got two broken ribs. We won 2–1, and Joe got his shoes.

For those three Cup Final victories we received £25 a time. Oh yes, and somebody gave my wife and me a couple of plastic macs.

The third final for Newcastle, against Manchester City in 1955, presented a problem for Cowell and his second wife Elsie. They had between them three children from their first marriages – their first spouses had died – and needed a third winners' medal so that the children would have one each. Elsie's brother George Prior had been a full-back with Sheffield Wednesday, so she had grown up with the game.

Cowell was the first Newcastle player ever to receive a testimonial. It raised £4,500; he came off the books in 1956, his career ended when he was carried off, on his wedding anniversary, during a tour match in Germany. The injury being received abroad, he received no compensation; and, with three children, he was out of a job. He managed to find a position running an off-licence for £11 a week. All those friends who had been eager for tickets during the champagne years, businessmen in the city, quietly evaporated: there were no offers of employment for yesterday's hero.

For this first final of Cowell's in 1951, the club gave the players' wives ordinary tickets outside the main stand at Wembley. Harvey's wife, Ida, said there was no way she was sitting out there; the players threatened to refuse to catch the train to London. Stan Seymour, the chairman, doggedly said the club would field the reserve team, but in the end relented; and the club tried to do things in style, with a private coach attached to the end of the London express.

'We went to Buxton up in the Peaks for a week's training beforehand, and talk almost every night was what we were going to do about the two Stanleys, Matthews and Mortensen,' Cowell recollects. 'The plan was that Matthews would be left to the nearest man. Bobby Corbett and Charlie Crowe, our full-back and wing-half, would try and handle him between them. In fact it was my man (Perry) who did the damage on the day. Bobby Corbett had one of his finest games ever. He was the kind of fellow who didn't know when he was beaten.'

Blackpool had encountered serious misfortune several weeks prior to the final when Allan Brown, a centre-forward of reknowned courage, damaged a knee against Huddersfield; and all the attempts of trainers and physiotherapists could not get him fit in time. Further bad luck followed when, one week before the final, George McKnight was picked for a try-out against Sheffield Wednesday. He damaged a knee too, and this meant that Bill Slater, an England amateur international, would have to be drafted into the side.

SM: We'd been chasing the double of Cup and League. We'd had a run of twenty games without defeat in the League, and finished third with fifty points behind Spurs and Manchester United. We were really confident this time, in spite of the two injuries. We were in excellent form and Newcastle had been going through a poor spell. The final, however, was disappointing, for us and probably for anyone who was not a Tyneside supporter. There was not much football up to half-time, and we went down to the dressing-room knowing just how much the first goal would now mean.

Five minutes after half-time, Mudie fed the ball to Stanley. For one of the few times in the match he was able to beat Corbett, and cut through to the goal-line. Seeing Mortensen in position, Matthews pulled the ball back: but too fast. Mortensen stumbled, Robledo won the ball, and raced towards the Blackpool half. His through pass ran to Milburn, just over the half-way line. Blackpool had been using an off-side trap to counteract the threat of Milburn's speed, and this moment showed what a dangerous tactic this could be. As Milburn received the ball, the Blackpool defenders hesitated, appealing for off-side. Milburn checked, glanced over his shoulder, heard no whistle, and set off at speed: on and on, down the middle of the field with the ball at his feet. He was a thrilling figure, this powerful athlete, entirely on his own, racing down an empty pitch towards the waiting, trembling Farm. The goalkeeper, with little option, advanced to meet him, to attempt to narrow the angle. Milburn struck the ball a blacksmith's blow from about fifteen yards out, and turned for the congratulations almost before the ball was in the net.

If that goal seemed decisive, within barely five minutes Milburn hit a second, which Henry Rose of the *Daily Express*, never one to underplay a moment of drama, proclaimed as an historic moment. 'When Geordie soccer fans who were at Wembley grow old, and take a sentimental soccer journey back over the years, they will tell their wide-eyed grandchildren of the greatest goal they ever saw,' reported Rose.

The diminutive Ernie Taylor, who would subsequently be transferred to Blackpool and earn another winners' medal with them, initiated the goal. Receiving a pass from Bobby Mitchell on the right about twenty-five yards from goal, Taylor seemed to have no escape, hemmed in by defenders. Unexpectedly, he suddenly back-heeled the ball to Milburn, who was close at hand a few yards behind him. With the casual yet instant action of a man who might have been taking a ball rolled to him by the trainer during shooting practice, Milburn hit a left-foot drive that was a blur as it sped past an immobile Farm and into the top of the net. Blackpool were finished.

On the day they had played disjointedly, Newcastle as a team. The luckless Slater had looked out of his depth, while Mudie had failed to reproduce his consistently outstanding form in the League. Mortensen could hardly be blamed, for he never received the kind of pass upon which he depended to carve the opposition apart. Matthews, facing the frustration of a second failure, had, as they say, worked his socks off: taking free-kicks, throw-ins, shooting with both feet, even twice heading the ball. Yet Corbett had played him with intelligence, and, on a bad day for the rest of the team, Matthews had been unable to engineer the prize for which he and a million of his supporters so longed. The England selectors, responding as usual to the most recent outstanding goal they had seen, announced that evening through Arthur Drewry at the winners' banquet that Milburn would be recalled to the England team in place of Mannion against Argentina at Wembley a fortnight later. Their loyalty to Milburn would last for two matches.

'It was a bad game for us, we never got going,' Bill Perry, Blackpool's outside-left, recollects. 'There's nothing worse than losing at Wembley, worse than a semi-final. I've never felt so bad. It had happened twice to the two Stanleys and Harry [Johnston].' With the coveted winners' medal again eluding him, and with a leg injury keeping him out of the Blackpool side for almost three months the next season, Matthews seemed to have passed into limbo. So much so, that when Stoke enquired of Blackpool whether they were willing to release Stanley to rejoin them, he said he was agreeable. The Blackpool directors, it seems, were also in favour of accepting the approach by Frank Taylor, Stoke's manager, but Joe Smith still had his eye on the foot of the rainbow. And said 'no'.

An ageing manager with faith in an ageing genius; though there were times during the next two seasons when neither could give too much encouragement to the other. Stanley continued to be bothered by injuries, and in 1951–52 Blackpool finished ninth in the League and were eliminated from the Cup at the first hurdle. Nor did fortune smile on them early in the 1952–53 season; though by the time it came to the start of the Cup for First and Second Division clubs, with the third round in January, Stanley was showing something of his old form. 'I saw them in the third round, and the word beforehand was that Stanley wouldn't be playing,' Geoffrey Green remembers. 'But he did: and took Wednesday to pieces.' Blackpool won 2–1, then defeated Huddersfield 1–0 and, after a replay, Southampton 2–1. They were drawn away to Arsenal in the sixth round. In his autobiography, Harry Johnston wrote:

Against Huddersfield, at home, only a forty-yard lob by our left-back Tommy Garrett, which fell into the Huddersfield net two minutes from time, won us the match. Not even Tommy would claim he meant to score. We had our finest hour at Highbury, when Allan Brown played one of his greatest games – and in the process lost his second chance of playing in a final. That day, Arsenal were so preoccupied with Matthews that Stan came in at half-time and said, 'I think I'll just stick to the touch-line, they seem to be liking my company out there today.' Thus, with Matthews as decoy as the man Arsenal dared not leave, Brown became the match-winner. With two minutes to go, he raced through to shoot the winner; but even as he shot, he lay still and silent under the Arsenal goalkeeper, Kelsey, who had flung himself forward to try to block the shot. His body crashed into Allan's left leg, which broke in two places. We could have all cried as Allan was carried off. Already we had played much of the season without our other match-winning forward, Mortensen, and now Brown had gone. It was a sad Blackpool party which left London for home. We had scored a wonderful victory, but at what cost.

There was again to be an dramatic conclusion to the semi-final, against Tottenham at Villa Park. With a minute to go, and the score 1–1, the studious Ramsey, who had played twenty-five consecutive matches at right-back for England, misjudged a back-pass to his goalkeeper. Mudie, with swift anticipation, intercepted and glanced the ball past Ditchburn before he could reach it. Ramsey hung his head in dismay. It was harsh punishment for a man who brought to football, as player and manager, a carefully applied intelligence.

For the third time in six seasons, Blackpool were through to the Cup Final, and with Mortensen recovering his form and confidence after spending weeks out of action with cartilege trouble, the club and their followers were once more optimistic that they could succeed: this time against Bolton Wanderers. There was nothing especially alarming about Bolton. They had finished fourteenth in the League, seven places behind Blackpool, and in reaching the final of the Cup had a moderately easy passage against Fulham, Notts County, Luton, Gateshead and Everton. Notts County had taken them to two replays, while they had only got through by the odd goal in seven against Everton in the semi-final.

SM: My fan-mail in the days and weeks leading up to the final was enormous. People who'd never seen me play, or in fact never even seen a football match, sent me their good wishes. I received hundreds of mascots and thousands of letters, and they overwhelmed me. Complete strangers called at my home to wish me well, and phone calls came through day and night from all parts of the country. It was good to feel that I had so many people behind me in this third attempt to achieve a winners' medal. To me, however, it was just as important to get to Wembley on football's greatest day as to win. Of course I wanted a medal, but it is always better to have played at Wembley and lost than not to have been there at all. I was feeling fitter and stronger in the build-up towards the final than I had been for three or four years.

Brother Jack's memory is that it had not been, by any means, a carefree season for Stanley. The knee injury had continued to be bothersome, and at one stage he had been to Sheffield for a manipulative operation under anaesthetic. 'Afterwards, a nurse came into the ward, when Stan should have been coming round, and there he was, still half-dazed by the anaesthetic, standing beside the bed, swinging his leg and testing his knee to see how it was,' Jack recalls. 'It was the week before they played Sheffield Wednesday at home. Stan played, and scored.'

There was one anxiety still to come before the kick-off. In the last few days of training, Stanley had sustained a slight thigh injury, hardly an improbability for a man of thirty-eight. After breakfast on the morning of the match, he faced a fitness test on the lawns of the team's hotel. Although less than fully fit, and in spite of the fact that there were still no substitutes permitted – Cup Finals were repeatedly marred by injury – he decided to take the risk. Smith calculated that the inclusion of Stanley was a psychological advantage over the opposition. Stanley was given an injection in his thigh at the Stadium, and as he headed out of the tunnel on to that expanse of lush grass, in front of the eyes of millions, no one knew of the gamble which had been taken by the very man upon whom all attention was concentrated.

Commentators were, before the match, by no means unanimous in their previews that Blackpool were the probable winners; even though almost everyone in the land was hoping, sentimentally, that this venerable figure would at last be rewarded with the major prize. Archie Ledbrooke, for example, wrote in the *Daily Dispatch*: 'For many people, the match is looked forward to as the event that may crown Matthews' career with a winners' medal. How many, I wonder, think with equal concern of the equally long and honourable, if not so distinguished, career of that other Stanley – Bolton's goalkeeper Stanley Hanson?' Ledbrooke went on to point out that Bolton's attack of Holden, Moir,

Lofthouse, Hassall and Langton was potentially the line of all talents. Moir was an outstanding captain partnering a young winger, Holden, who could out-run many full-backs. Hassall and Langton were a left-wing pair of England internationals of knowledge and experience, Hassall equally adept in defence and attack. And at centre-forward Lofthouse, who had replaced Milburn as England's centre-forward, had earned the accolade 'Lion of Vienna' with an exceptional performance in the 3–2 victory over Austria the previous May, scoring two goals. Johnston, for all his experience as veteran of club and country, would need equanimity and guile to resist the relentless power of Lofthouse, who said before the match:

Many people have been saying that Bolton are lucky, that we are not a great side. My response is that we have always had eleven good players, and that we have improved as we played each round. With due modesty, I thought that in the first half of the semi-final against Everton we played some very fine football to get a four-goal lead; though maybe with a margin like that we slackened in the second half. I think that our half-back line of Wheeler, Barrass and Bell has proved to be the real reason for our appearance in the final. Our goalkeeper, Stan Hanson, is one of the best Bolton have ever had. We all hope Bell will be able to lend the support necessary to help Ralph Banks at left-back keep the great Stanley in check.

Ralph Banks was thirty-three. A former Sunday school player, he made his debut for the first team on Christmas Day, 1940, before being called up with the 1st Loyals North Lancs regiment. He was in the second wave of support landings at Anzio, was then withdrawn to go to Palestine, and arrived back in Bolton in 1946. The final would be his last match for Bolton, though he did not know it at the time, before he was transferred to Aldershot. His story at the Hampshire club would not be a happy one. The club tried to cut his salary, he refused to play – having his rent to pay – and sued them in the county court before leaving to play with non-League Weymouth. A bricklayer by trade, he built his own bungalow in Dorset; and was finally put out of the game when playing with Dorchester Town in 1961; a girl on a moped crashed into his car when he was pushing it in the dark, rupturing his knee, and he found himself unemployed, with £100 compensation.

Wembley was not going to frighten Banks. At Anzio, lying in a trench, he had placed his binoculars on the ridge, and a shell blew them to pieces. Defending his platoon's position in a farmyard, his captain, who was from his home town of Farnworth in Lancashire, was accidentally killed from behind by his own machine-gunner. Banks was instructed to ride with the body, either side of a donkey, back to HQ;

under fire again, he threw himself off the donkey into a ditch, and when he raised his head again found the nose-cone of one of the shells resting between his legs. He is one of history's millions of anonymous heroes. Playing at Wembley, for a fellow who had signed on at Bolton for 35 shillings a week (£1.75), was a bit of a bonus.

'We tried to find a pitch that would compare with Wembley in the couple of weeks before the Final,' Ralph recalls. These days he is back living in Farnworth in a bungalow – which he built – in the same road as his younger brother Tommy, who also played for Bolton, and then for England at the time of the World Cup Finals of 1958. 'Bill Ridding, our manager, wanted us to play our normal game. I'd only had one previous match against Stan, at Blackpool that season. He was all right if you could stand in on him, but at Wembley he went deep, much more than he normally did. With Taylor supporting him so well, and then when our left-half Bell was injured early on and went on the wing, it was often two against one. With Stan, you had to stop the ball getting to him, and even if it was fifty-fifty he wouldn't really go for it. I'd done all right in that first game at Blackpool. I wasn't worried about the final, I was more bothered about my shins, where I used to get cramp, and with that spongy pitch, I massaged them well with oil beforehand.'

There was a much greater anxiety gnawing away at Lofthouse. He had played against Matthews often enough to realize that so long as Stanley was on the pitch, no team was ever safe. 'Just think what Bolton faced that day,' he reflects. 'Everybody in England, except the people of Bolton, wanted Stanley to get his medal. We had a huge emotional barrier to break down, just as we did when we played against Manchester United in the 1957 final, after they had been devastated by the Munich crash. I was thinking beforehand about whether our defence could cope with Stanley's accuracy. You never saw him place a cross inside the six-yard box, where the goalkeeper might reach it, always half a yard outside, tempting. As a forward, the cross was always coming towards *you*. His strength was getting to the line, which was the key to his game. He was a perfectionist, always trained on his own, working at his sprints. He was a remarkable man.' Lofthouse's anxieties were to prove well-founded.

For me, a schoolboy of eighteen just about to take my 'A' level examinations prior to going to university, it was a day of intense emotion, and probably the most profound of all the many sporting experiences I have had the opportunity to enjoy, even as a journalist travelling the world of sport for over thirty years. I had followed Stanley's career, at a distance, ever since I was old enough to comprehend a radio commentary. In the immediate post-war years, I had lain on the lawn under the apple tree, listening to Raymond Glendenning as he described scenes and events and great names in a way which, to a schoolboy in rural England, had a special, magical quality, and had left me addicted for life to this annual spring ritual. The reality was something even better and this, wonderful to behold, was my second final at Wembley. I had been able to obtain a ticket, as captain of my school team, through the County Association. The previous year I had been there to see Newcastle beat Arsenal, and that had been an indelible baptism. As a winger, I had 'affiliated' myself to Stanley while he was still at Stoke, and when he was transferred, I dutifully transferred my allegiance. Imagine the grief, therefore, of a youngster enduring those two previous Cup Final defeats. As I headed down Olympic Way that sunny day in May 1953, it was with strangely mixed feelings: on the one hand a huge, bursting expectation of seeing the match in which my idol would triumph, on the other an inner fearfulness that I would not be able to endure sitting there and seeing him fail. There was that same sensation one has prior to academic examinations: wishing that one could make the clock leap twenty-four hours and wake up afterwards to know the outcome. Though I could not know it, Harry Johnston had something of the same mood. He was later to write:

At two-fifty, I picked the ball up and led the lads out into the fierce glare. My mouth was dry. I gazed anxiously up into the stands, where my wife and relatives would be. Surely we couldn't fail for the third time? I looked over to the touch-line, and there was Allan Brown, grim-faced, probably more pent-up than we who were playing, and alongside him the other Blackpool casualty, Hughie Kelly, who had chipped an ankle bone. How they would have loved to have been playing. How we would have loved to have had these regular first-teamers with us.

This was the line-up:

BLACKPOOL: Farm; Shimwell, Garrett; Fenton, Johnston, Robinson; Matthews, Taylor, Mortensen, Mudie, Perry.
BOLTON WANDERERS: Hanson; Ball, Banks; Wheeler, Barrass, Bell; Holden, Moir, Lofthouse, Hassall, Langton.

Johnston and Moir led their teams to the centre of the field, to be introduced to the Duke of Edinburgh, who, inevitably, paused momentarily on his way down the ranks for a word with Matthews. From my seat on the far south side of the stadium, I can remember feeling, with passionate subjectivity, how horribly smart the Bolton team looked in their shiny satin shorts and white shirts, alongside the tangerine of Blackpool. Ralph Banks recalls: 'When he got to us, the Duke paused,

looked at our shorts, and said, "You all look like a bunch of pansies." '
Ralph still keeps his kit, never used again or washed to this day, neatly
pressed and folded in his bedroom.

There was edginess among the Blackpool team during the prelimi-
naries, as though Robinson and Fenton, the Blackpool wing-halves,
momentarily questioned their capacity to meet the demands of the
occasion, Taylor and Mudie whether they could escape the grip of
Wheeler and Bell. Whatever their feelings, there was immediate disaster. With no fewer than nine of the team which had been at Wembley
two years before against Newcastle, Blackpool were one down within
75 seconds. Their goalkeeper George Farm, who two weeks before had
played superbly on the same pitch for Scotland when they drew 2–2,
was now totally deceived by a low cross shot from the right by Lofthouse.
Johnston had early been caught out, not concentrating; Lofthouse shot
speculatively, the ball dipped, screwed through Farm's grasp, and flew
into the net off his shoulder. Such a reverse knocks the floor from
beneath any team, and soon Bolton could have been two up, when a
shot by Lofthouse struck a post. Now the game took another equally
important turn, this time against Bolton.

Bell, their left-half, tore a muscle, and this confronted his team
with a problem infinitely more serious than that facing Blackpool. They
compounded it with a serious tactical error, switching Bell to outside-
left and Hassall to wing-half, and moving Langton inside. As Morty
told me:

It was the biggest blunder of all time. I don't think we would ever
have won ultimately, but for that. If there was one thing Matthews
hated, it was the opposing winger on his flank tackling back. I've even
heard him tell wingers to go away and get on with their own job,
when he was particularly frustrated. By moving Bell to outside-left,
Bolton had sacrificed one of their means of checking Stan. Frankly, he
played a mediocre part in the game in the first-half, and really only
came into things later on.

Against ten and a half men and a rearranged formation, Blackpool
equalized ten minutes before half-time, though rather luckily. Mortensen, breaking through the middle, hit a less than formidable left-foot
shot and Hassall, attempting to cover, ran across the line of the ball
and helplessly deflected it into his own net. That should have been
sufficient to give Blackpool the platform from which to win the match;
but Farm was again at fault minutes later. Too slow in coming off his
line to met a cross from Langton, he allowed Moir to lunge in and score
with a header. Up in the grandstand, I was almost too miserable to
watch, and at half-time I wandered around, down below in the bowels

of the stadium, clutching the cheap and useless 'pirate' programme I had ignorantly purchased in the street, wondering what fate now held in store. The answer was something even worse.

Early in the second half Bolton went further ahead, the injured Bell somehow getting airborne to head home a cross from Holden on the right. Two down, with only twenty minutes to go, Blackpool were looking dead-beat. It was now that we were to experience one of the most emotional and remarkable transformations in the history of sport, culminating in a climax of nerve-shredding tension.

Suddenly, belatedly, Matthews started to come into the game. Sensing this surge in his partner's motivation, little Taylor also began to play with a perception that would rake the muscles of an ailing Bolton defence. Taylor was the powder-monkey to the cannon of destruction that now ranged up and down Bolton's left flank.

When Hassall dropped back to wing-half, he wasn't really working, and I was shouting at Langton to come back and help, because he'd run about and impede Matthews [Banks recalls]. I kept shouting at Billy Moir to get someone to deal with Ernie [Taylor], as Hassall was out of position and wasn't doing it. But Moir did nothing, he thought we had it won at 3–1. I was now getting cramp in my shins, as I'd feared, trying to hang on to Stanley. He was phenemonal over ten yards, and it was almost impossible to do anything with him once he had the ball. I was off the field [for treatment] four times in the last fifteen minutes, I just couldn't feel my legs. I shouted at Moir at one stage to swap me with Ball, our right-back, but by now he was partially injured and hopping about too. We were in a right state.

With panic now beginning to run through Bolton's rearguard, Blackpool reduced the lead to 3–2. Matthews, now at his most mesmeric against a stricken defence, sending defenders spinning like ninepins, sped away on yet another pass from Taylor. Stanley recalls. 'Morty and I knew each other's game so well, and he had that knack of knowing just where the ball was. On that second goal, I was really just aiming for the far post, beyond the goalkeeper, intending to stretch him. Hanson must have taken his eye off the ball for a split second, which was a lucky break for us.' Stanley had raced down the wing almost to the goal-line before sending a high, curling cross over the goalmouth. The Bolton defenders beneath turned to follow it as it sailed towards the far post; Hanson clutched at it with his fingertips and it spun away, straight to Mortensen, who was lunging feet first towards the left-hand post.

'I yelled at Hanson to let it go,' Banks says. 'I could see that the ball would have gone out. What the goalkeeper did was to keep it in. It was desperate. Another yard and the ball would have been out of play and Mortensen would have missed it.' Instead, the ball was in the back of Bolton's net, and now a deafening sound was coming from Wembley's 100,000 crowd, the roar of people who could barely believe the drama that was mounting before them. Morty says: 'I think in fact Stan put the ball a shade too close to the goalkeeper, but for a split second Hanson looked at me, and fumbled. As I slid in beyond him with an outstretched foot, I thought the ball was going to go beyond me, wide of the post, but I caught it with my studs and it just crept in.'

There was still more than a quarter of an hour to go: Bolton were not yet beaten. Yet strangely, as though hypnotized, they did nothing to re-shape their defence. As Taylor said: 'They handed it to us, they should have moved Wheeler, their right-half, who was a good defender, to the left side, and also switched their full-backs. Our hero in fact was Morty. The idea that the match was won by one man is nonsense.' There had always been a trace of resentment towards Stanley in Taylor, yet although he and Mortensen were now actors with a critical role in the plot, it was the spell of Matthews that was freezing Bolton's limbs.

'I had no feelings at all at that stage,' Stanley says, 'my concentration was good, and I knew it was essential not to panic.' With only three minutes to go it was still 3–2 to Bolton. At this point, Blackpool gained a free kick on the edge of the Bolton penalty area, on the left. 'I was tripped,' Mudie says, 'that was *my* contribution to our victory. As we took the kick, I felt that if it went in, the way things were, we'd get six in extra time.' Mortensen placed the ball and, with the crowd in a frenzy, prepared to take the kick. It was now that poor Bolton made one final mistake to contribute to their burial. As Mortensen recalls:

As I put the ball down, I couldn't see the goal behind the defensive wall. Ernie said to me, 'There's no gap,' but I said, 'I'm going to have a go.' As I turned to walk back, I could see Ernie Shimwell, our right-back, moving up to take a position on the far post, in case I crossed the ball. When I turned round, one of the Bolton players had moved off the right hand end of the wall and taken up a position on the other end, to keep an eye on Shimwell, and now I could see the left post. This convinced me I should have a belt, and the moment I struck the ball I knew it was in.

Of all his many remarkable goals, this was probably the most important. There have been few players in the modern game who could strike a ball so hard and simultaneously so straight as Mortensen. Denis Law was another; it requires a particular skill, with the knee, ankle and foot exactly in line and knee over the ball. Most players who try to strike the ball as hard as Mortensen did in that instant, tend to pull it. Barely able to believe it, as the ball hit the net I was unknowingly beating the man seated in front of me repeatedly over the head with a folded newspaper.

In the main stand, behind the Royal Box on the other side of the field, the Matthews family was equally close to hysteria. Jack was sitting with his brother, Arthur, his wife, their mother, and the Vallances. When Mortensen made it 3–2, Mrs Vallance had fainted. As Jack recalls, 'Someone drew Jimmy Vallance's attention to this, and Jimmy said, "Oh, bugger it" and just left her, and carried on watching the match. She came round, and when Morty scored again, she fainted a second time.' Jean says: 'At 3–3 we were all crying, and someone offered mother a brandy. Granny was sitting there intent but not saying a thing.'

Ralph Banks, whose mind was in a spin, was busy thinking that it shouldn't have been a foul against Holden when he brought down Mudie. 'I was in the defensive wall, and I think it was Wheeler who changed ends,' he says. According to the referee there was, with the score 3–3, less than a minute of injury time still to go.

Of those agonizing last ten minutes, Lofthouse recalls: 'I had no sense of panic, only tiredness. I spent the time just watching Stanley. He stood there, toes turned inwards, looking like a little old man – until he moved. In that final spell, he could do it, and he *knew* he could do it.' As the Blackpool players hurried back to the half-way line, Matthews looked round at his team and clapped his hands, slowly, three times, as if to say 'Come on, time is short now, but it's not over.' Those of us who half an hour ago had supposed Blackpool could never win were now merely thankful that, after this spectacular equalizing goal, we and our hero could draw breath and prepare for extra time. Not so.

From the kick-off, Bolton lose possession almost immediately: ship-wrecked men adrift in a leaking life-raft not knowing which way to paddle. Instantly the ball flies once more to Matthews. Now follows one of the most photographed and debated goals in history.

Matthews receives the ball level with the 18-yard line, a few yards to the goal-side of Banks and the centre-half Barrass, but kept on-side by Ball, the right-back, who has moved centrally to cover. Matthews now does what he has done ten thousand times before over the past twenty-one years: pauses, the ball at his feet, in order to compel Banks and Barrass to come to him, which they obligingly do. The usual sway to the left, ball on the right foot, as though to come inside, then in an instant gone past Banks on the outside, now in a position midway between the touch-line and the penalty area line.

Mortensen, as he has done a thousand times, is moving away towards the left-hand side of the penalty area; while Barrass abandons any thought of covering Mortensen, to move across to the right-hand side of the penalty area, in the hope of jockeying Matthews. Perry, meanwhile, is moving in from the left-wing, coming across behind his inside-forward, Mudie, into a central position; Hassall is racing back beside Banks in a vain pursuit of Matthews.

Matthews is cutting in towards the goal area; and is now three or four yards clear of Banks and Hassall. Ball, commendably for a defender trying to react intelligently in such crisis, has raced back and is already on the goal-line, with Hanson crouched anxiously on the near post. Barrass, arms and legs spread in a desperate attempt to smother the tormenting menace now facing him eight yards away, is just inside the edge of the goal area. Mortensen, from a yard outside the goal area, is watching Matthews' approach; and Perry is now in line four yards or so behind Mortensen. Matthews takes a glance upwards, and reads the situation in a flash: a pass pulled back to Mortensen will in all probability be blocked or deflected by Barrass. Matthews' concentration is total, head down over the ball, like a potter moulding his clay.

Now leaning at such an angle only he has mastered over the years, arms spread in perfect balance, he pulls his pass backwards beyond Barrass at an angle of thirty-five to forty degrees. As he does so his left foot, his anchor on the soft turf, slides; and with the ball gone, he slips down on to his left knee. It will be argued later, by those who seek to denigrate his achievement in this moment of glory, that he slipped before he passed, that the slip was contributory to his and Blackpool's moment of fortune. Yet photographs clearly disprove this, for his studs still held at the moment the ball was on its way. I can vouch for the likelihood of his falling in such a position at such an angle on this turf; in almost the same spot eighteen months later, playing on the wing for Cambridge against Oxford, I dislodged a piece of turf, almost the size of a chair seat, with my grounded foot when making an acute centre.

As Matthews falls and Barrass turns, having just failed to intercept the ball, Mortensen checks a yard inside the goal area: the ball is going behind him, too far behind him, almost back towards the penalty spot. Straight to Perry. Holden, Bolton's right-winger, is likewise doing his best in this moment of crisis, and has come back to shadow Perry. But now, having placed himself goal-side of Perry, he has no chance of reaching the pass that is speeding on to Perry's *right* foot. It will also be claimed afterwards that the ball runs almost beyond Perry; that he has to hook it through nearly 180 degrees. This is not so. As it comes to him and he places his left foot in preparation to shoot, he is able to have half an eye on the goal, and at the moment of impact he is almost square on to the goal. The angle between pass and shot is probably sixty degrees. As he meets the ball, there are eight players clustered in and around the goal area: Hanson and Ball, poised on the goal-line like a couple of relay runners waiting for the baton; Mortensen static, and Matthews sitting on the ground watching; Barrass, Banks, Hassall and Holden all vainly moving towards the ball, like men hoping to grasp a rabbit bare-handed.

Perry shoots. Hanson and Ball lunge helplessly on the line as the shot streaks beyond them into the left-hand corner of the net, almost striking the net stanchion. Mortensen wheels away in triumph, Perry throws out his arms in acclaim; while Bolton's defenders stand looking at that ball in the back of the net in utter resignation, their resilience and their spirit finally crushed. The roar that swells up from the stadium, a roar that has been riding a crescendo for the last five minutes, now has an intensity that threatens to shake the girders from their rivets. Blackpool, indeed the nation, celebrates; Matthews, in the most extraordinary of circumstances, has his medal. And Mrs Vallance is in a permanent faint.

The stadium is in pandemonium. People lose hats, scarves, umbrellas, and probably some of their children, in an ecstasy of celebration. Thousands are in tears, tens of thousands are limp with emotional exhaustion. Such an event could not have been achieved by design for Coronation Year. As Blackpool wearily go forward to climb the steps and collect the Cup from the Queen, Johnston dashes over to Johnny Crosland, Blackpool's twelfth man, to collect his teeth. If he has to shake hands with the Queen, he wants to be properly dressed. The Queen is having quite a year, what with Hillary and Tensing ascending Everest, and Gordon Richards about to win the Derby on Pinza.

While all thought at this moment, in the stadium and indeed throughout the country among those following the match, was for Matthews, thought should be reserved for those who helped to make it happen: Mortensen with his three goals, Taylor with his selfless service to the master on the wing, Perry with his final stroke of execution. 'I had to hook it a bit,' Perry reflects.'Morty says he left it to me, but that's not true, it was out of his reach. Ernie changed the run of play. He didn't get the credit, but he was the main man. Although I scored the winning goal, strangely I didn't get much satisfaction from the game. I'd contributed much more in the semi-final against Spurs. Of course Stan was special, the *ability* he had. If a player had a choice of pass, me or Stan, they'd give it to Stan, knowing he'd get to the line and take two opponents with him. For speed, I'd beat him every time over fifty yards, but never over five or ten yards. His dedication had always been a lesson to anyone, he'd come back to the club in the afternoon and work alone with the ball. That was rare, especially at his age.' Perry arrived in Blackpool from South Africa, at the age of nineteen, in 1949, and scored more than a hundred goals for them from the wing, an achievement by a winger equalled only by Peter Harris of Portsmouth. Perry was not, on his own admission, particularly clever – 'but quick, I used to go and watch Billy Liddell at Liverpool a lot, I think he was similar to me.'

Ralph Banks is as philosophical today as he was at the time. 'On the winning goal, Stan went past me on the outside, along the line, and Barrass went to smother him. I might as well have been off the field by then. When we came down from the Royal Box, Malcolm [Barrass] threw his loser's medal in the air, and lost it in the sand behind the goal. Back in the dressing-room, it was terrible. Ridding [the manager] didn't say much – there wasn't much he could say. Stan had come over to me at the end, and we were just about to shake hands, when Joe Smith dragged him away for the celebrations. I thought it nice when Stan was interviewed afterwards and said about me, "Ralph doesn't kick you all over the place." I never was a thumper. I beat him a time or two before the cramp came on, but then it were murder.' He loved his time at Bolton, he says. All of it. 'It was a good club, they used to give us a treat at Blackpool, take us to stay in a nice hotel. There was no falling out. We were a fine team. It got to where you didn't have to look at the notice board.'

Lofthouse looks back almost nostalgically: 'When it was all over, I felt it couldn't have gone to a better man. There were no recriminations in our dressing-room. I don't think a bullet would have stopped Stan in the last seventeen minutes. Ernie may have been the man of the match, in a sense, but it still needed Stan's judgement. It was such a friendly match, in a way. There were seven Lancashire clubs in the First Division those days, and before the match we were all talking together with Blackpool, chatting away about families and holidays. Not mentioning the match, of course!'

In a daze of euphoria, I and a friend – the son of the doctor of Johnny Lynas, the Blackpool trainer – wandered around for an hour and a half, long after everyone had finally drifted away from the stadium, searching for the car of the schoolmaster who had brought us to the match. It did not seem to matter to us at the time whether we found him or not. I was anxious to read the papers in the morning: to confirm that every trembling detail of the afternoon was true. I could never then have agreed with the view, expressed some years later by Danny Blanchflower in the *Sunday Express*: that Stanley's last twenty minutes were far from being his best, and that the final was mostly bad football. True, there had been mistakes on both sides, particularly those by Farm which enabled Bolton to lead 2–1. Blanchflower is one of those who claim that Stan slipped on the final pass for the winning goal, but he should look again at the picture-stills, and the Movietone news clips.

He claims Morty's equalizing free kick was luck, yet he earned his luck by the way he struck the ball.

What none of us had known, nailed to our seats by the drama inside Wembley, was that at almost exactly the same time as Stanley was creating history, a British Airways Comet, on a flight from Singapore to London, had crashed in a storm after taking off from Calcutta, killing all forty-three on board. In Monday morning's papers, Bolton denied that Bell, their left-half, had been injured before the match and should not have played. Bell said that the previous injury was different, and in no way contributory to the muscle pull he suffered in the final. Praise for Stanley, predictably, knew no bounds as the papers wallowed in sentimentality. It can fairly be said that never was it more justified. And the England selectors, with their characteristic Pavlovian reaction, promptly recalled the 38-year-old hero, who had been out of the England team for more than two years, for the forthcoming tour of South America and New York. If nothing else, the selectors knew how to seek popularity. Stanley, as ever, took it all in his stride, with no more than a murmur of satisfaction and gratitude. In his by-lined comments in the *Sunday Express*, he said that one of the most touching moments was the spontaneous and ungrudging congratulations of the Bolton players. Football was like that in those days. When players were, however wrongly, still paid only a few pounds for performing, they retained a sense of proportion in victory and defeat. 'We went to the team's hotel afterwards for dinner, and then caught the nine-thirty train home.' Jack recalls. Dinner was early in those days. 'The team then went off to the Café de Paris. Mother was invited, but she wouldn't go'.

'I know she was pleased, the way she looked at me,' Stanley says.

9. EXPOSED

'*THE* greatest tribute to Stanley Matthews, the Houdini of soccer... is that he can go to any ground and make a monkey of a full-back, and still be loved by the crowd. No one ever tires of watching him: no one is ever bored by his methods: no one has ever quite discovered just how he mesmerizes his way beyond two or three players who have given their oath they will stop him that day, come what may. Stanley is inimitable. Football has never had anything quite like him. Even Alex James, whose play was similar, was not honoured by so much attention from opponents... No planned tactic can stop him, save the switching of so many to look after him that the rest of the Blackpool line must get goals. And the agile Matthews brain is rivalled by the agile Matthews feet, which take him out of harm's way easily when the fiercest tackle is in mid-air. That Matthews can do almost precisely what he likes with the ball and with opponents is the greatest mystery of football. He is the sleight of foot artist doing his turn almost in slow motion, and still concealing the trick of it. Watch him in the film of the recent Blackpool cup tie and you will wonder (still more than you do when you see him in the flesh) how he can meander through a defence as though it did not exist. Matthews is an enigma in other ways, too. He is the most undemonstrative player in the game: he says less on the field and off than any other. He plays soccer as though in a poker school, a school, by the way, in which he is never seen with less than a full house. What is his secret? Footballers and fans have been trying to answer that and no one, least of all Matthews himself, has ever supplied the answer. As far as anyone can judge, he blends ability, adaptability, variation of pace, variation of policy and agility, with wonderful balance and a guile which takes him where the inspiration of the moment takes him. On top of that, he has the greatest ace of them all: the knowledge that the full-back who takes him on is half beaten before he steps on the pitch. The Matthews physique is just not there. A stranger, pitchforked into any ground when Matthews is performing, would take one look at his hunched up figure and slight build, when the ball is on the other side of the park, and would say: "That man is not only an unlikely looking footballer, but is obviously a little bored, or a bit chilled". How deceptive is appearance. How often does Matthews take and give a charge and remain upright? No doubt his stamina and his timing were passed down to him in part by his professional boxer father. Matthews senior must have been something of a sporting character, too. One of his fights at the old National Sporting Club was so fierce and unyielding that the referee, father of the old England cricket captain, J.W.H.T. Douglas, sent both men to their corners before the end and said: "There will be no winner, or loser." *

LESLIE EDWARDS, *Liverpool Echo*

THE belated invitation of the selection committee to go to South America was in vain. Concerned about the strain for which he had had an injection immediately prior to the final, Stanley thought it unwise to accept. It was likely that the long trip, and matches on unfamiliar ground against Argentina, Chile and Uruguay, would neither assist the team, enhance his reputation, nor allow him to begin the start of the next season fully fit. The following weekend he went to Dublin for a charity match, and had to coast his way through that at half pace. England headed across the Atlantic, drew 0–0 with Argentina, beat Chile 2–1 and lost by the same score to Uruguay. It was on this trip that Tommy Taylor, the tall Manchester United centre-forward, who would be one of the victims of Munich, made his debut alongside Lofthouse; while Johnny Berry, so dangerous on the wing for Birmingham and subsequently bought by Busby, made his first appearance on England's left wing. Berry would survive United's crash, though afterwards was never the same man.

The opening international match of the 1953–54 season was against Wales, in which Quixall, a rising young star with Sheffield Wednesday, who would fail to fulfil his immense teenage promise, replaced Broadis at inside-forward; Finney and Mullen were on the wings. England won 4–1. An air of false security insulated the English team and the British football public. After a fortunate draw with a fine Austria side in 1951, newspapers had continued blindly to claim that 'British is Best'; and a 6–3 victory over the United States on the way home from the summer tour had erased some of the memories of humiliation in Belo Horizonte. Rous relates in his autobiography the continuing absurdity of selection committee meetings: the manoeuvring of individual members of the committee to get their personal preferences included in the team; their resistance to Winterbottom's pleas to play some particular club pair together to exploit their familiarity with each other. Teams were still being selected one position at a time on a show of hands; so that it was possible for England to take the field with eleven wholly unrelated players. In the first four matches of the 1953–54 season there were thirteen team changes.

Following the Wales victory, England played a FIFA XI to mark the ninetieth anniversary of the FA. The FIFA team was given the exaggerated title of the Rest of the World, when it was selected exclusively from western Europe: Austria, Italy, Spain, Sweden, Yugoslavia and West Germany. The Cambridge University team with which I was currently playing went to the match, and some of the skills which we saw, primarily from the visitors though at times also from Matthews, Mortensen and Quixall, were a revelation. Kubala, who in his time would gain international caps for Hungary, Czechoslovakia and Spain, was sheer delight. There was seemingly nothing he could not do with the ball, no matter how it came to him; FIFA's other midfield players, Vukas, Cajkovski and Ocwirk, a master at shielding the ball from the tackle, were endlessly inventive.

England spent an embarrassing afternoon attempting to tie down these elusive Continentals. After only five minutes Vukas, who formed a Yugoslav left-wing with Zebec, was brought down in the penalty area, and Kubala scored from the kick. England had their moments: one of them three minutes later when Mortensen burst through to equalize. Thereafter, FIFA toyed with England's defence for a while, and Boniperti, the Italian right-winger, scored with two unstoppable shots, England's full-back Eckersley being overrun. Only a misunderstanding between Zeman in goal and his right-back Navarro allowed Mullen to reduce the margin before half-time. Matthews had been recalled on the wing, yet, even from Mortensen, was receiving little service, the preoccupations of Wright at right-half being almost entirely defensive. However, it was Matthews who created the opening in the second half for Mullen to level the scores again. Both sides had further chances, with FIFA always the more decorative team in spite of their unfamiliarity with each other; and Kubala once more put them in the lead. Just when it seemed that England was about to experience its first home defeat, a penalty was awarded following a collision between Mortensen and Cajkovski, and Ramsey's careful shot preserved the unbeaten record for a few weeks more.

In November, following a 3–1 victory over Northern Ireland at Goodison Park, with goals from the Bolton partnership of Lofthouse and Hassall (2), England were due to play Hungary. Rous had seen the Hungarians impressively win the Olympic title the year before, in Helsinki, and had promptly invited them to play in London. Hungarian football had been steadily developing for fifteen years. Before the war they had some 15,000 registered players; now there were more than 100,000. Moreover, they had long ago recognized the importance of coaching, and had 900 qualified coaches training their young players. Arthur Rowe, at this time the manager of Tottenham and later the coach of Pegasus, the combined Oxford and Cambridge team which twice won the Amateur Cup, had played in Hungary before the war, and was well aware of the threat which they posed to the alleged invincibility of the English.

Since 1945, Hungary had won over eighty per cent of their mat-

ches, were unbeaten at home, and unbeaten anywhere in the past four
seasons. Several English journalists had been on a spying mission to
Budapest beforehand to run their eye over the Hungarian team; not-
withstanding which they remained confidently ready to forecast an
England victory on the morning of the match. Their number even
included the eminently experienced Charles Buchan, who wrote in the
News Chronicle: 'I think we have the men to beat the brilliant Hungarians.
This is the best team England have put in the field this season . . . .
The clever ball-control and close passing of the Hungarians do not
alarm me in any way. Close marking by the half-backs is the answer.
Our defenders should prove equal to the task. I have little doubt that
Eckersley will cover centre-half Johnston and his partner Ramsey, and
ensure that no openings are left as they were against FIFA. Do not
expect a goal flood.' As forecasts go, this was delta minus.

Only two men in England, it seems, were fully attuned to the
danger impending: Rous, and Geoffrey Green of *The Times*. In a BBC
radio discussion beforehand, Green, who had not seen the Hungarians
yet was instinctively aware of English shortcomings during the FIFA
match, said that 'one of these days we shall wake up and find six goals
in the back of our net. I believe Hungary will beat us 4–2.' Green's
perceptively accurate forecast was aided on the day by what was – not
just with hindsight – an inept selection. Although the defence, and
Matthews on the right-wing, remained unaltered, the other four forwards were changed. Finney was only missing on the left-wing at the
last minute because of injury, his place being taken, quite inexplicably,
by George Robb. A year before, Robb had been an amateur international playing with Finchley in the Athenean League, and he now
had had one season as a professional with Tottenham. His virtue was
that, as a member of the British Olympic team, he was the only England
player to have seen the opposition; and may have advised them what
they were about to encounter. The three inside-forward positions were
taken by Mortensen, recalled in place of Lofthouse; Ernie Taylor, who
replaced Quixall; and Sewell of Sheffield Wednesday, who had played
four times two seasons previously. Yet in spite of muddled thinking in
the selection of the attack, it was the defence that would be found
wanting. In a hand-out before the game, the Hungarians had provided
the information that when England first played Hungary, 'the English
goalkeeper had so little to do that he sat on the cross-bar smoking his
pipe'. That was in 1901, when England won 4–0. The positions were
about to be reversed by the following teams:

ENGLAND: Merrick (*Birmingham*); Ramsey (*Spurs*), Eckersley (*Blackburn*); Wright (*Wolves*, capt.), Johnston (*Blackpool*), Dickinson (*Ports-

mouth); Matthews (*Blackpool*), Taylor (*Blackpool*), Mortensen (*Blackpool*), Sewell (*Sheffield Wednesday*), Robb (*Spurs*).
HUNGARY: Grosics; Buzanky, Lantos; Bozsik, Lorant, Zakarias; Budai, Koscis, Hidegkuti, Puskas (capt.), Czibor.

Seemingly dazzled by a candle when facing the sun, the selectors' choice of Ernie Taylor, for his first and only cap, was extraordinary: never mind his contribution to Blackpool's Cup victory. He was going to share, with Wright, the job of opposing a player about to demonstrate that he was currently the most dangerous in the world: Puskas. It was, maybe, a reassuring self-delusion that England's right-side triangle of Johnston, Matthews, Taylor and Mortensen would find some neutralizing co-ordination; yet, in the event, the England team would play almost as though blindfolded. The unique success that the Hungarians were about to achieve was the more startling because they themselves, conditioned to decades of acknowledging English leadership, questioned their ability to do so. Laszlo Felaki, the only journalist accompanying the Hungarian team to London, was the specialist of *Nep Sport*, the national sports paper, and his forecast was cautious. 'It is much more difficult for us than the Olympic Games,' he said beforehand. 'We would be happy to get a draw. This would be a good result for us. Not one of the Hungarian players has ever been in England before, nor seen an English team play. Our players are great ball artists, but I believe our defence will be the weak link.' A fortnight before, the Hungarians had played a less than effective draw with Sweden; and though they had run up a hat-full of goals in practice matches against factory teams, they retained a conditioned perception of England's invincibility.

Their left-back, confronting Matthews, was Mikhalyi Lantos. I was recently able to talk to him in Budapest about that eventful day on which he and his ten colleagues were to become national heroes for all time.

We respected England as the home of football, and we'd heard of Matthews, of course [Lantos says]. Some of our experts had been to England beforehand to analyse the opposition, and I was told about this right-winger who was thirty-eight. I was assured that his age was irrelevant, that he was a master of dribbling and very quick. But I was still wondering what I would find. We knew we were a good side, having beaten Sweden, the 1948 Olympic champions, by six goals in the Olympic semi-finals, and then Yugoslavia 2–0 in the final. After the recent draw with Sweden in Budapest, when Puskas missed a penalty, it had been a long journey through Austria and Switzerland by train, with a stop-off in Paris for an informal warm-up match. We'd been through our plans against England fairly carefully with Gustav

Sebes, our coach, though the way we were going to play was little different from normal.

We played a 3–1–2–4 formation, though with a lot of flexibility. Buzansky, Lorant and myself were the back line, Zakarias was a defensive wing-half in front of us, and the midfield players were Hidegkuti, even though he wore No. 9, and Bozsik. In front, there were the two wingers, Budai and Czibor, either side of Koscis and Puskas. Czibor and Budai both came back deep when the opposition had the ball; but when we were attacking, Bozsik and Hidegkuti would both move forward to join the four at the front, so that we could attack with six.

I was surprised to be told that Matthews never headed the ball, and I was fascinated to see such a man and be playing against him. I was twenty-five, and had previously been a stopper centre-half when I was in the Under–23 side with several of the same team. My club, MTK, had bought me as a centre-forward. I was a strong kicker and Bukovi, the MTK coach, who was the creator of the 4–2–4 formation, converted me to full-back. One day when Bukovi was absent at a match, the national left-back, Biro, who had fifty-three caps, switched himself to centre-forward. He had an ambition to play there, but the team lost 3–2. Biro got the sack, but I now had the position at left-back.

One of our aims at Wembley was to exclude Wright from the play, as much as we could, to bypass him by the interchanging of our midfield players, and we succeeded in this. But Matthews I found a problem. I'd prepared myself beforehand to try to get to the ball before him, but found I couldn't do this, and had to drop back, leaving Matthews to be challenged either by Zakarias or Czibor. There was a great similarity in dribbling skills between Matthews and Garrincha of Brazil, the same speed off the mark. Garrincha scored more goals, but I found that Matthews had a much finer awareness of the position of his colleagues.

It did not take long for England to discover a measure of their opponent's skill. To be precise, fifty seconds. Leo Horn, the Dutch referee, blew his whistle and immediately England conceded a throw-in. Instantly the ball flickered towards the England goal in an allegro of silken passes: from Bozsik to Hidegkuti, a couple of dummies, a side-step, and Hidegkuti had the ball past Merrick and in the net with a shot that England's goalkeeper hardly saw. From the moment Dickinson conceded the throw, not an England player had touched the ball.

SM: It was Hidegkuti who was at the root of all our problems. He was playing as a deep centre-forward, in reality in midfield. You can't afford to leave a player of such ability on his own. I must admit that my own mood beforehand was that we'd win, I never imagined that we could lose at Wembley, even if they *had* scored twelve goals in their practice in Paris. Harry Johnston didn't know whether to go with Hidegkuti, or stay and cover the middle. I shouted at Billy Wright that we should put Taylor – anybody – on Hidegkuti. Blackpool had had the experience when playing in Stockholm of having to deal with a deep-lying centre-forward, Liedholm, when we were two down after twenty minutes; and we'd pulled back a forward, McCall, from inside-left, and he had checked the flow. This is what we should have done now, to let Harry stay deep.

I don't know whether Walter discussed this with Harry at half-time. He may have done, but he seemed to spend much of the interval talking to George Robb. It's difficult to know how we might have done better, because they overran us so swiftly, and this meant that their defence was full of confidence. I didn't do that much against Lantos, as I remember. I felt rather out of it, though when I am on the field I have no sense of whether I'm dangerous. I only know that on that occasion I hadn't any confidence. Morty was our best forward. I was sick with disappointment afterwards, though there's no doubt they were easily the better team. The press hammered us, and it was even suggested that we should go to ballet lessons! Yet Hungary had eleven great players, and I don't know who could have beaten them at that time. The third goal by Puskas, when he controlled the ball and shot almost in one movement, was remarkable.

After a quarter of an hour there had been briefly the illusion that England might save the day. A fine intervention by Johnston gave him the chance to put Mortensen away, and with Sewell slipping into a gap while Hungary were expecting Mortensen to shoot, Morty slipped him the pass for an equalizing goal. Hungary's answer to this was to score three goals in eight minutes through Hidegkuti, Puskas and Bozsik. As Stanley has said, it was the goal by Puskas that left English football open-mouthed in wonderment.

Wright went into a tackle on Puskas inside the penalty area as the ball was crossed from the right. As the ball and Wright's boot arrived almost simultaneously, Puskas controlled and dragged the ball back, away from the tackle, under the sole of his foot and in one continuous movement struck a shot with the same left foot into the roof of the net. Even the ranks of Tuscany could scarce forbear to cheer. The game was little more than half an hour old, and Hungary were 4–1 in front.

In the thirty-seventh minute, Mortensen, ever eager, again cut clear and this time scored himself. Such slim hope as England might have retained of saving the game was dashed when Grosics made a phenomenal save from a header by Robb just before half-time. With a great team, Hungary were additionally fortified by a great goalkeeper. England were done for. Further goals by Bozsik and Hidegkuti in the second half, and a penalty by Ramsey, completed the score of 6–3. The news throbbed throughout the football world for the next twelve months. It was a watershed in the international game.

A million post-mortems would be conducted in football clubs and ordinary households up and down the land. The English had at last had their eyes opened to the march of the game the other side of the Channel. Was it a matter of Hungarian skill, or tactics, that had to be equalled? And how could this be achieved? Writing at the time, Stanley had said:

All the old stars had to fight their way to the top, and they were learning all the way. That is why they were good. Where are those youngsters we thought would pitch us older players out of the game long ago and keep up the old standard of British football? The ability is not there nowadays, and the will to learn is missing. Far too many youngsters appear to know it all before they start. Some of them will not listen to advice, even from senior professionals, and, to many of them, training beyond the minimum is irksome.

We had more competition for places in our day. Albert Geldard played for Everton at sixteen. If you got in the team, you were mature by twenty-one.

When I was a boy I played football every evening after school, sometimes with teams of twenty a side, sometimes with only half a dozen. Anything for a game. When the ground was waterlogged, as it often was during the winter, I used to kick a tennis ball against our garden well. My ball control can be traced back to that small rubber ball and the garden wall. A footballer cannot see too much of the ball when he is young. I would set young players to it every day, and keep them at it until they reach the age of nineteen. There appears to be a greater sense of discipline among players on the Continent. Discipline is what we need, and if any youngster doesn't like the idea, let him get out. Young players must learn that they only get out of football what they put into it . . . .

The reaction of the England selectors to the disaster was predictable: eight changes against Scotland in the spring at Hampden, including five new caps. Ramsey had played his last match, Staniforth and Roger Byrne coming in at full-back, Clarke at centre-half, Ronnie Allen and Nicholls in attack. Finney once more replaced Matthews on the right wing. In spite of this lottery of alterations, England won 4–2; and, with more optimism than confidence, set off for a summer tour of

Yugoslavia and Hungary prior to playing in the World Cup finals in Switzerland. The British Championships had again been a qualifying group for the finals; and this time Scotland agreed to accept their qualification. The only change by England in Belgrade was the replacement of Clarke by Owen, the Luton centre-half. England lost by the only goal, and now faced the all-powerful Hungarians in Budapest.

When we discovered that Matthews was not even in the party, we were delighted and astonished [Lantos recalls]. He had been one of the best in London: he was the player who had created the goal-scoring chances. We were equally astonished at seeing Merrick in Budapest, not on account of his being a particularly bad goalkeeper, but because we knew he would have lost any self-confidence against us. Another error in Budapest was that of putting Owen, the centre-half, tight on Hidegkuti, because this completely opened the middle of England's defence for Koscis and Puskas . . . . The final score could have been fifteen. I got the first from a free-kick. We'd won friendlies against Scotland 3–1 and 4–2, and at that time we thought they were better than England.

These were good times for us in many ways. We could take almost anything we wanted back through Customs – nylons, watches – though sometimes we had to sell a few things to the Customs officials. I finished with MTK in 1962, and then had three years as coach of Olympiakos in Athens. We won the championship twice and the Cup once. Then I came back to coach a small mining town in southern Hungary, Komoto, and we won the Second Division championship. Eight of our team had never even seen the Nep stadium.

Sebes, who created our great national side, was disliked by many officials because he selected those players *he* wanted. He had his own way. That's often not the case, and that's why many of our best coaches, such as Baroti, Stefan Kovacs and Ferenc Kovacs, have had much of their success abroad. Me, nowadays? Now I'm someone in the family; someone *here*, someone *there*, a grandfather doing the odd jobs.

Lantos smiles with the satisfaction of an old man who has experienced fulfilment; and his reflections cast doubt on the tactical wisdom of Winterbottom.

There were yet more changes in the England attack in Budapest, five including the switching of Finney from right to left, bringing the total during the current season to twenty-two changes in seven matches in the forward line alone; chaos by design. It was hardly a surprise that England crashed 7–1. With their tail between their legs, they set off for Switzerland. Public pressure now forced the recall of Matthews, who replaced Peter Harris for the opening match against Belgium. With such an unsettled team, they did well to hold the Belgians to a 4–4 draw. Coppens, Belgium's centre-forward, was a constant thorn in England's defence, with Owen no answer to the problem at centre-half. Matthews, prompting memories of his performance years before in Brussels, led the Belgians a dance and made enough chances for the match to have been won comfortably.

We hadn't really learned much since 1950 [Billy Wright admits]. We were still playing as individuals rather than as a unit, because our domestic game was used to chances being created by individuals rather than by collective play. Even after the Hungarian defeats, people continued thinking for some years that the 6–3 defeat was just a 'one-off', and tended to overlook the slaughter in Budapest. There was still the misconception that ours was 'the best league in the world'. In the World Cup in '54 our forwards were a bit better, but the defence was worse. Stan was incredibly fit for thirty-nine, exceptional, and he did well for us out there.

For the second match, against Switzerland, a radical change was made that for once seemed sense: Wright was switched from wing-half to centre-half. It was a change that probably should have been made years before, because passing the ball was never one of Wright's strengths, and his continuing selection at wing-half, great competitor and leader on the field that he was, had kept out of the team other and possibly better wing-halves, such as Nicholson of Spurs. McGarry of Huddersfield now came in at right-half, Taylor replaced Lofthouse, and with Matthews carrying a knock from the first match, Finney once more switched flanks, Mullen coming back on the left.

In a temperature of over one hundred degrees, England qualified with an uneventful 2–0 victory free of alarms. In addition to Matthews, Lofthouse, who had scored twice against Belgium, was unfit, and replaced by Taylor. Geoffrey Green wrote: 'England, in a world sense, represents a Third Division side that has found its way into the last eight of the FA Cup.' In that last eight they would meet Uruguay, one of the four best teams of the finals.

'That was the vital match,' Stanley recollects. 'Unfortunately, poor Merrick in goal let one in early on the near post. When your goalkeeper's making errors, it's difficult for the rest of the side. We were on top for the last twenty minutes, but couldn't maximize it. We really did have a bit of a chance.' Lofthouse and Matthews were back, Finney was on the left, Wilshaw and Broadis at inside-forward. Winterbottom might complain that the selectors had prevented the experimenting with young players such as Quixall and Nicholls of West Bromwich from being developed; yet the belated return to the older men had produced some effectiveness, and dignity. Lofthouse echoes Stanley's feelings. 'We could have reached the final with that team,' he says. 'It was bad goal-keeping that finished us against Uruguay. That was the first time I'd ever seen Walter agitated. We gave Uruguay two or three goals. There was a lot of joking in the squad about Stan's age. We asked him if Albert Quixall was his elder son.' He could have been.

It was another blistering afternoon for the match with Uruguay, and in the contrast of English and South American styles it was the English, though defeated, who had looked the better team. Wright had found his role in the heart of defence; and Matthews, defying his own years and the youth of his full-back, played one of the most varied and tactical games of his whole career, drifting from one side of the field to the other as he sought to set his colleagues free. Borges put Uruguay in front, only for Matthews to send Wilshaw through at the start of a move which saw Lofthouse equalize. Uruguay pulled back eight men to stem the English tide; Lofthouse and Wilshaw both went close. Now came the first set-back. Varela, Uruguay's centre-half, hit a speculative long-range shot which Merrick seriously misjudged; and England were 2–1 down. In the second half, England continued to call the tune, and with several Uruguayans showing signs of injury or fatigue, England were poised to draw level. Instead, Merrick failed to react to a shot by the brilliant Schiaffino which most international goalkeepers might have saved; and England were 3–1 down. They swept into attack, Finney scored, and they were back in the match. Now pounding the Uruguayans, they again seemed likely to equalize. Matthews hit a post, and had another shot turned away by Maspoli in goal. With a quarter of an hour to go Ambrois, for the third time, found Merrick wanting, and England's fine performance ended with wretched elimination.

In another quarter-final, in Berne, Hungary won what had developed into a shameful brawl with Brazil, then defeated Uruguay, and met West Germany in the final. Earlier, they had outplayed the Germans. Now, with Puskas unfit, and possibly ill-advised to play, Hungary suffered their first reverse in four years, and lost to a team shrewdly organized by the legendary Herberger.

10. EVERGREEN

*I*T is complained that the Matthews life had veered from that of the dedicated footballer into something grotesquely compulsive, like a circus act preserved into aged ponderousness. The answer is the same answer that must be given to those who question his greatness even as a young player; whatever name you care to give it, the Matthews act worked. He compelled attention, which was very often his principal value when he was playing for England. It did not matter, least of all to Matthews, which of his side put the ball in the net. Football is not just a game. In a sense, Matthews' clinging to his playing days was very like the manner in which he played an individual match. When he moved with the ball, shuffling, leaning, edging ever closer to the defender, he was always the man teetering to the very brink of disaster, and we waited breathlessly to see whether this time he would fail or whether yet again he would come swaying back at the last possible moment to run on clear and free. This was how his career was for years. Could he carry on past forty? He played for his country at forty-two. Every season after that had to be his last. Or just one more? Would this be the very last game? Back he came for another. There was the courage of manhood here, of the very English, stubborn, contrary, self-determining kind... the response he drew from crowds was very different from the one George Best gets. I think, for one thing, we were always afraid for Matthews, the non-athlete; the sadly impassive face, with its high cheek-bones, pale lips and hooded eyes, had a lot of pain in it, the deep hurt that came from prolonged effort and the certainty of more blows. It was a worker's face, like a miner's, never really young, tight against the brutal world even in repose. We admired him deeply, urging him on but afraid for him, too, as he trotted up yet again to show his shins to a big young full-back and invite the lad to make a name for himself by chopping old Merlin down. The anxiety showed in Matthews too: again like the frail miner's fear of the job which must always be done, not joyfully but in deeper satisfaction, for self-respect. As Matthews said, "It's my living." In communicating this frailty and this effort, Matthews went to men's hearts, essentially to inconspicuous, mild, working men's. He was the opposite of glamorous; a non-drinker, non-smoker, careful with his money. He had an habitual little cough. He was representative of his age and his class, brought up among thrift and the ever-looming threat of dole and debt. For as long as he was one of the world's fleetest movers he never had exuberance. He came from that England which had no reason to know that the Twenties were Naughty and the Thirties had Style. *'*

ARTHUR HOPCRAFT, *The Football Man*

SM: For most of my later years, I had a constant unspoken battle with the reporters. For one game, I'd be OK, two games maybe. Then, if in the third I was so-so, out would come the cry that I was too old. An old player will never play really badly or too disappointingly, because of experience. I was lucky in my friendship with Arthur Millwood, the osteopath at Manchester, who knew how to treat my injuries and helped to keep me going. The problem was that when I reached my last games for England after forty, if things went wrong, I was the first one dropped. By then I'd realized that I didn't need to train so much, and to avoid feeling jaded on Saturday, I would try to take Wednesdays completely off – no match or even training if I could avoid it. Other people always think they know your business better than you do. I remember once, with Blackpool, we were playing Spurs in London, and I'd been to Ipswich the day before for some autograph signing in connection with the Co-Op. I didn't arrive at Tottenham until after two on the day of the match, and some reporters saw me and found out where I'd been. Mel Hopkins, Tottenham's left-back, followed me all over the field that day, even when the ball was dead. We lost 2–0, and the next day the papers were saying, 'What right has he to be tiring himself out going to Ipswich?' I found that the best way to deal with reporters, the next time you saw them, was to shake hands and be really nice, and they tended to be disappointed, supposing you hadn't read their report.

Emerging in the Blackpool team in the latter part of the Fifties was a young full-back called Jimmy Armfield. These days Armfield, after a playing career as Blackpool and England captain and manager of Leeds, works as journalist and broadcaster. The young Armfield found himself fascinated by the discipline and condition of a player old enough to be his father, who could still give a lesson in skill on the field to anyone in the club.

The fitness of body and mind was channelled, an exclusive occupation [Armfield says]. Stan was never one for backing horses at one o'clock on the day of a match. He'd be sitting there changed by two-fifteen, concentrating, conditioning himself for the match. That was something valuable that he taught me. Before a lot of games, you would hear his retching, being sick in the bathroom, trying to bring his wind up. 'It's feeding time at the zoo,' the other fellows in the dressing-room would joke. It was his nerves, before he got on the pitch. If you ever wanted to talk to him about anything, the place to be sure of finding him was the beach at eight in the morning. He'd be out there in ordinary trousers, wind cheater and cap, doing his deep breathing and sprints. In club training he didn't do weights, but was always asking, 'Do we have a ball today?'

In the autumn of 1954, following the disappointment of the World Cup, Stanley was included in the Football League side to play the League of Ireland in Dublin. His inside-forward was Don Revie, currently making a name for himself as a deep-lying centre-forward – in effect an inside-forward – with Manchester City. The precocious Johnny Haynes of Fulham, against whom I had played for England Under–18 Schools when he was in the FA Youth XI, was inside-left between Lofthouse and Finney. The Football League won 6–0, and this forward line, with Pilkington of Burnley replacing an unfit Finney, was selected for the first international match of the season against Ireland. Haynes and Revie scored the goals in a 2–0 win, but Revie was dropped for the next match at home to Wales, a 3–2 victory.

I was a flop in Belfast [Revie wrote in his autobiography, *Happy Wanderer*]. It was my own fault. I played too close to Stan, and there were times when I must have got in his way. The truth is, I suppose, I was trying to play with him, as you would with a winger who chases the ball, whereas Matthews is a law unto himself. I was of course trying to live up to something, because my old boss, Raich Carter at Hull, has gone down in soccer history for his wonderful association with Matthews. I understand Raich had a simple formula. He gave Stan the ball, then wandered to take up an open space in the penalty area ready for a crack at goal when Stan sent the ball over. The experience of playing with Stan against Ireland was rather chastening, and I couldn't see myself being picked again.

Stanley played well enough in the victory over Wales, Archie Ledbrooke reporting: 'Once again Matthews showed what a great player he is, especially at Wembley. His centre for Bentley's first goal, made with barely room to swing a boot, was a model. The ball fell on Bentley's head, so that he did not have to move as he nodded it home. This was the first goal of Bentley's hat-trick.' A month later England were due to meet West Germany, the World Cup holders, at Wembley. The team selected was Williams (Wolves); Staniforth (Huddersfield), Byrne (Manchester United); Phillips (Portsmouth), Wright (Wolves), Slater (Wolves); Matthews (Blackpool), Bentley (Chelsea), Allen (West

Bromwich), Shackleton (Sunderland), Finney (Preston). Allen was the dextrous centre-forward of a West Bromwich team that had unexpectedly defeated Preston, and Finney, in the Cup Final. This had been the one conspicuous failure in Finney's illustrious career. Personally, I was sorry that Slater, studious left-half for Wolves though he was, had been preferred to the gifted Barlow of West Bromwich, who had gained his only cap a couple of months before in Belfast.

Germany came to Wembley with a team being remodelled by Herberger and containing only three of the side that had won the Cup: Posipal, the captain, Kohlmeyer at full-back and Liebrich at centre-half. Kohlmeyer has now been dead some years, but Liebrich has a clear memory of Germany's humbling experience that autumn afternoon at Wembley:

> My style was fairly similar to the English game, and with this being my tenth international, I was not expecting an especially hard afternoon [Liebrich says]. We planned no particular change of tactics, but the performance of Matthews that day put him at the very peak of international players, someone like Maradona or Beckenbauer. As soon as he had the ball, he dominated us. From the touch-line, Herberger told us to try to stop the ball getting to Matthews, and told Kohlmeyer to retreat when Matthews did have it, as that was the only possibility. I went over to the left to try to halt him, and twice he went round me as if I wasn't there. At half-time we didn't alter our tactics, but kept trying to play our own game as the best method of breaking England's domination. It was an honour to play against Matthews on such a day. Byrne made a great impression at left-back, and so did Seeler for us in his second international, though he missed a couple of chances.

At inside-left for the Germans was Jupp Durwall, at twenty-seven not in the flush of youth; some twenty-odd years later he became national team manager following Helmut Schoen, who succeeded Herberger. Playing on the left side, he vividly remembers Kohlmeyer's embarrassment:

> I was inside-left, and so many times I tried to stop Matthews, yet I hadn't a chance. It was terrible for us, it could have been five or six instead of 3–1. Kohlmeyer was saying to me, 'What can I do against this man, what's happened to my concentration?' In the dressing-room afterwards, Kohlmeyer didn't say a word, he just sat on the floor with his head in his hands, and he was still there after the rest of us had dressed, and we had to wait for him in the bus before we could leave. He was in a daze, I've never seen anything like it. When Matthews was dribbling, he was not looking at the ball, he was looking at

Kohlmeyer or Liebrich. He was so special, and a great sportsman. Yet he played so many opponents out of their team. Kohlmeyer was one of them. When Muenzenberg, our full-back who had played against Matthews before the war, saw this performance, he said, 'Maybe I should still be playing at fifty.'

Seeler had not even been born when Matthews first played for England, yet the following morning the newspaper correspondents were struggling to find words adequate to describe this performance of a man two months short of his fortieth birthday. My own recollection is like that of watching a father showing off when playing football with his small sons on the beach and never letting them have the ball. The German defenders kept taking huge swipes at Stanley's legs, yet the ball and he were never there. He moved about the field as though with some magnetic attraction for the ball. I had heard crowds laugh when he tormented a full-back in League football, yet this is possibly the only time it has ever been heard in an international match, and poor Kohlmeyer was several times reduced to hoofing the ball high into the crowd when Matthews was not even within yards of him, simply because his nerve had gone.

Frank Coles wrote in the *Daily Telegraph*: 'England's decisive victory over Germany at Wembley not only bore further evidence of the gradual restoration of our national football standards, but the stark truth for all Continental teams that supremacy and mediocrity these days are narrowly divided. Yet through the changing scenes of international football, the genius of Stanley Matthews remains a radiant beacon. He won this match for England just as nearly twenty years ago he inspired the 3–0 defeat of Germany at Tottenham. For Matthews it is a dazzling decade, and that he is still as spritely and skilful at a time England seek to win back lost glories is one of the most remarkable stories of modern sport.' Lofthouse, in a commentary for the *Daily Dispatch*, said: 'Stanley showed once again with his fifteen- and twenty-yard bursts that he is one of the most remarkable players the game has ever known. Once or twice he seemed deliberately to invite Kohlmeyer to a direct race, and he won each sprint with ease. The crowd were pleased every time Matthews had the ball, and you could hear the excited chatter of expectation whenever he was put in possession. It was a lovely game to watch, and in my opinion the level was of a very high standard. I don't think much better than this was seen right through the World Cup competition in Switzerland.' Cullis, by now manager of Wolves, said in the *Express*: 'Thank heaven for Matthews. He scares the daylights out of the Continentals. England can drop him at her peril . . . . Any First Division side here would be lucky to have Werner Liebrich, the German centre-half. He is world class.'

Bob Ferrier of the *Daily Mirror* thought that Germany were a moderate team, but that Matthews was 'immense, indescribable', and went on to quote Herberger as saying afterwards: 'When Germany played England in 1938 Matthews was the menace, the outstanding player of the match. In sixteen years he has forgotten nothing.' Helmut Schoen was at that time Herberger's assistant, later succeeding him and managing Germany in four World Cup final competitions. Now retired and living at Wiesbaden, Schoen reflects: 'Stanley was unique. There has never been a better man in that position. He was not a fighter, he was a *player*, and that was why I liked him.'

In *The Times*, Geoffrey Green wrote: 'The German covering was gallant: there could have been more goals. Liebrich at centre-half was the hero. His fair head was everywhere, just as it had been against Hungary [in the World Cup final]. It was a day of perfect sunshine for the crowd of 100,000, with not a cloud. The prince of all was Matthews. Majestically, he glided across the afternoon. Poor Kohlmeyer, supported by Harpers and anyone else at hand, tried to play him all ways: sliding tackles, lunging, retreating. But always that outside flick, having anchored the defender on the other foot, would carry Matthews clear. As a variation, Matthews would go inside, or merely beat him by acceleration. Here was a tour de force by the greatest player in football . . . and not far behind Matthews was Shackleton.' Absurdly, this would be the last of Shackleton's five caps spread over seven seasons: a player of almost unlimited technique who profited or ultimately suffered, according to your view, from a belief that the game was as much about entertainment as victory. On this occasion he scored one of the goals, Bentley and Ronnie Allen the others. 'Stan and Shack were poetry, they didn't just play football,' reflects Jack Matthews.

The renaissance of Stanley's ability in this season was truly astonishing. Armfield recalls an occasion early in 1955 when they played Arsenal in London. Stanley had not been in the party that travelled south from Lancashire. At mid-morning on the day of the match, there was Stanley to be seen in the lobby, with a tan, in a cream suit. Joe Smith, surprised but delighted, said as an aside to another player without even looking at him, 'You're not playing', and turning to Matthews asked: 'Where have you been?'

'I told you I was going to South Africa,' Stan replied. 'I knew you didn't listen.'

'When did you get back?'

'Overnight.'

'Are you fit?'

'Of course.'

Stanley proceeded to play one of his best games ever for Blackpool in a 4–1 victory. There was a moment in the second half when for ten seconds he stood stationary with his foot on the ball and not a single Arsenal player had the courage to go and try to take it off him. 'The Highbury crowd gave him a standing ovation,' Mudie recollects. 'He was applauded off the field. He'd had Lionel Smith against him, then they switched Wally Barnes across to take him on, Alex Forbes had a go, then Mercer, eventually Don Roper. There were five players trying to stop him and nobody could do a thing. It was the greatest game I ever saw him play, and afterwards he just got in the bath as if nothing had happened. He simply didn't realize what he had done.' Tom Whittaker, Arsenal's manager, and Joe Smith had equal admiration. 'I've never seen him play so well – at forty years of age, it's a miracle,' Whittaker said. And Smith added, 'I've seen Stan play brilliantly many times, but never anything like that.'

England's next match was the annual springtime encounter against Scotland, the uneven year being at Wembley. The selectors played their usual private game of shuffling the cards and came up, as so often, with an odd hand: a new left-back, Meadows of Manchester City, and right-half, Armstrong of Chelsea, for each of whom this would be the only international appearance; the recall in attack of Wilshaw, Lofthouse and Revie; and, for the first time, at left-half, the phenomenal and ill-fated Duncan Edwards of Manchester United, ahead of whom in a gloriously meteoric career lay no more than eighteen caps before United's plane crash.

The Scottish left-back, on an afternoon when they were to be almost ritually slaughtered by Stanley and his colleagues – though most memorably by Stanley – was Harry Haddock, aged twenty-five:

I'd been a wireless operator, and joined Clyde in '49, part-time [Haddock says]. My next job was with the Glasgow Corporation Transport, driving buses in the days when buses were moving further and further out with the spread of the Glasgow suburbs. I loved it – marvellous days – after three months' training. You had to learn how to correct the bus with the handbrake when it started waltzing around in the wet. I had had an early football injury, and thought I was finished, but Willie Kinlock, the physiotherapist at the local hospital, said, 'Give me a month, and only pay me if I succeed.' Originally, I was a wing-half, renowned for my long throw. I once hit the cross-bar with a throw-in from ten yards back from the eighteen-yard line, and that with an old wet leather ball. Although I was shortish, five foot seven, I had strong thighs and could leap to about nine feet for a header. After we lost that match at Wembley, I went on tour with Scotland to Yugoslavia, Austria and Hungary. I was injured in the first match, missed the second, but was back for the third against Hungary in Budapest. I had played up against their winger Sandor in the match before we met England, now I had him again. I knew if I could pin him down, I could make him get rid of it. By half time he was substituted.

I was still in the squad for the World Cup finals in '58, and came in for the second match against Paraguay. I eventually finished with Clyde in '63. When I played at Wembley, Matthews was only a name, though I'd seen the '53 Cup final on television. On the day of the match, Scottish FA officials were saying to me, 'Go at him, he's got no left foot.' I tried this the first time, Stan went inside me, and shivered the cross-bar with his left foot. Don't let anyone tell you he had any deficiency other than heading. With his skill, he had no need to head. To this day, I believe I should have allowed him more to go down the touch-line. My asset was speed, to be able to get in a second tackle after recovering. At Wembley, I once made three tackles on Stan between the half-way line and the goal-line, and he still crossed the ball!

He'd walk towards you, with the ball on his right foot, feint to his left, and you'd go with him to your right. He'd touch the ball the other way, and be gone. You'd see it, and could do nothing. I knew that's what he'd do, and I wanted him to do it, to force him down the line, because I thought I had the speed, if I was still on the inside, to stay with him. But he lost me. The game in those days was more physical, yet not as dirty as it is now. Stan had a fantastic match, but I never tried to injure him, and the extraordinary thing was, once he'd gone past you, it seemed he'd forgotten about you. Football's an entertainment sport. People don't pay four quid to see me kick Matthews. I'm still repeatedly asked, 'How did it feel?' That day was something special for me, and for a lot of other people, and although we lost, it's something I treasure and no one can take away from me. It was marvellous to discover that he was so brilliant yet still just like any other fellow.

I was sorry we lost badly, but it might have been different if I'd been allowed to play the way I would have preferred. In those days you did as you were told. I'm sorry there's not the camaraderie in the game that there was then; nowadays footballers seem to be in opposition all the time, whereas then you were just opponents for an hour and a half. I was always a part-time professional, and the game for me was always a pleasure. I went to shake hands with Stan at the end and he said, 'The ball was running for me today, I think.' He wasn't big-headed, though he had enough reason to be. He had a fantastic reputation up here because of what he'd done to Scotland over the years, and when he played in a charity match in the early Eighties, when he must have been nearly seventy, twenty thousand people turned up at Grangemouth, which is thirty miles from the city centre.

Whenever he played up here, there were men taking their children to see him in case it was the last opportunity.

Annoyingly for me, I was playing for Cambridge University on the day of the Scotland match, and gave my ticket to my twelve-year-old brother. (It was the afternoon that Churchill resigned as Prime Minister, to be succeeded by Eden.) There was at the time a national newspaper strike, so that the only printed record of the match appeared in the *Manchester Guardian*, which was not involved in the dispute. Of England's 7–2 victory, in which Wilshaw scored four and Stanley had a hand in all seven, Don Davis ('Old International') wrote:

With Phillips of Portsmouth injured in training, Armstrong of Chelsea was included at right-half at the last moment. Duncan Edwards, gaining his first cap, became the youngest player in history for England at the age of eighteen years and six months. Scotland relied on the team which did well but was beaten by Hungary in December, making one change. This was one of soccer's bloodiest massacres. The Wembley turf shone like watered silk. The fumbling of Martin, the Aberdeen goalkeeper . . . aided the rejuvenation of Matthews. Martin's blunders in the second and twenty-fifth minutes, when he dropped centres when unchallenged, allowed Wilshaw to bundle the ball in. The second goal by Lofthouse came from a beautifully lobbed pass by Revie, Lofthouse beating Davidson of Partick on the turn to smash the ball in. Reilly made it 2–1. Now Martin came out to the edge of his own goal area, groped at Revie, missed, and Revie was able to stroke the ball into an empty net. Matthews made the fourth for Lofthouse. Matthews demonstrated the rarest of virtues – the spectacle of a veteran of matchless skill and limitless resources playing with all the freshness and sprightliness of youth – not short bursts, but great sweeps of the field. He holds the game up, does he? Ask Haddock. Ask Cunningham. They needed someone to hold them up before the end, yet both were scrupulously clean right to the finish. Matthews moved so fast that his own forwards were often hard pressed to keep up with him. All three second-half goals by Wilshaw were due to Matthews . . . . Not since Washbrook's record 160 in his first innings for Lancashire has any young colt stepped up into high company with such ease as Edwards.

Lofthouse, who in that match scored two of his thirty goals for England besides the 441 that he struck for Bolton in 654 matches, recollects: 'Stanley set up all our goals. The talk always comes back to him, doesn't it, even these days? When you went out with him, you were a goal up before the kick-off because the opposition had planned

all week how to stop him. He could create goals from impossible positions. And I've seen him change his boots twice in one match – only
Stan could do that.' The teams on that day of Scotland's destruction
were:

ENGLAND: Williams (*Wolves*); Meadows (*Manchester City*), Byrne (*Man-
chester United*); Armstrong (*Chelsea*), Wright (*Wolves*), Edwards (*Manch-
ester United*); Matthews (*Blackpool*), Revie (*Manchester City*), Lofthouse
(*Bolton*), Wilshaw (*Wolves*), Blunstone (*Chelsea*).
SCOTLAND: Martin (*Aberdeen*); Cunningham (*Preston*), Haddock
(*Clyde*); Docherty (*Preston*), Davidson (*Partick Thistle*), Cumming (*Heart
of Midlothian*); McKenzie (*Partick Thistle*), Johnstone (*Manchester City*),
Reilly (*Hibernian*), McMillan (*Airdrieonians*), Ring (*Clyde*).

England now departed on a summer tour of France, Spain and
Portugal, losing the first and last and drawing in Madrid, Stanley
playing in all three. The match against Spain, in front of 125,000 in
the Bernabeu Stadium, is remembered by Lofthouse as the dirtiest
international match he ever played in, the worst offender being the
Spanish left-back Campanais. At one moment in the match, Stanley,
driven to an extreme of indignation was heard to mutter, 'I could spit
at you' – which was as far over the top as Stanley had ever been known
to go. 'I wouldn't have liked to be him,' Lofthouse recalls. 'He was
jumping around, everyone was kicking him. When we thrashed Scotland, I know that Eckersley would have kicked him that afternoon, but
Harry Haddock didn't. Full-backs *did* feel proud to have played against
him, proud just to have been associated with him. But not Campanais!'
    The defeat by Portugal was forgettable; but France, who had
recently defeated West Germany, Spain and Sweden, were a developing
team that would reach the World Cup semi-final three years later, and
won only by a penalty by Kopa. Marche, the French captain and left-
back, clung to Matthews like a leech, though England were unlucky
not to break down the French defence.
    Stanley returned home, free of injury, for another of his evergreen
seasons with Blackpool. Playing against Charlton at The Valley on 1
February, his birthday, Stanley treated a 40,000 crowd to a calculatedly
individual performance in a 4–0 victory. Beforehand, the crowd had
sung 'Happy Birthday to You', but it was they who received the gift of
a matchless display. Arriving at Kings Cross station, Stanley had read
in the evening papers, Jimmy Armfield recalls, that a new full-back,
Townsend, was intending to make it an unhappy birthday for him.

    That was a red rag [Armfield says], and he put on a one-man show,
    though Ernie Taylor was trying to outdo him. It was raining, and

muddy. We were winning 3–0 when there was a penalty near the end. Ewan Fenton never missed penalties, but the crowd was shouting, 'Stan-ley, Stan-ley.' Neither of them took it, in fact, because Taylor grabbed the ball, made a tee in the mud, and put the ball on top of it. Looking at Sam Bartram in goal, Taylor pointed to the side of the net where he was going to put it. Bartram dived that way, Taylor sent it the other, and Bartram chased him half-way back to the half-way line – they were both Geordies. Stan was the only man I've seen who, when he tormented a full-back, was not putting on an act. It was part of his intention, and when he reached that point, it was the killer for any team. That's why such crowds came to see him, and even in the Midlands and South they objected if their own full-back started knocking Stanley around.

Stanley had played in the autumn international against Wales, in which England had suffered one of their rare defeats in Cardiff, losing 2–1. This had convinced the selectors for the twentieth time that he was too old, and once more Finney had been switched to the right wing against Ireland, Spain and Scotland, with Bill Perry, Stanley's Blackpool colleague, receiving his initiation on the left. Such was Stanley's form with Blackpool, and such was the public demand for his reappearance, that the selectors yielded to popularity – too often was Popularity the first name on their team sheet – and recalled him for the springtime match at Wembley against Brazil, preferring him to Finney. Brazil's full-backs for this match were Djalma Santos and Nilton Santos. Several of their team had been in the World Cup quarter-final two years before and were now part of a side being reshaped for the World Cup two years later in Sweden, where they would win world-wide admiration with their exhilarating victory. Nilton Santos, who now faced Matthews, was the captain, quick and aggressive. Describing him in his book *One Hundred Caps*, Bill Wright wrote:

Nilton Santos was very different in appearance from Djalma. His skin was lighter [Djalma was black], he was taller and less heavily built. Yet his approach to the game was every bit as aggressive, and I have seen him complete a movement by shooting at goal on more than one occasion. When I first saw him I was deceived by his air of casualness. I thought a really fast winger would be able to lose him. Yet, in later years, I always noted that no matter how fast the winger, Nilton was always alongside him waiting for the right moment to tackle. Stanley Matthews, marked by Nilton, had a hand in all four of the goals scored by England against Brazil at Wembley in 1956 – but this is no yardstick of Nilton's ability. Stanley is a law until himself. Nilton and Djalma, their individual abilities strengthened by their deep understanding of each other's play, remain the finest pair of full-backs I have ever seen.

Had it not been for the emergence of Pelé, only seventeen when he devastated Sweden in the 1958 final, Didi, Brazil's black midfield player, would probably be regarded as the finest of all players in Brazil's history. Like Pelé, he had the fluid, supple movement and ball control of all the great negro players, the difference being that he did not score the overwhelming waterfall of goals that flowed from Pelé. Didi was in the team at Wembley, and a revelation at that time for English eyes. Today he recalls:

It was one of the first occasions that I'd played outside Brazil. Wembley made a great impression on us. We had sincerely hoped for a large crowd, but never thought it would be a full house. This was a trip to Europe in preparation for the next World Cup, and some of us were very nervous. A few days earlier, we'd lost 3–0 to Italy, and didn't want to be defeated again by England. It was the last game of this tour, and at the very least we wanted to go home having given a good performance. I warned my colleagues beforehand about Tommy Taylor and about Matthews. I told Nilton, a colleague of mine with the Botafogo club in Rio, to pay particular attention to Matthews. I remember that England scored twice before the game had hardly begun, but we managed to equalize, Paulinko and I scoring soon after half-time. But England got another two with a splendid performance, and deserved their victory. Matthews was astonishing. I never thought that a player of forty-one years of age would be able to do what he did on the football pitch. I'd told Nilton, who was one of the best players of Brazil and to this day is considered to be the best marker in the history of Brazilian football, that he should be especially careful and not be influenced by Matthews' appearance or age. Yet I only know that on that afternoon Nilton gave one of his weakest performances. Not because he played badly. On the contrary. The play of Stanley Matthews, who gave a complete exhibition of his genius, must take the glory for this. He did not score any goals, but he was the creator of almost all of them. He was, for me, an extraordinary player. I would say he was in the same class as Garrincha or Julinho. He was the most like a Brazilian or Argentinian player, something rare in England, and he has not been equalled to this day.

Under the headline, 'Triumph of the Old World over the New', *The Times* carried this report from Geoffrey Green:

Marshals and scarlet Caesars have won their victories on land, but few could have equalled in colour and dramatic contexts this triumph of the Apolleonic English game over the Dyonisaic dance of Brazil. Wembley yesterday saw as varied and as exciting a show as has ever touched its velvet surface since the early days of the Rodeo. Here was everything: football, a touch of the three-ring circus, a dash of the bull-ring, and at the end of it all a huge and undisputed triumph for the original masters of the Old World against the champions of the New. A 100,000 crowd loved it from the first moment, though before the close there were many painful moments to live through.

A thousand and one things vibrate in memory, but where to start? Best perhaps is to tell the sequence of events simply. Winning the toss and taking a broad south-westerly wind on their backs, England crashed through to a two-goal lead by Taylor and Grainger within the opening five minutes. Here was something to set all England dancing. That lead they still held preciously and with much authority at half-time, though for spells the Brazilian virtuosos had seemed to need only the inspiration of a goal to set their intricate fires alight.

LONG WAY TO GO

Within ten minutes of the second half the picture had changed utterly. Paulinho and Didi, with strange goals, rocked the Englishmen to their heels. Now it was 2–2, with the balance of inspiration changed and a long, long way to go. But in the end it was the particular artistry of Stanley Matthews, backed by the iron spirit and direct skill of his colleagues, who saw England home.

Supplementing his already rich contribution to England's opening goals, it was now two centres of his from the right, each pitched to the far posts with pin-point accuracy, that were headed home by Taylor and Grainger, so that finally the grand young man of English football, aged forty-one years, left the scene of most of his greatest triumphs with yet another crown about his head. Yet during that dramatic last half-hour, he and a hundred thousand people had stood by to watch England miss two penalties into the bargain and all but throw the match away.

So in the end full justice was done and none could quarrel with the verdict; indeed, the sentence passed on the Brazilians should have been more severe. England this day played as if their very lives depended upon it. They did exactly what was required to disrupt the superb Brazilian artistry. They tackled swiftly, like lions, they refused to be drawn out of position defensively, and they used the long through pass for the sudden switch to attack, using Haynes in midfield as the hub. It was fast, direct, accurate, and full of finishing drive, and it is a long time since one has seen an English side move with such power to dominate maestros of the calibre of these Brazilians.

GREAT RIGHT BACK

Make no mistake, these Brazilians are maestros individually. There surely is no greater right-back in the world today than D. Santos, his control and use of the ball being equal to anything any forward could wish to attain. Didi, at inside-left, is a supreme artist, quick as a black panther, a man who, for a spell of twenty minutes before half-time, threatened to take the match and wrap it round his little finger. There was, too, the lightning support in attack of Dequinha, from left-half.

These were the ringmasters who took the eye. But it was in defence in depth, in teamwork, and in the creation of the final and destructive opening which stamps great sides that Brazil failed. Of the two goals they scored one was a freak bearing some dark magic about it. The other came from a mistake by the junior Matthews, who seemed unsighted under the English cross-bar, but a mistake it was.

For the rest, it was all lovely patterned approach, a colourful picture in design and content, but no finishing touch to the picture behind Wright and his backs within the English penalty area. These ebony Brazilians, wearing shirts of daffodil colour and the briefest of pale blue shorts, might have belonged to a wood in springtime. Their gyrations, too, told of dance steps in wild woods with a special relish for flexibility and flourish. But this day it all faded against the solid oak of England.

The English half-back line, in particular, won the highest laurels. Wright, Clayton, recovering wonderfully from Didi's inspired spell, and the giant Edwards, were magnificent. They, together with Hall and Byrne behind them, made all the Brazilian frills count for nothing in the end, and to them must go the major praise for the victory. But the forward line, too, reacted in just the right way, with a clever mixture of the long pass and a change of the attacking point.

Here Taylor, at centre-forward, gave full effect to the tactical plan by his authority over Pavao, both in the air and with his speed over the ground. Haynes, the linchpin of attack, was quick to spot this chink in the South American armour, and he cleverly varied his tactics accordingly to keep the Brazilians moving the wrong way, ever fearful of the pass to Stanley Matthews

SUDDEN SPASMS

Matthews, in point, came into the pattern only in sudden spasms, but when he did danger trembled as he moved either inside or outside N. Santos. In the final analysis indeed, quite apart from the vast roar of expectation he drew from the company when on the move, he had a foot in each goal, and that was something to savour.

England began with a surge as in the days of Mortensen at centre-forward. Within seconds Taylor caught the tide that carried him through the battle. He broke clean through finely, but shot too high and too soon with the roar of goal already on the wind. But within two minutes he had set it right. A fine move put England ahead. Edwards to Matthews, a lovely square pass to Haynes, a forward touch, and Taylor hit the roof of Gilmar's net a thundering smack.

Three minutes later England were two up. Matthews, falling into defence, began it near his own right corner flag. A saucy flick through Canhoteiro's legs found Hall; Hall's long through pass saw Taylor again sweep past Pavao, and there was Grainger up to shoot home from Haynes's final touch. So it remained at half-time, though Taylor, with a great shot, had hit a post. England two up, but Brazil not yet out of it by a long chalk.

Now rain began to fall, and with the sudden change the battle changed too. A new hazard was thrown in, and for the next half-hour the packed terraces lived either on the crests or in the trough of waves of excitement. With eight minutes gone, and now the wind behind Brazil, N. Santos joined a swift attack down the left. Over came a centre, and Paulinho on the right let fly almost on the by-line. The angle was the acutest possible, but the impossible happened. His shot struck Byrne, ricochetted back in an awful parabola across a helpless defence, and spun over the England goal-line.

LEVEL

This gave Brazil a straw to clutch. Within another two minutes they were level as Didi, taking Wright's half clearance, surprised Matthews (R.) from twenty yards as the goalkeeper merely turned a rising shot inside his own goalposts.

Now followed the rodeo, the circus, and all the rest. All we needed was an earthquake. Brazil, moving the ball about in close circles, seemed to have saved their day. But now their volatile temperament failed.

With half an hour left Haynes's cross free-kick from the edge of the penalty area was handled by an excitable defender. Penalty. But could the French referee make his point? It might have been carnival time in some South American city as he was jostled by the Brazilians. One player annexed the ball and made off with it like some third form schoolboy who had decided to go home with the only plaything and spoil everything. In due course Atyeo, the least distinguished of England's forwards, had his penalty kick saved, and no wonder. But why Atyeo as the intended executioner, one wondered.

But now Matthews came to the rescue, and a perfect centre by him from Haynes's inside pass was headed back by Atyeo for Taylor to nod England into the lead once more at 3–2. Then came another penalty for hands, stopping Taylor and Atyeo going through in a duet.

This time Byrne failed to beat Gilmar on his left side. The agony of it all.

Yet once more Matthews helped to settle something we should all have been spared. Hall found him with a short pass, another centre followed, and the alert Grainger stamped his first game for England with another goal, a swift header past Gilmar. England, with seven minutes left, were home at last amid gusts of excitement and a stormy afternoon now wore more than a wrinkle or two on its damp ground. Teams:

ENGLAND: Matthews (R.) (*Coventry City*); Hall (*Birmingham City*), Byrne (*Manchester United*); Clayton (*Blackburn Rovers*), Wright (*Wolverhampton Wanderers*, capt.), Edwards (*Manchester United*); Matthews (S.) (*Blackpool*), Atyeo (*Bristol City*), Taylor (*Manchester United*), Haynes (*Fulham*), Grainger (*Sheffield United*).
BRAZIL: Gilmar; D. Santos, N. Santos (capt.); Zozimo, Pavao, Dequinha; Paulinho, Alvaro, Gino, Didi, Canhoteiro.
REFEREE: M. Guigue (France).

Committed to a coaching trip to South Africa, Stanley missed the summer tour of Sweden, Finland and West Germany, but was back in the side in the autumn against Northern Ireland. England, too, were now preparing seriously for the World Cup, and the selectors at this stage were not excluding Stanley from their consideration. There was no disappointment in the 1–1 draw in Belfast in front of a 58,000 crowd, for this was the finest side in Ireland's history, that would go on to achieve noble deeds in Sweden, reaching the quarter-finals. The team on this occasion was: Gregg; Cunningham, McMichael; D. Blanchflower, Casey, J. Blanchflower; Bingham, McIlroy, Jones, McAdams, McParland. Stanley scored one of his rare goals, in spite of being opposed by one of his least favourite full-backs, McMichael of Newcastle, and from McParland's long throw McIlroy vollied the equalizer. Three consecutive victories followed at home against Wales, Yugoslavia and Denmark, in each of these Stanley now being partnered by Brooks, a powerfully fast but not particularly erudite inside-forward from Tottenham. The selectors experimented with Finney twice at centre-forward; the regular inside-forward, since mid-way through the previous season, was Haynes. The 5–2 victory over Denmark was the beginning of England's series of qualifying matches for the World Cup finals. With only half an hour to go, the Danish amateurs were holding on at 3–2 down. Two powerful drives by Edwards, added to a hat-trick by Taylor, finally floored the Danes. It had not been a happy match for Stanley because, unknown to anyone except his family, he was suffering acutely from intestinal trouble that had plagued him for years, and on the day before the match he had driven over from Wolverhampton to Stoke for some comfort at his mother's house, and returned to give a comparatively poor performance.

Nonetheless, he kept his place in the team at home to Scotland four months later, albeit with yet another inside-forward partner, Tommy Thompson of Preston; one of eight partners with whom he was asked to co-ordinate during his last sixteen appearances for England over a three-year period. Scotland were in front in the first minute when Ring, the Clyde winger, intercepted a pass from England's right-back Hall, cut inside, and drove past Hodgkinson with his right foot. It was well into the second half when Kevan, a big, lumbering inside-left from West Bromwich who was playing in his first match, headed the equalizer. In between there had been much drab football, and seven minutes from the end another of those fulsome drives by Edwards from twenty yards gave England victory and the British Championship crown.

For their second World Cup qualifying match, England now faced the Republic of Ireland at Wembley: with another four forward changes. Matthews was now partnered by the blustering Atyeo of Bristol City, who scored two goals in a 5–1 victory. Geoffrey Green reported: 'Half of the 52,000 crowd was a sea of Irish green. Clayton at wing-half supported Matthews well, but he got little from Atyeo who was playing as a double centre-forward alongside Taylor in a 3–3–4 formation. Finney, on the left wing, remains a paradox who has yet to reach his full height at Wembley.' Green considered that the half-back line, or midfield, of Clayton, Edwards and Haynes lacked balance. Matthews set the ball rolling in the ninth minute, beating two men – one of them Cantwell, the West Ham left-back – before giving Clayton the chance to set up a goal for Taylor. In their return tie with Denmark in Copenhagen a week later, England found themselves drawing 1–1 with only twenty minutes to go. They saved their blushes by scoring during a ten-minute spell while the Danish centre-half Hansen was off the field, receiving treatment for an injury suffered in a collision with Taylor. Atyeo scored, and England were safe. Finney, constantly brought into the game by Haynes, made a fourth goal for Taylor, but Matthews was again starved of the ball by Atyeo. On that day in Copenhagen, an exceptional international career spanning 23 years and 84 appearances came to a close. When England went to Dublin and luckily escaped with the 1–1 draw which was sufficient to take them to the World Cup finals, Matthews was absent. The selectors, driven by their latest whim, had switched Finney to the right for the last time, in a debate which had raged for eleven years, in order to include on the left wing David Pegg, another of Matt Busby's rising young flames; and another who would perish within nine months.

Should Matthews have been retained, at the age of forty-three, for

the World Cup the following year? Many, with and without qualification, argued that he should have been: one of them his rival and
friend, Finney. In the event, the right-wing in Sweden would be filled
by Bryan Douglas, the weaving, jinking little player from Blackburn,
who possessed much of Stanley's elusiveness, but none of that capacity
to intimidate psychologically an entire opposing team. Douglas would
even lose his place for the first-round play-off in which England lost by
the only goal to the Soviet Union. In his book *Finney on Football*, the
man who regrettably was injured in the opening match against th Soviet
Union in Sweden, and missed the next three games, wrote:

If I were England's sole international selector Stanley Matthews would
have been in the 1958 World Cup party in Sweden. I know he is an
old man by normal soccer standards, but nobody should ever attempt
to compare Stanley with the ordinary mortals of football. He is a law
unto himself, the Peter Pan of the game, the ageless artist who, shrug-
ging aside gratuitous annual advice to retire, is still with us . . . and
playing as well as ever. The *Daily Express* report of the 1948 match
between Scotland and England at Hampden Park suggested that the
Scots had seen the last of Matthews as a power in international soccer.
How could they have known that, *seven years later*, Stanley was to be
the architect of one of the most humiliating hidings ever inflicted by
an English team on Scotland. . . . Would Brazil, or Russia or Austria,
have been able to fathom the Matthews mystery had he been in an
England shirt in Gothenburg? I know I still would certainly prefer to
have him on my side than playing against me. And I'm not concerned
if he is fifty years old.

Edelston and Delaney wrote in *Masters of Soccer:* 'A player in his
twenties who was as good as Matthews was in 1958 would certainly
have been picked for the World Cup.'

When I recently discussed the performances in Sweden with Billy
Wright, he said:

We drew the second match against Brazil, and were the only team in
the competition they didn't score against. It was the first time, in that
tournament, that Walter had had a tactical assistant. Bill Nicholson,
who was just about to take over at Spurs, had been to watch Brazil
and said that it was imperative to stifle Didi. Bill Slater was given the
job and went with him everywhere. In the third match, Bobby Robson
had the chance to score the winner when it was 2–2, and missed. That
goal would have put us in the quarter-final. In the play-off against
Russia, Broadbent replaced Robson – and what a player Broadbent
would have been at any other club than Wolves. Cullis made him

work, up and back, and never allowed him to blossom. Football was changing. Systems were coming into the game. After the World Cup in 1962, I went on a coaching course in Switzerland with Walter, and Gustav Sebes told us: 'The game is altering, we will no longer have teams like Hungary, Brazil and England at the top. Tactics will take over.' The game would be the poorer for it.

'Silchester' of the *Manchester Guardian* had argued before the 1958 finals: 'On every Saturday of the football season some few hundreds, or perhaps thousands, of the people who watch football, do so, in fact, "to see Matthews". In a few days he will be forty-three years old: it would seem his days as an English international player are ended, yet, as outside-right for Blackpool, he continues to attract as many spectators as ever. Some watch him as a new experience, others out of relish for fine football, others for nostalgia's sake. None of them is likely to be disappointed. . . . It is therefore small wonder that, as the final rounds of the World Cup competition approach, many football followers are wondering whether Matthews will again win back a place in the English team. Undoubtedly he must be considered.'

He probably was; and, disappointingly, for history's sake, was left out.

For Stanley, there was compensation of a different kind in the making. Stanley junior, aged thirteen, was showing promise of becoming an excellent tennis player. From 1960 to 1962 he would be British Junior Champion, the only boy to be so three times, and in the third year he would also win the Wimbledon Junior Invitation title. No effort or expense was spared by his father towards helping him achieve his ambition. Regularly Stanley senior could be seen at tournaments, trying to remain anonymous behind dark glasses, trembling like a leaf with sympathetic expectation The best resources available in private lessons and coaching from George Worthington, the Davis Cup coach, were finding reward. Yet ultimately, having finished runner-up to Mark Cox in the Under-21 championship, Stanley junior failed to make a lasting impact on the senior game. He moved instead into coaching, and now has a successful school in America. Reflecting on his son's career, Stanley says: 'I think my reputation did put some pressure on him, no doubt about it. Maybe, too, his service was not quite strong enough, and he tended to double fault. I know it worried him a bit, being in my shadow, and I hoped he might overcome it. Yet he's made a most satisfactory career in America, so his early success has been beneficial.'

11. REVIVAL

'*MANY* a Huddersfield Dad must have been wrestling with the same problem today. Stoke City were at Leeds Road, and Matthews was due to play. Now it is not possible for any mere mortal to forecast the date when Mr Matthews will finally hang up his boots, but logically (and to put it no higher), that date is now somewhat closer than it was, say, twenty years ago. Therefore, the thought that today's might be the great man's final appearance at Leeds Road (the Huddersfield ground) must have occurred to many fathers of small sons, and they may have conceived it to be their duty to cart the offspring down to the ground to witness the historic occasion. "We're going to Leeds Road this afternoon," they may have started to tell their sons, "so that you can see Stanley Matthews on his last visit here; then in years to come you will be able to tell your children that when you were no more than knee high to a corner flag, you saw the greatest player of all time." But then, even as they were announcing the day's programme, doubts may have assailed them. The great thing in family life (we are told), is that parents must be trusted absolutely by their children. But what would happen to that precious trust if, Matthews being Matthews, this did not prove to be his last appearance? Suppose Matthews has no intention of retiring for several years to come? Suppose (and it is a very welcome thought), he goes on and on coming to Leeds Road? One can imagine that five-year-old son growing up with a very troubled mind... "It's ten years now since Dad told me that Stanley Matthews was playing at Leeds Road for the last time – but he's there again this afternoon. It seems pretty clear to me that I can no longer rely on anything dear old Dad tells me," ...and with this complete breakdown of mutual trust and confidence in the parent-child relationship...'

READER'S LETTER, *Huddersfield Examiner*

BLACKPOOL continued to be a force in the First Division. Though knocked out of the Cup in the third round in 1958, they finished seventh in the League behind Wolves, the winners; and the following season reached the sixth round of the Cup, going out to the eventual finalists, Luton, after a replay, and were eighth in the championships, again behind Wolves. Joe Smith's £11,500 investment had been provident indeed; Stanley seemed to have reached a condition in which he would never age. When he had signed for Stoke in 1931 as an apprentice, a three-bedroomed house in London cost £550, or £25 down. Interviewed by Alan Hoby of the *Sunday Express* at the start of the 1959–60 season, and asked whether, at 44, this might be his final 'final' season, Stanley said:

I don't honestly know. It's too early to say, but I'll admit I am a bit worried. I don't know at the moment whether I shall be fit for the start. Naturally I want to play, as it would be the first time I have missed the opening since I first began playing League football at the age of seventeen. I feel marvellous, bodily. Other than kicking the ball, I have been training hard, but last September I twisted my right knee-cap trying to get to the ball too quickly. The whole season I felt it. I could do very little training, only one day a week, and then play on Saturday. During Blackpool's Cup run last season, the grounds – heavy one match, frozen the next – knocked the knee to bits. But I'm stubborn. I'll give myself another test soon. The next few weeks will decide whether my battle of patience is won or lost. Set-backs are a challenge.

An additional difficulty facing Stanley was that Blackpool now had a young alternative, Arthur Kaye, transferred from Barnsley and with a rising reputation in the England Under–23 team. Stanley could no longer regard the position on the right wing as his own, even if fit; less than effective performances, those in which he might for his own benefit decide to coast a little, would no longer be sufficient. Billy Walker, in his autobiography *Soccer in the Blood*, wrote:

The very structure of League football makes the weekly competition the toughest in the whole world, and enthusiasm alone is bound to burn itself out. In this week-by-week, and sometimes almost day-by-day contest, people marvel that Stanley Matthews and Tom Finney have kept playing so long, but that is because Matthews, like all good players of experience, knows how to save his legs. Such players do not bound all over the field for ninety minutes; they know, as good boxers know, when to coast, when to take it easy, when it is not necessary for them to be in the hurly-burly. But they know also when to be in the right place at the right moment and turn what might be a mêlée into a polished exhibition. If such a player plays full out for only twenty minutes, he has still done as much as any of the youngsters who are bounding around like startled elks for all of the ninety, and looking for more places to run when the game is over.

The development of defensive play by all players in the coming years would counter-act Walker's argument. Stanley's knee continued to be bothersome, so that by the start of the following autumn, 1960–61 – Blackpool having the previous season finished only eleventh in the League and been eliminated in the fourth round of the Cup by Blackburn and Douglas – Ronnie Suart, the new Blackpool manager, was ready to release his veteran winger: *if* Stanley wished to continue playing, which he did. Clandestine moves had begun once again, for a return to Stoke. When this became known, Stanley now being in his forty-sixth year, the suggestion was ridiculed by many of the newspapers. 'Don't Do It, Stan. Retire With Pride – Now' was the headline over Desmond Hackett's commentary in the *Daily Express*.

George Birks, accountant and key figure in the Stoke Supporters' Club, recollects: 'The club was in the doldrums, back in the Second Division for some years. We'd gone beyond the depth. One wet Friday night, the gate was 4,000. We felt Stoke was hitting the skids. When Tony Waddington made an approach for Stanley, I just prayed that it would happen. And it did. Even at that age, and until he was fifty, he could still give forty-five minutes, physically, in any game, and intelligence and experience for the whole of it.' Waddington was backed by Albert Henshall, vice-chairman at that time. Henshall had been in Blackpool, where his wife was recuperating after illness, had seen in the evening paper that Stanley had been left out of the Blackpool team, and sensed that a return to Stoke was on the cards. A meeting with the Blackpool directors was arranged; yet extraordinarily Stoke had to argue their case, Blackpool claiming a £3,500 fee for the man who had contributed so hugely for fourteen years to their greatest achievements, and to spectator attendances they would never see again.

Those who might think Stanley was financially artful should know that at this moment, in the period immediately following the abolition of the maximum wage, he was being paid £25 a week, while the rest of the first team were on £30–£35.

SM: I couldn't believe that Blackpool's chairman, Albert Hindley, refused to waive a transfer fee after all those years. My knee had been painful for much of the past couple of years, and Arthur Millwood had been treating it regularly. I don't think Stoke knew about this, but Blackpool did, and they evidently thought £3,500 would be more useful. I'd talked to Waddington for half an hour, and asked him to make me an offer. He suggested £50 a week, with £25 appearance money, and a two-year contract. I said, 'No, make it a year, two years might boomerang on you.' A friend of mine said I was a fool, that I should have got a five-year contract for £100 a week, because the moment I signed, Stoke got their money back in ticket sales. I'd been in Toronto in the summer of '61, playing with Danny Blanchflower, Jimmy Hill and others, and I was getting £100 a week there. Ronnie Suart had even used me as the bait to fix up a pre-season friendly in Eire, so maybe I was worth more than I asked from Stoke. Yet my motivation in going was not money, but the fact that I just wanted to keep playing, that I loved the game. Of course you have poor games at that age, but if I hadn't thought I could do something, I'd have packed it in.

So it was that on Saturday, 28 October 1961, Stanley Matthews made his reappearance in his home town in the colours of Stoke City. Waddington, the man who engineered it, had served as a radio telegraphist in the minesweeper HMS *Hound*, which sailed with the Russian convoys and participated in the D-Day landings. Playing football for the Navy, he received a knee injury which led a surgeon to tell him, two days after the end of the war, that he would never play professional football again. Two hundred matches later, he was obliged to agree; and stepped out of Crewe Alexandra's team to join Stoke as youth team coach, subsequently becoming one of the League's youngest managers in 1960 at the age of thirty-five. His much criticized defensive tactics, that became known as the 'Waddington Wall', averted relegation for a team that had previously lost twelve matches out of thirteen. Now, early in his second season, he had achieved the signature that would transform the team, the club and even, to an extent, the city.

I'd sat on my dad's shoulders among those 80,000 at Maine Road to watch Stan for the pre-war cup-tie against Manchester City, and was hooked for life [Waddington reflects]. When I was a 'nothing' player, I went to stay at Stan's hotel once, just to give myself a bit of a fillip. But in 1961, he'd reached the point where he was not even playing in Blackpool's reserves. For the first time in his career he was on the side-lines. From the first day I joined Stoke, there was constant talk of 'bringing back Stan'. When we managed to stay in the Second

Division, Don Revie had rung me up to congratulate me. I'd signed Jack Mudie from Blackpool, and his five or six goals had saved us. I tried to get Tom Finney, but he'd packed up. I always believed in having a player the crowds wanted to watch, and we desperately needed to bring back the public, because we were down to eight thousand or less. Finney couldn't sign because he'd already drawn his annuity from the League's Provident Fund. Then, one day, we were playing in London and found ourselves staying at the Russell Hotel together with Blackpool. Stan was there, but didn't play, and was fed up with being messed about. Our chairman suggested I make the approach. When he signed, my idea was to give him his first match away from home, so that the pressure would be off, but Stan merely said 'Why?' So he played at home against Huddersfield. The expectation was that Ray Wilson, who was the current England left-back, would dominate him, yet Ray just couldn't cope. It was mind over matter. It surprised me, the extent of it.

Stan is a strange man in many ways. Quiet, detached, a loner. Yet when he got his strip on, he instantly inspired confidence in others, even the older players. The intelligent thing I did was not to let Stan carry the team on his shoulders, but to find others who would help. We finished that season OK, and then I was able to persuade Dennis Viollet from Manchester United and Jimmy McIlroy from Burnley, both internationals, to join us. I exploited Stan to the maximum, not only for publicity and headlines, but in getting other players to come to Stoke. Viollet, a marvellous player, said that he came to watch us play against Leicester in the Cup, and what a crazy idea it was for them to have tried to mark Stan out of the game. Dennis said, 'I don't know what you want me for, but if I can play alongside that man, it's a great moment in my career.' [Viollet was half Stanley's age.]

Stan wouldn't discuss the terms of his contract, he just signed the forms and said, 'You fill in the details.' He revitalized the club, *and* he did something great for the game. He was the only really old player I signed; the others were all experienced, yet he was the one who set it going. Even at forty-six, he still killed the ball stone dead without looking at it, never gave it to a player in a bad position. People tend to think of him as being a dribbler, not a passer, yet he had such vision, he could see everyone *all* the time. He'd worry about his injuries a bit. On the train going to a match, Stan would get up, walk up and down, feel the aches in his legs. As we approached the station he'd be grimacing, but would then walk to the ground. Never a taxi. And when he arrived at the ground he would say, 'Do you know, the pain's gone,' and he'd go out and inspire another victory. He'd usually reject the suggestion of a fitness test. He was the Pied Piper: wherever we went, there were hundreds of kids waiting for us. Towards the end, he started to have a bit of back trouble, and I didn't want people to start laughing at Stan Matthews. I don't know what will happen when he can't travel anymore, he's got to be on the move. Wherever we went, everyone knew him. Every door opened, and Stan would stroll in. It was incredible to watch it.

That October day, when Huddersfield came to town, must have been nostalgic for Stanley. Not only were his mother and the rest of the family there in the stands, but so much of the club was the same as when he left it: the same eighty-year-old dressing-room where he had laced his first boots, swept the floor as a £1-a-week ball-boy. Only the old pot-bellied water heater that had stood in the centre of the room had gone. And outside, waiting to give him a roar of welcome, was gathering a crowd of 35,288, almost five times the average attendance which Stoke had been attracting that season. Waiting in the other dressing-room was Ray Wilson.

'Two weeks previously I'd been to Stoke for a celebrity game, Neil Franklin's testimonial as I recall, and there were about seven thousand there,' Wilson recollects. These days he seldom goes to football, living a peaceful life in the hills above Huddersfield, walking his dog, when he is not attending to his undertaker's business.

I could sense the club was dying [Wilson says]. There was no confidence, and if you can't put on some style in a friendly match, what chance have you? Two weeks later Stan had signed. Now the atmosphere was electric. The build-up, even over here in Huddersfield, was receiving more attention than we'd get for a quarter-final in the Cup. National newspaper photographers, and all that. Arriving at the Victoria Ground, it was like arriving at Goodison Park for a Derby game against Liverpool when I was with Everton.

Stan was *the* name, before and after the war. I went twice with my uncle Eric to try and see him at Chesterfield during the war, and each time he couldn't arrive. I'd never seen him on the field till that moment. I really did worry about it the week before. I only had my name taken once in my career, for arguing, so I wasn't going to clatter him, to try and bend him and then be the big bad wolf. There was no talk in our dressing-room beforehand, but as soon as we got outside on the pitch I felt we were intimidated. The Stoke guys were really fired up, they had nothing to lose.

On the night, we never played! Stan played like a man of his age would, mostly knocking the ball off to others. Whenever the ball came to him, the crowd erupted. Once, I slid in quick, got the ball off his feet, never touched him. The whistle went. A foul! As we came off at the end, I jokingly said to him, 'I coughed twice in the second half and nearly got booked!' He had shielded the ball ever so well. I'd have liked him to have had even more of a go at me than he did, just for the experience. The nearest thing to him was Garrincha, who I played against in the World Cup the next summer – the jink, the side-step. Only those two could beat me from a standing start, though others could do it on the run. Garrincha was exactly the same as Stan, he'd get across your line once he was past you, so that you couldn't get back at him.

Mind you, the game has changed so much over the past few years. An example of that came the next year in the quarter-final of the World Cup. Brazil had a corner, and Garrincha scored their first goal with a free header, there was no one back picking him up, such as Bobby Charlton, who was our left-winger. That wouldn't happen now, it would be a very different game for the likes of Stanley and Garrincha. Stan's strength, of course, was that he had no self-destruction button in the way a lot of famous players like Garrincha and George Best have had. What would give Stanley a problem nowadays is that either he would have a man-for-man marker between his shoulder-blades all the time, or a full-back who never committed himself.

Wilson's point leaves begging the question that many full-backs in Stanley's day tried desperately not to commit themselves, and still fell over.

For Stanley, it was an emotional reunion with the people of his youth, with some of those who had seen him set out thirty years before: those that were still alive. Jack, his father, was long gone, but his 75-year-old mother was there in the grandstand, loyal as ever. Years had passed since she last saw him play, other than on television. There, too, was Harry Loffil, aged eighty-six and for forty-two years the club's head groundsman. 'When Stan joined the club in July, you could not get him to pick up a match stick, but give him a football and a spell of training and he was a changed person. Many times I had to tell him about walking around with his hands in his pockets. But I soon got him out of his bad habits . . . he was only a kid.'

SM: I was so happy to go back. It was where I'd started, the same wooden floor in the dressing-room, the same boot-room where I'd clean the boots. And the reality now? I knew I was still pretty fit, I thought I could help, as long as I didn't get injured again. Their depressing position, nineteenth in the Second Division, never crossed my mind, yet I'd never imagined that there could be such a crowd as there now was. It was comforting beforehand, when I was so nervous, that Jackie [Mudie] was there. It was the first time I'd really had evidence that I had such drawing power. I wasn't expecting an easy time from Ray Wilson, or any of the other Second Division full-backs, not for a moment. And I soon found them coming in as hard as ever, some tougher than the First Division, like the Harris brothers of Chelsea. But I was still pretty quick, I still had confidence. I was going to be as much harassed in the Second Division by outside-lefts as I was that first night by Ray.

One of the changes to which Stoke players had to adjust was getting used to passing the ball to Stanley *when he was marked*. Most of them were accustomed to playing the ball away from a tightly-marked colleague. They had never met someone who could control a ball with a single touch and then take on his marker. Indeed, this would be, just as it had been for the past thirty years, Stanley's value to his team: that he drew opponents to him without surrendering the ball, thereby putting them out of the play while he remained in it. Stanley had less of the ball than he would have wished against Huddersfield, but that did not prevent Stoke winning 3–0, in front of a euphoric crowd. As Geoffrey Green reported:

Stoke City's match against Huddersfield Town on Saturday was sup-posed to be a collective game of football. In a sense it was, with Stoke gaining a valuable 3–0 win which keeps them a stride or two away from the quicksands that suck down to the Third Division. Yet it was a game largely between two players: Stanley Matthews, cast as the reluctant middle-aged hero in the red and white stripes of Stoke, the other young Wilson, the Huddersfield and England left-back, the unwilling villain. Transcending all else, however, this was a communal celebration, a relief from greyness. It was the day Mr Matthews returned to his birthplace after an absence of fourteen years.

Peter Buxton relates that before the match Stanley had been at the North Stafford Hotel, lying in his room for hours under a towel, like a boxer. Once the door had opened, and it was Betty, his wife, but Stanley asked her to leave. 'If his mind was not quiet,' Buxton reflects, 'it would show in his play. There was great will-power there. I think Wilson was paralysed by the occasion. I'd thought the build-up might fall flat, and be a fearful anti-climax, but it exceeded everything you could have hoped for. Matthews had a passing hand in all Stoke's goals by Adam and Thompson (two). At the finish, many of the crowd, including some of those in the directors' box, were in tears.' There were, however, those who thought that for such an emotional night, and with some of the decisions by the referee adding to the visitors' problems, Wilson and his colleagues also deserved the highest credit: they had behaved themselves impeccably.

The attendance proved to be no one-night wonder. Crowds continued to leap dramatically. For the next match away to Swansea, the crowd of 20,000 was double that which Stoke had attracted to Vetch Field the previous year. Likewise, the crowds were double for their visits to Middlesbrough and Rotherham; and were up nearly fifty per cent for their home matches with Southampton and Sunderland. Suddenly the pulse of the club and the town was racing. Billy Russell, a local who played 150 times at right-half for Chelsea and whose son was an inside-forward for Sheffield United, said of Stanley's return: 'Before Matthews came back, this place was a cemetery with electric lights. The old man has worked a bloody miracle. When he was signed by Stoke, I thought it was a ridiculous stunt, and I was so wrong.'

Within a few weeks of Stanley's arrival the lord mayor, Alderman Hancock, was saying: 'He has given the team and the city a new pride. Everywhere folk are talking about Stoke.' The week before Matthews was signed, Stoke's home match attendance have been 8,409. For their opening cup-tie against Blackburn in the new year, police restricted the attendance to 49,500. Mrs Bobby Howitt, the wife of the Stoke skipper and right-half, observed: 'People are asking us out again.'

Exhilarating days they were, both for Stanley and the team which he had transformed.

The two years at Stoke were two of the happiest of my whole career [Mudie says]. I think Waddington was lucky, because Stan's presence helped bring in the money and then other players. We had a marvellous forward-line when Viollet and McIlroy arrived, together with Don Ratcliffe, a local player, on the left-wing. The next season Viollet scored twenty-two goals and I got twenty. The team fused with the crowd. I've seen three different people in Stan in my time. At Blackpool he was a bit of a private person and seldom accepted social invitations; then at Stoke he mixed more, and would join in with the laughs. Now, in his seventies, he is different again. Much more sociable and relaxed. But we weren't looked after by Stoke the way we should have been. When we had a celebration dinner after promotion, we had to pay for ourselves. We were promised an overseas tour, taking our wives, but it never happened. Waddington wasn't straight with me. He said we were all getting the same: then I found I was on forty pounds, and Viollet and McIlroy on fifty.

These idyllic memories – Mudie's or mine or anybody else's – are not sentimental, not distorted by time, affection and nostalgia. It did happen. Repeatedly, over a period of two and a half seasons, Stanley inspired victories and occasionally rescued his colleagues from defeat. And he continued to compare favourably with some of the best that the country could still produce. Two months after his first match, Stoke were at home to Southampton. The visitors' right-winger was the then England Under–23 player, Terry Paine, who would soon be in the senior national team and subsequently in the World Cup squad of 1966. On the day, an objective assessment was that the older man was the better of the two. Stoke won 3–2, and though Paine was Southampton's most effective forward, Stanley had turned the match in Stoke's favour, entirely on account of thirty years' experience. There were those who said he was yet again worth recalling to the England team; even more so a month later, following Stoke's two cup-ties against Leicester City.

Stoke were drawn away, and a crowd of 30,000 was cheering Leicester on to victory with twenty minutes to go. Leicester were leading by the only goal of the first half by Riley, who had headed home a low cross from Cheesbrough. For seventy minutes, Norman, Leicester's 24-year-old left-back, had been led all over the field by Matthews as he darted this way and that. Now, with Stoke facing defeat, Stanley took a free-kick when fouled yet again by the desperate Norman. Threading through a sea of Leicester heads, Matthews' kick found Mudie; and Stoke had earned a replay. What a match that was to be! Not only were there 38,000 spectators at the Victoria Ground but, two weeks short of his forty-seventh birthday, Stanley Matthews scored the all-important first goal. It came in the twenty-first minute, when he sprinted for a through pass from Ratcliffe, beat the tormented Norman for speed, and calmly shot past the advancing Gordon Banks and into the net. It was the kind of goal he had no right to be scoring at such an age, and the crowd erupted in applause. From that point Stoke went from strength to strength, winning 5–2. It was Matthews' first goal in the FA Cup since 10 January 1953, when he had scored in the third round victory against Sheffield Wednesday, at the start of the run which took Blackpool to Wembley and the Cup. Stoke now went out to Blackburn in the next round.

When McIlroy had arrived, as Waddington pieced together a team that could win promotion the next year, there was another fine tactical mind in the forward line: 'the missing link', Waddington said at the time. The first match with McIlroy and Matthews together as a right-wing pair was away to Norwich, who were then among the favourites for promotion. Most of Fleet Street were there for the occasion – and Stoke lost 6–0. Things could only get better.

Playing with someone of his reputation, I always wanted to impress him with my own ability [McIlroy says]. Yet I found his confidence rubbing off on me. His confidence was unbelievable for forty-eight. He was unique. By the time I was thirty-six, it was my concentration that was going, not my physique. Stanley still had *total* concentration at fifty. My time as a professional was something irreplaceable to me. Whatever else I would do, I'd just be passing the time: though now I enjoy my life with the grandchildren, and the golf. Standards, today, are not what they were, and they were slipping even by the time I got to Stoke. At Burnley, we used to be coached by Bill Dougall, a Scot, who demanded a proficiency you would never find today. If we were practising shooting, with me pulling the ball back from the line, and the player shooting had to check even the slightest, Billy would say '*Nearly* a good one.' We were doing the same thing at Stoke, with George Eastham pulling the ball back for Ritchie to shoot first time. Ritchie had to check, and I said, 'It's almost a good one.' George was quite cross. 'It was great,' he insisted.

In the promotion season with Stoke, arguably the finest period in Stanley's career, he played in 35 of the 42 matches. By the turn of 1962, Chelsea's young team looked all set for the championship with a six-point lead; but in 1963 they stuttered, making various slips, and when they lost at home to Stoke in May, Stoke moved critically to the front, in a battle which ended with Sunderland failing to stay ahead of Chelsea.

Stoke clinched promotion on the final day, when they won at home to Luton, Matthews scoring the second goal in a 2–0 victory. McIlroy collected a ball in midfield, saw Stanley setting off out of the corner of his eye, and flighted a pass over the head of the defence. Going like a whippet, Stanley outpaced everyone, went round Luton's goalkeeper Baynham, and rolled the ball into an empty net. At the instant McIlroy won possession Stanley had seen the Luton defence was square, and his run had made the pass for McIlroy. So much for those who suggest he could not have played in the modern game. The defeat sent Luton down to the Third Division; and there can be no doubt that the Stoke fire brigade had played a hand. In the early hours, they had been busy hosing thousands of gallons on to the pitch so that the dry conditions of late season would not jar one particular 48-year-old knee. Many was the manager who had been surprised upon arriving in Stoke on a fine day to find the pitch quite damp.

SM: It was a great satisfaction to have proved over almost the whole season that I could still do it. I can't tell you what it felt like, to know that I was not being carried by the others, that I was justifying my inclusion. If I wasn't, I'd have packed up there and then. It was *experience* that enabled me to do it. An experienced player seldom has a really bad match, and I tended to be at my best in the last twenty minutes of a match rather than the first twenty. Mind you, I got a bit of moral support that season from my right-half, Eddie Clamp, who joined us from Wolves. Eddie had a reputation for being a stern man, and if my full-back was dirty, Eddie would give him a warning, and afterwards would say in the bath, 'I looked after you all right, didn't I?' When we beat Luton, I spotted that there was a chance to go for a ball from Jimmy, but it seemed to me I had plenty of time when I went round the goalkeeper to the left, and scored with my left foot. Afterwards, there was a big crowd on the pitch and we all went up into the directors' box. But I never thought of myself as a hero.

Stoke did. The champagne flowed for days on end. On two occasions, thirty years apart, at the ages of eighteen and forty-eight, Stanley had helped take Stoke to the First Division: in recognition of which the Football Writers' Association for the second time elected him their Footballer of the Year – never mind that Law and Charlton had won the FA Cup with Manchester United, or that Everton, led by Alec Young, had taken the League championship. The *Evening Sentinel* wrote in its leading article after victory over Luton:

For Stoke this was a Centenary year dream come true. For Matthews it was the crowning achievement for the club which he had served with great distinction at the beginning of his career and which he has rejoined in these latter days in the role of football's elder statesman. Football is essentially a team game, but it is surely true to say of Matthews that he has been the inspiration, indeed the architect, of Stoke's triumphant battle to win their way back to the summit flight of English football. . . . The outstanding season which is now closing has rebuilt among local football supporters a fund of goodwill. This entitles the club to call upon the continued loyalty of the crowds in the testing time to come. Directors, management and not least the players themselves, know only too well what an important role is played by the crowd in keeping a football club up to scratch.

Waddington, a shrewd buyer and wheeler-dealer for entertaining players, would keep Stoke in the First Division for thirteen years, including victory in the Football League Cup in 1972, reaching FA Cup semi-finals in 1971 and 1972. He knew how to get the most out of nearly every player he bought; and was known to ring Stanley late at night in bed to ask him what he thought about selection for the coming day. Waddington handled his board of directors with equal shrewdness: this could be because he occasionally listened to their boardroom conversations via the holes for the boiler-room central heating pipes immediately below. He also had charm, which he used with particular effectiveness on the press.

As further players were tempted to join Stoke, such as Peter Dobing from Blackburn, a most talented forward, and even eventually Gordon

Banks, the World Cup goalkeeper, profits rose and Stoke were able to build a new £150,000 stand. The old dressing-room would disappear. But not before Stanley had established further landmarks. In the fifth round of the Cup against Swansea in 1964, he became the oldest player ever to score in an FA Cup tie. Having been awarded the CBE in 1957, the New Year's Honours of 1965 elevated him to a knighthood: the only footballer to have been thus honoured while still playing. The Prime Minister of the day was Harold Wilson. Consulting with his senior civil servants about the award of a knighthood to an active professional footballer, Wilson encountered some opposition. Surely, it was asked, Matthews already had the CBE?

'Who has the final decision?' Wilson inquired. 'You do,' nodded the Whitehall gnomes. 'In that case, he receives it'. No sporting honour has been more deserved or more roundly acclaimed.

On 6 February 1965, five days after his fiftieth birthday, Sir Stanley Matthews became the oldest player in history to appear in the First Division, when he played in the home match against Fulham. It was his 710th League match, and his first for more than twelve months. The knee had been troublesome again. The reason he was recalled by Waddington was not merely to enable him to record a moment in history. 'Stoke were short of players, so he gave me the chance,' Stanley says. He had played thirteen fewer peace-time League matches than Billy Meredith, who had played until he was forty-nine. The only older player than Stanley to have appeared in the League was Neil McBain, at the age of fifty-two for New Brighton in 1947. That had been in an emergency, when McBain, the manager, having retired some while previously as a player, stepped into the Division Three match when his goalkeeper failed to arrive.

Stanley's half-centenary appearance on the field was not a gimmick. From the defence-ridden tactics which had sullied their reputation in two Cup encounters with Manchester United, Stanley restored them for that day into an attacking unit. A crowd of 28,000 was there to see him take part in a veteran's duel with Jim Langley, the 36-year-old Fulham left-back. Langley, with a sense of occasion, played with a marked degree of courtesy, but that was of little influence in Stoke's victory by 3–1. Langley was in no position to do anything mid-way through the second half when Matthews made the pass that enabled Ritchie to put Stoke in front, after having been one down. The whole of the Potteries must have heard the acclaim as the goal was scored.

The Fulham team contained players of the standing of Cohen, who would be England's right-back when winning the World Cup the following year, and Robson and Haynes, members of the World Cup team of 1962. The two sides on that historic day were:

STOKE CITY: Leslie; Asprey, Allen; Palmer, Kinnell, Skeels; Matthews, Viollet, Ritchie, McIlroy, Bridgewood.
FULHAM: Macedo; Cohen, Langley; Brown, Dempsey, Robson; Key, Marsh, Leggatt, Haynes, Howfield.

It was Stanley's final match, and a farewell Testimonial was planned for 28 April, eleven weeks later. The preparations for this were confused by various snags, the chief of which, it is evident from talking to many of the parties involved, was a degree of envy on the part of Stoke's directors. For various reasons, the Testimonial could not be organized by the club, so a committee of friends was formed, including George Birks, Charlie Chester and Peter Buxton. At one stage the club alleged that FIFA were opposing the match, on the grounds that it was planned to oppose a Sir Stanley Matthews XI with an overseas team of famous international players, which would contravene FIFA regulations. Among those opposing the match was thought to be Harry Cavan, the Irish FA representative on FIFA's executive committee, with the intention of blocking the proceeds which were expected to reach £30,000 after expenses had been paid. Sir Stanley Rous, who by now was president of FIFA, denied that he was obstructing the match, and at one stage Buxton had to threaten to take the whole issue to the international court in The Hague. The mayor became involved, indeed just about everyone. Half the civic officials of the city of Stoke seemed to be involved. Finally, the match went ahead. And what a night it was.

Josef Masopust, who had been captain of the superb Dukla teams of Prague, and of Czechoslovakia, in the 1960s when they had reached the 1962 World Cup Final, later wrote:

Matthews' farewell match was in many ways different from a normal match. Our team of stars, for instance, had no coach, in spite of which we went for training the day before, and Stanley went with us. Pluskal gave heading practice to Van der Boer of Belgium. Kubala of Hungary and Stanley practised crossing. Puskas, Johanssen of Denmark and I practised passing. And in the end we played five-a-side. I was able to observe what a transformation had taken place with Stanley.

When he had come to welcome us on our arrival, wearing civilian clothes, slim and with greying hair above a high forehead, one could see in his face the fifty years of his life. Yet when he changed into playing kit and put on his boots, it was as if suddenly he became younger. Even at fifty, on the field he was still young. It was remarkable to see what training and a strict lifestyle could achieve. And then that remarkable match started. Nobody felt the necessity to gain points, nobody's legs were hampered by defensive tactics. We played only for joy of the game, for the beauty of football. And Stanley proved that he deserved all the honour given to him. His run had not lost its speed, his technique was still the best. He was playing up against Karl-Heinz Schnellinger, who at that time was with AC Milan, and was rated among the best of European professionals. Yet even that outstanding German defender had to bow before the mastery of the Matthews dribble and the deceiving sway of his body. After the match was over, the fans gave the retiring footballer a warm and wonderful ovation. It was not applause for the game, or for the goals. It was thanks for everything that Stanley Matthews had done for football. All the players stood in a circle in the middle of the field holding hands, and bagpipers played 'Auld Lang Syne'. It was a moment one never forgets. Stanley's chin started to shake, he bent his head to hide how moved he was, but the tears betrayed him. They ran down his cheeks and fell on to the green grass, the turf that had meant so much for him.

The crowd was 35,000, and they came from all parts of the world: from Australia, Canada and the United States, paying over £300 in air fares, and from almost every country in Europe. Television was beaming the match to a hundred million viewers from Moscow to County Mayo; and so many were those who wished to take part in tribute to the greatest player of the game, alive or dead, that two matches had to be played. In a preliminary match between post-war favourites led by Harry Johnston and Wally Barnes, there were included: Bert Trautmann, George Hardwick, Neil Franklin, Don Revie, Stan Mortensen, Nat Lofthouse, Jimmy Hagan, Tom Finney, Jimmy Scoular, Danny Blanchflower, Jimmy Dickinson, Bill McGarry, Jackie Mudie, Jackie Milburn, Ken Barnes and Arthur Rowley, with Denis Howell the referee. For the main match, in which the International XI beat Sir Stanley's XI 6–4, the squads, from whom several substitutions were made during the course of the game, were:

INTERNATIONAL XI: Yashin (USSR), Johanssen (Denmark), Schnellinger (West Germany), Plouskal (Czechoslovakia), Popluhar (Czechoslovakia), Masopust (Czechoslovakia), Henderson (Scotland), Kubala (Hungary), Di Stefano (Spain), Puskas (Spain), Van den Boer (Belgium), Sorensen (Denmark), Ritchie (Stoke City).
STANLEY'S XI: Waiters (Blackpool and England), Cohen (Fulham and England), Thompson (Wolves), Haynes (Fulham and England), Flowers (Wolves and England), Baxter (Rangers and Scotland), Matthews (Stoke and England), Greaves (Spurs and England), Gilzean (Spurs and Scotland), Douglas (Blackburn and England), Jones (Spurs and Wales).
REFEREE: Arthur Ellis (FIFA).

Di Stefano might rightly claim to have been the equal of Matthews, in control, judgement, balance, in all the crafts of the game. He had originally come from Argentina to Spain to play for Barcelona, was then stolen by Real Madrid, and had been the architect and inspiration of Real's five consecutive victories in the opening years of the European Cup. I have seen a few moments of Di Stefano on the field which extended all superlatives of description in the same way that Stanley did. Yet even Di Stefano, although he might have scored dozens of the greatest goals ever in some of the greatest matches, had never commanded quite that authority and certainty that Stanley did when he took the ball slowly and menacingly towards a defender. A day or two before the Testimonial match, Mudie had been in London with Stanley when Di Stefano and Puskas had come strolling along the pavement towards the hotel where Jackie and Stanley were staying. Upon seeing Stanley, Di Stefano and Puskas had flung their arms around him in a Latin embrace that had been no histrionic gesture, but an act of spontaneous affection and respect. Jack had thought to himself that the greeting by such players towards Stanley spoke more than a thousand headlines.

Among many tributes carried in the match programme, that from the Hungarian FA had said:

If we speak about the great personalities of football, the name of Sir Stanley Matthews is among those worth mentioning. His career, from Stoke City to Blackpool and back to Stoke, is well known in Hungary, in spite of the fact that unfortunately he never played here. In Hungary, Sir Stanley is appreciated and admired, not only for his long and successful sporting activity, but for his example of sportsmanship and real humility. On the occasion of this rare jubilee, we take the opportunity to congratulate him by wishing good health and prosperity to the number one player in the world today.

The Duke of Edinburgh sent a personal message in which he said: 'No one can estimate the immense contribution which Stanley Matthews has made to football and good sportsmanship in every part of the world. He has become a legend in his own time, which is a distinction reserved for only really great men.' Yashin managed to get his expenses paid twice: and Stanley left Stoke City for the second time with the club owing him their promised contribution to the Testimonial. It would be two years before he received it.

SM: Thirty-three years of playing in first-class football had come to an end. Charlie Chester said afterwards there wasn't a dry eye in the house. They say the crowd applauded me all the way back to the dressing-room, but it's difficult to see what other people are doing when your own eyes are full of tears.

12. CONTENTMENT

*W*E live in a time when the cupboard is bare of class wingers; Peter Thompson, of Liverpool and England, yes, but not quite: something is missing; Cliff Jones, of Spurs and Wales, yes, a lovely manner and superb in the air; George Best, of Manchester United and Ireland, a Beatle-haired, invidious mover with a flair for fast cars, yes, a seemly, splashy colourful dresser who is probably the best we have in the country now. But there was a time after the war when wingers lined up in far more profusion, independent and devastating as a select band of archers...

Matthews is one's winger in a lifetime and there cannot be anyone to replace him, with a League career which started during the year I was born and finished on a misty day in 1965 at the Victoria Ground, Stoke, against Fulham, and a masterful performance it was. Stanley came down to the hotel before the game to meet the Fulham players, and everyone treated him like a retiring professor, respectfully, with a touch of humour. It seemed to bring out the extrovert in Johnny Haynes, who smiled broadly as Stanley shook hands and walked around with his neat suit and natty tie, a quiet, gentle person in a room of youthful players. Stanley, the Wizard of Dribble, the Old Master, his hair glued back over his head, came out of the palid, smoky, bricked blur of the Potteries, and gave us thirty years of genius, spanning games and games and games that cannot be forgotten, and the men who helped him acknowledge this, with wonder and admiration: Raich Carter, Ernie Taylor, Wilf Mannion, Stanley Mortensen and others.

Once, sitting on the touch-line at White Hart Lane where the photographers were, I could have touched him as he wiggled up the bye-line. Those hands held out slightly, the shuffle, the spurt, and then there was the heaving and straining and pushing and shouting as the Spurs defence jostled to put the ball away and stop Mortensen and Perry from the *coup de grâce*. And Stanley always going through on the outside, coming again, and Withers in trouble again, not knowing whether to go forward, not knowing whether to take the bloke and make a fool of himself again, or hang back; and others trying to help him, but Stanley was too fast for them, going on to meandering runs in mid-field, spreading out the passes with delicate prods across the mud, and when he was near the goal we could hear the delicate slap, slap of his boots on the ground which you never hear from the terraces because of the noise. "Bloody marvellous," said the photographer. "How old is the bloke now? Sixty?" *

JOHN MOYNIHAN, *The Soccer Syndrome*

*P*ARTING from Stoke, which should have been a graceful affair, with the directors touched by gratitude for the renaissance which Stanley had generated within their club, was instead uncomfortable. Sections of the club were riven with envy of his fame, and of the money which had been raised by his Testimonial match. The directors, now enjoying their seat in the First Division, wished to be the star turn. The manager, Waddington, was understandably anxious lest Stanley should turn round and take his job. What, of course, should have happened was for Stanley to be made a director or vice-president, whereby he could have helped maintain and spread the reputation of a club for which he had already done so much. Yet there would then have been resentment in the boardroom; there had already been objections, publicly unspoken, about the way Stanley's name would open doors, and the way invitations to overseas tours would stipulate 'if Stanley Matthews is in the party'. Charlie Chester, Stanley's friend of many years who had stage-managed with style the Testimonial match, had suggested other ideas.

'My plan was for him to go on a three-year tour of exhibition matches around the world', Chester says, 'to play one-match "Tests" against a whole succession of countries where he had been loved and admired for years. I was prepared to give up my career to be the manager of such a tour, I was the showman who could have put it on.' Yet Stanley hankered after staying in English football, and when Port Vale, his first love, offered him the chance to go to Vale Park in Burslem as manager of their Fourth Division side, Stanley accepted. Feelings within the Potteries were mixed. Many thought that, in view of the huge demonstration of public affection at his Testimonial match, he should have remained with Stoke; but he knew deep down he was not wanted by either the board or the management. Waddington was ten years younger than he, and had met with nothing but success in his four years as manager: much of which he owed to Stanley. Yet in Stanley's last season, Waddington reduced his wage to £25; and when, in the first week of his move to Port Vale, Stanley asked for two complimentary tickets for a Stoke home match, Waddington told him: 'Sorry, the directors don't want you here.'

Others in the Potteries were happy that, showing no flourish of self-importance, Stanley was willing to immerse himself in a lowly role among the grass-roots of the game. The motive was noble: the reality was to prove loaded with pitfalls. Port Vale, not surprisingly, had no money, indeed, were heavily in debt. For several years Stanley, the allegedly mean man, drew nothing of his salary, in spite of the fact that he was working a fourteen or fifteen hour day, getting up at five in the morning at his home in Blackpool so as to be at Vale Park by breakfast-time. Besides managing the club teams, he was travelling all over the country in pursuit of young players for a Youth Development policy. He had pursuaded the Port Vale directors that, since there was no possibility of buying players, the only solution was to find youngsters who cost nothing. He was lucky to have Reg Berks as chief scout, with a talent for spotting young players, and they travelled hundreds of miles together. But it was here that Stanley was heading for trouble, unknown to himself.

Over a couple of seasons Port Vale infringed two League regulations. Neither was particularly serious, but the penalties that would be inflicted on the club aroused disproportionate publicity: Sir Stanley Matthews, the man who hitherto could seemingly do no wrong, was now involved in alleged scandal. For a League Cup tie against Chester, it was agreed at a board meeting, attended by the chairman and the secretary, that a bonus should be paid if they beat Chester. This proposal was duly minuted, the secretary having said that such a bonus was within League regulations. In the event, Port Vale lost, and no bonus was paid. Such a bonus would in fact have been illegal, being outside the players' previously negotiated contract. For the time being, however, it was no more than a line in the minutes book, of no apparent relevance.

However, Port Vale were running into a more immediate financial problem. It was a regulation that for each young player's registration a fee of £500 must be paid to the League. In his scouting around the north-east, still the most fruitful ground for young players, Stanley had been particularly successful; but the players he found had not been properly registered and no fee had been paid to the League. Yet the board should have been aware that, whatever the club's finances, they could not afford to ignore the registration fee. As bad luck would have it, the bonus irregularity came to light because of a problem with a boy who was dirty and undisciplined, gave continual trouble to the landlady with whom the club had arranged lodging, and was sent home. He complained to his former headmaster, and claimed he had been paid illegal monies. The Football League and the FA held enquiries over the registration fees, during which the proposed illegal bonus also came to light in the club books.

For whatever reason, the club secretary's paperwork, if nothing else, had been seriously adrift. While awaiting the result of the enquiries, Stanley had a couple of unpleasant brushes with Alan Hardaker, the General Secretary of the Football League, who resented Stanley's knighthood. Eventually, in March 1968, Port Vale were fined £2,000 by both the League and the FA and the club was expelled from the Fourth Division; re-elected in the summer only thanks to the loyalty of their fellow members. In the wave of bad publicity, Stanley resigned in disillusionment, still having drawn nothing in three years of the £75 a week salary that was due to him. With a club overdraft of £120,000, and with sixteen young players having had to be returned whence they came because the fees had remained unpaid, Stanley felt there was little more that he could do for the club.

'When I talked to him about what had happened,' Peter Buxton recalls, 'he was almost in tears. The youth policy was in a shambles, and Stan had been condemned for things that were really outside his responsibility. It is a cross he's had to bear. He was particularly upset about losing Ray Kennedy, one of the boys from the north-east. Kennedy was a particularly fine player, who went on to make a name with Arsenal, in their Double-winning team in 1971, and then with Liverpool. Quite unfairly, he later wrote that Stanley hadn't recognized his ability, which was absurd.' Port Vale were in such a plight that they could not even pay off the salary owing to Stanley at £100 a month. Eventually, under a new chairman, he was given a cheque for £3,000, with £6,000 owing to this day.

There was another, more emotional problem tormenting Stanley at this time: the recognition that his marriage with Betty, which had been in difficulties for some years, was finally at an end. During his travels he had met, in Czechoslovakia, Mila, married to George Winter, one of Prague's more prominent artists. She was Cultural Assistant of the American Embassy, a multi-linguist who had interpreted for Stanley on several visits of his to Prague. By 1968 they wished to share a life together. Stanley was thrown into confusion by this dilemma, sensitive to the headlines which he knew would be provoked at home by the news of an end to his existing marriage.

The return to Stoke had put additional strains on the marriage. Betty was less than happy about him playing for a Second Division club, and disliked motoring back and forth to Stoke for matches. When Stanley went to ask Charlie for his advice, Charlie, unaware of the extent of the ties that had developed between Stanley and Mila, and the fascination for Stanley of her wholly different life-style, told him to come to his senses. It was, however, too late for that kind of talk; Stanley was looking for reassurance that he was doing the right thing, which he received from his eighty-year-old mother. Ada had long been aware of the gap that had developed within his marriage. At Stoke, some of the players had been vaguely aware of the difficulties, and that Stanley was worried about his image. The situation came to a head when, in August, 1968, he was caught in Prague by the Russian invasion, and succeeded in making his way out of Czechoslovakia, with Mila, via Yugoslavia. By now, Mila and he had decided that they would set up home in Malta, and a perplexed Stanley came home to break the news that he wanted a divorce.

Friends and relations are of the opinion that unhappiness at home may well have been part of the motivation which kept him training and playing until he was fifty; though such had been his preoccupation and devotion to the game, and his self-discipline in maintaining his fitness, that Jackie Mudie considers Stanley must at times have been a difficult man to live with. Certainly the game had always been his life, and in Malta he continued to play weekly for the local Post Office team. For a brief time, he was manager of a Maltese club team competing in the European Cup Winners Cup, and in 1969 there was the bizarre possibility that he could have returned to the game, at the age of fifty-four, against Real Madrid in the Bernabeu Stadium.

SM: It was the first round, and, needless to say, we were short of good players. Before the match, I sat in the dressing-room thinking to myself, 'Imagine playing here!' I'd have loved to appear again in that famous stadium, and I was sorely tempted, but we had a couple of young British players in the squad who were desperate to play, and although I was fit and had been playing regularly every Wednesday evening for a college side, I gave way and picked the British boys.

Had he remained in England, could he have become a successful manager? My opinion is that it was unlikely, the way the game was developing with its over-emphasis on defensiveness and negative tactics. Where he could have been outstandingly successful was, perhaps, as a coach for the FA or one of the major clubs, working with junior players and instilling in them the necessity for working at skill, balance and concentration, which had been the key to his own success. I do not think he could have been a party to the scuffle of expediency – the determination not to concede points rather than to win them – which increasingly coloured what had become, by the 1970s, no more than 'industrial' football. The game as played by Matthews had been a relief from the drudgery of daily work for the spectators of his day: football had now become no more than an extension of work. It was his perception of this that persuaded him, and a number of the other famous players of his time, such as Carter, to denigrate coaching in general, and more specifically some of the attitudes of Walter Winterbottom which he had experienced with the England team. This was unfair on Winterbottom, and certainly Stanley's criticism at times led him into direct confrontation with the FA, who published rebuttals of his publicly expressed opinions. What Stanley rejected, and Carter too, was the suppression or erosion of natural talents in the pursuit of team play. The two facets are, of course, interdependent.

Sir Walter, who nowadays prefers not to become engaged in the public debate, was the initiator of almost all that was good in the establishment of coaching in England when he was the FA's Director of Coaching, simultaneously with his management of the national team. What has been wrong in England is that at all levels there has been a profusion of *bad* coaching, by schoolmasters, junior coaches, and even some League managers, who have never been *coached* to coach in the way that almost all foreign coaches have. Dogmatic, inhibiting tactical principles are drummed into young players, and even League players, which are individually and collectively damaging. No team was more coached, intelligently, than that greatest of all Hungarian sides by Gustav Sebes, never mind that they enjoyed the coincident occurrence of half a dozen exceptional individual players.

When Stanley was playing, [says Winterbottom], the England team was partially shaped to play to *him*. If that isn't coaching, heaven help me. Coaching is not a matter of some third person telling you what to do, it's helping you to find an understanding and advantageous relationship with your colleagues. Carter didn't want this. Coaching didn't exist in his day. When I was playing for Manchester United, Scott Duncan, our manager, hardly ever left his office all day. Hungary and other countries overtook England because their football at all levels had the advantage of a profusion of knowledgable coaches. We, the English, helped introduce coaching to amateur countries like Sweden and Holland, with men such as George Raynor, and look at the teams which the Dutch produced by the Seventies! It's a nonsense to say that coaching has no value, and it was nonsense, at the time we still had a selection committee, the way we picked our team.

One of the additional problems in England is that we have almost no club team that is wholly English. Another is that in Stanley's day, youngsters played every day of the week from dawn to dusk, so they learned to control the ball spontaneously. Nowadays there are so many alternative things to do, so many other attractions and pressures on young children, that it is necessary for them to be advised how to develop their skills. Most of the club managers in England in the Fifties were ignorant of what was going on out on the field. After the match against the FIFA side in 1953, when we drew 4–4, there was a meeting of managers. Jimmy Seed, of Charlton, whose centre-half Ufton had played on that day, complained that we hadn't marked FIFA's centre-forward. I asked who had been their centre-forward, and nobody could say, even though they'd watched the match. Nordahl of Sweden, who wore the No. 9, had played most of the time on the wing. In England, we were not reacting to the fluidity of thinking in opposing teams. None of our managers had been overseas, or knew anything about the Continentals' switching of positions.

There were players in the 1950s who were sensitive to the trends which were conditioning Winterbottom's thinking. Fine coaches would emerge from this period, such as Ron Greenwood, Dave Sexton and Malcolm Allison, all deeply influenced by what we had seen the Hungarians inflict on the pride of English football. I recall that at Cambridge, where our coach for three years in the mid–1950s was Bill Nicholson, for six months after England's 6–3 defeat we talked of almost nothing else but Bozsik and Hidegkuti. Trevor Ford, that fiery centre-forward of Sunderland and Wales, wrote in his autobiography, *I Lead the Attack*:

In the old days, players were ball artists. One reason why there are none today, and one reason for the dramatic fall in the number of players in League soccer who can beat their man, is that there is no organized coaching in the clubs. People read about Dick Chips, the United coach, but in reality he doesn't coach. He makes sure the team keeps fit, he looks after the balls, talks about the football stars of the Twenties. I've never had a day's coaching in my fifteen years in professional football. . . . The question of coaching must be tackled realistically. There are enough players who have been forced to hang up their boots who are thoroughly well equipped for the task. . . . Another glaring gap in the equipment of most clubs is the lack of a cine-film camera. The team should be allowed to see the film through to see where they blundered. An enormous amount can be learned in this way . . . far too many top-class men with years of highly valuable experience are flung on the scrap-heap, with no effort made to put their knowledge to good use in the game. An incredible number of our administrators have no real playing knowledge.

SM: The right kind of coaching is fine, but you can't drill players too much, you have to let them have their fling. When I'm training boys of twelve, I concentrate on their work at ball control and positional sense, and at playing five-a-side, not full-scale matches on full-sized pitches. Five-a-sides are essentially about ball control and accurate passing. Walter can talk about coaching, but I think he slipped up against Hungary. As soon as we arrived at Hendon Hall Hotel, he was going through tactics using billiard balls, but never said what we should do about Hidegkuti. Yet he'd seen him in Budapest, and must have known what a problem he would present. We needed to decide before the match whether Harry [Johnston] should stay or go, but we still didn't decide even at half-time.

I'm not impressed by all this talk that we wouldn't have been able to cope with the man-for-man marking that is now the rage. Finney, Carter and I had people at our backs all the time. I see matches nowadays where people get more space than we had. There aren't the full-backs today who can tackle. They all want to be attackers. Who does Sansom ever tackle? Anderson is the same: good at going forward. All the slow-motion that we see on television makes players seem better than they really are. While I agree with a certain amount of coaching for schoolboys, I disagree with the insistence on coaching and yet more coaching. Some of our greatest boxers, golfers, tennis players and athletes did things that the orthodox coach would frown on, but these champions had something the coaches never possessed. Natural ability. Of course players are fitter today, and you have to have tactics, but the problem begins at school age.

The difficulty for those who think like Stanley, who believe that the game essentially needs a freedom of expression, is that orthodox coaches, by their negative attitudes, have eliminated freedom from the game. It happened to Danny Blanchflower during his relatively brief period in charge of the Northern Ireland team and of Chelsea. As Danny has said: 'In those [pre–1960] days the game was full of talk about the great players and their personal magic. Nobody knew who the managers were. As a matter of fact, most of the international teams did not have a manager, they had a selection committee and a trainer. Now it's all different. The talk is about tactics and systems and managers and coaches. Does the fan today imagine himself as a manager instead of imagining he's Stanley Matthews?'

There must be some sympathy for the FA in their response to Stanley's public disapproval, though they were exposing themselves to further criticism when they published the following, in a 1960 editorial of the *FA News* which carries the unmistakeable stamp of Rous:

As an ambassador for his country, his [Stanley's] worth has been inestimable. When Stanley Matthews speaks or publishes opinions on matters concerning the game, his words are received with much more authority than they would be from almost any other player and indeed from many officials. Thus it is all the more regretted that at this time in his career he has chosen to say that the failure of English soccer is to be blamed on coaching, on the tactical thoughts of the team manager, and of a lack of ability of the team captain to crack the whip . . . we feel that his criticism of coaching is ill founded. He assumed that there is too much coaching going on in this country, yet we know that the average boy who leaves school gets no coaching whatsoever. Indeed, the majority of such boys are lucky if they get one game each week. How can we expect to draw level with world standards if the young player in this country gets only one fifth of the ball practice of the players in South America, Europe and Asia? Paradoxically, Stanley Matthews sees no anomaly in receiving fees to travel thousands of miles to foreign countries to demonstrate his skill and to coach players in these countries. It may well be that Stanley Matthews, since he has never attended any FA national coaching course, suffers from some common misconceptions on coaching and what it really sets out to do. To blame the England team manager now for the decline of England's performances seems less than gallant. Surely the time for Matthews to have made such criticisms was when he was active in the team.

To which the short answer must be that English football had never properly responded to the genius of the man, shown that they recognized the public-relations value of his reputation and skill in the way that foreign countries had for almost twenty years. When League football and English officialdom saw fit not to question a pittance payment of £15 in the close season to someone of such inestimable ability, who can blame him for having travelled the world, in response to appeals to impart his knowledge and give demonstrations of his ability for respectable fees? It ill became the FA to pontificate on the status and credibility of their team manager, in answer to criticism, when for so long they had wilfully restricted the authority of that manager. When appointing a professional manager to replace the selection committee for the first time in 1962, there was no mention of the fact in the annual *FA Yearbook*, though there were two pages of opinion from the new FA Secretary, Dennis Follows. For the FA to suggest that Stanley should have attended preliminary FA coaching courses was like requiring Margot Fonteyn to attend junior classes at Sadlers' Wells.

So Stanley's knowledge and experience were largely lost to the English game from the mid–1960s onwards, as he continued his tours of Canada, Australia and Africa. It is an irony that after seventeen consecutive years coaching black children, mainly in South Africa but also in several neighbouring black nations, he should have been placed on the UN list of prohibited persons for maintaining links with South African sport. He was adored by the football community in Soweto, where he was known as 'the black man with a white man's face', so integrated was he with the attempt to help develop their game. The attempt at times by the South African Non Racial Olympic Committee to prohibit his involvement in the awarding of prizes and charity events in neighbouring black countries has been laughably self-destructive. Last year my wife and I, visiting Johannesburg for the opening of the National Soccer League season, drove around Soweto with Stanley to visit some of his old haunts. He was greeted with open arms, and embraced by the head groundsman at the main stadium in Soweto. He had been one of them, more welcome than he ever was at the head-quarters of the FA, who had made honorary members of some of his international colleagues of the 1950s, such as Wright and Mercer, but pointedly chose to ignore him.

When Stanley played in Lorenzo Marques, in Mozambique, in 1955, one of the ball boys was Eusebio, who would become goal-scorer for Benfica and Portugal, playing against England in the World Cup semi-final in 1966, and in the European Cup Final against Manchester United two years later. So great was the crowd at the airport that the team's luggage and kit was taken back inadvertently to Johannesburg without being unloaded, and the plane had to return to Mozambique.

SM: I first went to South Africa in 1954. They had seen me play against FIFA the year before, and invited me over for three matches in Durban, Jo'burg and the Cape, at £100 a match. In Cape Town, the hall porter told me there was a man outside to see me. He wasn't allowed in, because he was an Indian: Marcus Davis, who'd written to me the year before, enclosing a five-pound note which he wanted me to put on the Pools. Now he just wanted to shake hands. I was the first, I think, to go on football safaris, playing the following year in Ghana, Zambia and Tanzania. In Uganda, I met King Freddie, a charming host who was an Arsenal fan and had been educated at Oxford. The name Soweto sends some people into a state of shock, yet for three years I effectively lived there. Certainly, I travelled back into Johannesburg every evening, but during the day I was invited into so many homes and made so many black friends that the place as far as I was concerned became home.

Under an arrangement with the South African *Sunday Times*, which sponsored the project, Stanley set about creating in the early 1970s an all-black team of the best boys that could be found in Soweto. They played under the name 'Sir Stan's Men', and had fixtures in the various townships and homelands such as Transkei, and in Swaziland and Lesotho. Stanley had a black assistant coach, and training was in the afternoons, following school. Coca Cola were joint sponsors, and for the only time during the period of intense anti-apartheid activity in sport, a black team was taken on tour overseas, to Rio de Janeiro.

SM: One of the best players around then was Jomo Sono, who was similar to Pelé in his dribbling ability, and who later was by far the best player in the South African League. I had a lot of difficulty trying to teach them the laws of the game. One of them once asked me, 'If I hit the cross-bar and the ball goes in, is it a goal?' There was a lot of difficulty getting them to realize that they had to defend. They all wanted to be attackers. The trip to Rio was a great event. They were all kitted out in blue blazers, flannels and ties. They received passports, and a smart bag from Varig Airlines, who were taking us to Rio. At one stage some of them even threatened to go on strike before we left, demanding more pocket money! They claimed that I would be getting all the publicity even though *they* were playing the football. So I said, 'OK, we cancel the trip', and they soon changed their tune. As we set off from the airport, their eyes were popping, and many of them were shaking all over, with their mothers pressing last-minute bundles of food into their bags, so that they wouldn't be hungry on the way. They didn't think much of the airplane meals, because they preferred mealie. There'd been opposition from SANROC and from FIFA, but neither could do anything about it because we were playing no official matches. I wanted them to go to Rio to watch some *real* games, to see that some of the heroes with whom they were familiar actually did *defend* in their matches. Our kids were great little footballers, but they weren't a team, and they thought that defending was unmanly.

It was a wonderful experience for them, travelling everywhere freely, no restrictions, going to the cinema, though one of their odd habits was that they always wanted to eat before a match and I couldn't persuade them that it was better to eat afterwards. We took them training with the professionals at the Botafogo Club, and they were able to see what disciplined football was like. They met Zico, the World Cup player, and many others, and it was a great step forward; even if such matches as we played had to be unofficial and behind closed doors. It was a shame when the *Sunday Times* pulled out a year or so later, and the project folded. We'd given incentive and a focal point to some eight hundred schools. [This is something which SANROC and the UN Anti-Apartheid Committee on Sport conveniently overlook.]

Since those days Stanley has continued with occasional coaching, having a contract in Canada, where he has lived for half each year, and this took him to Mexico for the last World Cup in 1986. How much for him the game has changed in the sixty years since he signed for Stoke as an apprentice. His eyes mist over as he sits back and reflects.

SM: I've seen some players, haven't I? I think I was lucky to play before and after the war, to experience all the changes that took place, with boots and kit and the ball. You could never bend the ball, when I started, the way you can now, the way it's possible for Platini to screw a free-kick round or over the defensive wall. Before the war, the goalkeeper was the *least* important player, he never cost a big fee. The ball has made it so much more difficult for goalkeepers, and the standard today is much higher. Gordon Banks, for instance, had to be so much more competent at a wide range of skills than Frank Swift, covering the whole penalty area, acting as sweeper. In my early days, the goalkeeper used to lean up against the post when the play was at the other end. When Blackpool signed George Farm from Dunfermline he held the ball all wrong, but we cured him, and he became so competitive. He'd be cursing the forwards afterwards in the dressing-room if we'd done anything wrong.

In an international career of 23 years, Stanley appeared with more than one hundred England international players. These are his recollections on some of them.:

GOALKEEPERS: HIBBS (*Birmingham*). He was finishing as I began; he was small but agile. WOODLEY (*Chelsea*). He came off his line a little, more than some, and was good going down low. Maybe a better shot-stopper than Hibbs, whom he succeeded; Hibbs had a big reputation, though I never saw him at his best. SWIFT (*Manchester City*). Frank was one of the best. He was one of those to start throwing the ball out rather than kicking. He had huge hands like spades. A great personality on and off the field, and an excellent shot-stopper. He, Hardwick and Franklin held off the Italians in '38. He was daring, and sometimes would *head* shots away. DITCHBURN (*Spurs*). Ted was not far behind Swift, a really fine keeper. WILLIAMS (*Wolves*). Sound and safe. MERRICK (*Birmingham*). He disappointed us in the quarter-final in Switzerland in '54, when we were playing well and had a chance. He let in two, maybe three, at the near post, I think – and he still owes me eight quid for a bet on a big race.

FULL-BACKS: HAPGOOD (*Arsenal*). He was a classic, a great full-back. When I was eighteen, full-backs used to send a telegram when they tackled, but Hapgood jockeyed, and with a 51,000 home gate at Stoke one Easter-time, he buttoned me up. The next season, at Highbury, I took the ball straight at him and he had to back off. MALE (*Arsenal*). A fine right-back, and better than Cooper of Derby, whom he succeeded. HARDWICK (*Middlesbrough*). George was good with both feet, and an excellent captain. He was very quick. SCOTT (*Arsenal*). Small and quick, very sharp, a tiger in the tackle, used to slide in a lot. For a little fellow, he was good in the air. His real asset was his speed on the turn. RAMSEY (*Spurs*). A finesse player, he had the flair. He wasn't fast, but made up for it with positional sense. Always a thinker, he made great use of the ball, and would let you have it when you called, would give you a fast ball before your defender could react. He was one of the boys, and I liked him very much. He never had that artificial manner which came later. ASTON (*Manchester United*). Left-footed, strong. He was difficult to play against, he challenged you all the time. STANIFORTH (*Huddersfield*). Not fast, used his positioning to keep him out of trouble. BYRNE (*Manchester United*). A very good full-back, hard and quick. When he tackled, you knew all about it, just like Aston. He could have been the best ever, but for the Munich crash. ARMFIELD (*Blackpool*). Very fast, liked the sliding tackle, but a poor passer and header. He was a listener and learner.

CENTRE HALVES: CULLIS (*Wolves*). A fine attacking centre-half, yet a good tackler and a very sound captain. He knew what he intended to do, and would come out of a ruck of players with the ball, arms out, full of authority. YOUNG (*Huddersfield*). Strong as an ox, he hurt you in the tackle. FRANKLIN (*Stoke*). The best I've played with. He made it look so easy, a master. The way he played, wanting the ball, always passing, you'd suppose he couldn't tackle, but he could. He had all the time in the world, I don't know how he did it. Yet I can see him now. If he was playing sweeper these days, he'd never need to have a bath, he'd never break sweat. He was marvellous in Turin in '48. He floated about the pitch, playing the ball with both feet, and would beat opponents on the edge of his own area. What a player! JOHNSTON (*Blackpool*). A better wing-half than centre-half. WRIGHT (*Wolves*). A better centre-half than wing-half, he was fortunate that Walter thought so highly of him. He switched during the World Cup in '54 when Owen of Luton got cramp against the Belgians, and Bill stayed there. He was outstanding in the air.

WING HALVES: COPPING (*Arsenal*). Never shaved before a match to try and frighten the forwards. He was very dark – and he was tough. Great to have on your side. You can't have eleven gentlemen in a team. WILLINGHAM (*Huddersfield*). A terrier, small and aggressive. Mainly defensive, but a good passer. MERCER (*Everton & Arsenal*). With those spindle legs, he always knew where to be, where the ball was going, tremendous positional sense. He wasn't a close marker, but an all-rounder, aware and clever. COCKBURN (*Manchester United*). Another terrier, wouldn't give the opposition anything, would run for ninety minutes when others sagged. He looked frail, but was as strong as can be. DICKINSON (*Portsmouth*). Jim was a gentleman, very strong in the tackle. His distribution was not special, defending was the highlight of his make-up. A good marker of his inside-forward. MCGARRY (*Huddersfield*). Tough. CLAYTON (*Blackburn*). More style than Bill [McGarry], would come through a lot. WRIGHT (*Wolves*). I never really liked Bill as a wing-half behind me. His asset was tackling, stifling the inside-forward, and he wasn't such a good provider as Ramsey or Johnston. JOHNSTON (*Blackpool*). A toss of a coin, really, about his position, but I preferred him at wing-half. He was a fine captain for Blackpool, wasn't a good tackler, but strong in the air and used the ball well. EDWARDS (*Manchester United*). Brilliant. Big, strong, fast, and could blast the ball with both feet. He could do anything. We never saw him reach his best. It was impossible to get past him, and so hard to play against him. He used to smother little Ernie [Taylor].

INSIDE FORWARDS: CARTER (*Sunderland*). Raich was an opportunist. If he had a half-chance, the ball was in the net before you could blink. His timing was perfect. A brilliant passer and a great partner. We had an excellent understanding. Unselfish in spite of his skills. Seldom gave the ball away. He would boast, 'I'll hit the back of the net and make it hang there for two minutes.' HALL (*Spurs*). Stocky, with a marvellous shot. GOULDEN (*West Ham*). Had a magical left foot. The way he could dribble and twist and give a short ball was fascinating. When he shot, the ball was *controlled*. A footballer. HAGAN (*Sheffield United*). A dazzler, he could play right or left. MANNION (*Middlesbrough*). Wilf could turn on a sixpence, and liked to play the short game. He had an instinctive football intellect, a beautiful player who was a delight to the eye. Had a dummy which could shift anyone and on his day there were few to touch him. So nice and modest. MORTENSEN (*Blackpool*). As fast as a whippet. We had a wonderful understanding. One misjudgement between us in the '51 final, when I pulled the ball back too far for him, and he was too far forward, led instantly to Newcastle's critical first goal. Morty was so courageous . . . and usually he'd arrive ten minutes before the kick-off. SHACKLETON (*Sunderland*). A player of touch, an entertainer, who should have played much more for England. A wasted talent. BAILY (*Spurs*). Slow, but always buzzing, a great left foot. Liked to play the one-two, as with Spurs, and could score fine goals. HASSALL (*Bolton*). Tall, a pushing forward who would go for goal, but lacked the fine touch. REVIE (*Manchester city*). Clever, but not in the same class as most of the others. ATYEO (*Bristol City*). A very nice man. A hard player but not that skilful. HAYNES (*Fulham*). Excellent with the long pass, but expected you to run for it, even when you had no chance. *He* felt *you* should go. Could pass with both feet, hadn't a weakness when on his game. Difficult to have a playing relationship with him.

CENTRE-FORWARDS: DRAKE (*Arsenal*). Give him a through ball, and he ploughed through anything. Fearless and strong as a horse. He'd always get there, I can picture him now. Not surprisingly, he was always having trouble with his legs, was always bandaged up. STEELE

(*Stoke*). Had the pace and change of pace which made him a great player. He could shoot with either foot. He was unlucky to get a bad injury against Charlton, and didn't know if he'd play again. When he did, he'd lost a yard, and was never the same again. He was quicker than Lawton. Could have been the best ever. LAWTON (*Everton*). Unrivalled in the air. A short back swing for his shooting, if it was in the goalmouth he'd get it. Marvellous timing on his right foot, and the only man who could match Freddie [Steele]. MILBURN (*Newcastle*). To me, his best position was outside-right, because he had speed. Yet change of pace is essential, and Jack didn't have that. LOFTHOUSE (*Bolton*). If anyone gave one hundred per cent, it was Nat. A bull – he'd take the weight off other players. An enthusiast, always shouting, a fine man to have on your side. Very good in the air. TAYLOR (*Manchester United*). Tall and quick, good in the air, yet his assets don't stick in my mind. MORTENSEN (*Blackpool*). Centre-forward was his best position. Frail, but had a lot of guts. He was much quicker than Lineker today.

WINGERS: BROOME (*Aston Villa*). Frankie was a smallish fellow, finely built. He was quick, and could shoot and cross accurately. BASTIN (*Arsenal*). A wonder-boy at nineteen, and a renowned sharp-shooter. FINNEY (*Preston*). A great player. The secret of his game was that he had that unpredictable change of pace, the same as Cruyff. He kidded every full-back, and when he was outside-right – which he was too often for my liking – he could use his left foot on the inside and was a marvellous goal-scorer. Showed he could play anywhere effectively for England. [Seventeen outside-lefts were used by England during Matthews' career.]

When reviewing players across the years it is perhaps interesting to note the views of Charles Buchan, expressed in his autobiography *A Lifetime in Football*. He named two teams as his choice from all England players, before and then after the change in the off-side law in 1925. While most of the old timers' names mean little to today's readers, it is nonetheless worth repeating here the opinion of such an experienced observer as Buchan. His two teams were:

PRE-1925: Hardy (Aston Villa); Crompton (Blackburn Rovers), Pennington (West Bromwich Albion); Veitch (Newcastle United), Roberts (Manchester United), Grimsdale (Tottenham Hotspur); Simpson (Blackburn Rovers), Fleming (Swindon), Shepherd (Bolton Wanderers), Holly (Sunderland), Smith W. (Huddersfield).
POST 1925: Hibbs (Birmingham); Cooper (Derby), Hapgood (Arsenal); Edwards (Leeds), Cullis (Wolves), Weaver (Newcastle); Matthews

(Stoke), Kelly (Burnley), Dean (Everton), Walker (Aston Villa), Dimmock (Tottenham).

If Stanley has meant so much to so many for so long, he has meant most of all to the Potteries, and continues to do so. His affinity with Stoke, unblemished in spite of the hiccup at Vale Park, is such that he has now sold his apartment in Toronto and returned to Stoke for the remainder of his days. He was more moved than ever he would show by two events in 1987. In July, the University of Keele granted him an honorary degree, together with Alan Ayckbourn, the playwright, Professor Sir Francis Graham-Smith, the Astronomer Royal and director of Jodrell Bank, and Sir Brian Urquhart, the former Under-Secretary General at the United Nations. On a day of academic ceremony, the Chancellor, Sir Claus Moser, bestowed the honour upon these sons of Stoke in a crowded King's Hall. In his address on behalf of Sir Stanley, Professor George Jones said:

The ancient Chinese called it *Tsu Chu*, the Greeks had a word for it – *episkyros* – although my enquiries of our Emeritus Professor of Classics indicate that it could be better described as the Argentinian than as the English game, being played predominently with the hand. The ball was of leather, as it was in the twelfth century in England, when the play was in the street, causing an edict from Edward II in 1314: 'For as much as there is a great noise in the city caused by hustling over large balls, from which many evils may arise, which God forbid, we command and forbid on behalf of the King, on pain of imprisonment, such game to be used in the city in future.'

Plus ça change. . . . By the early years of this century football had reached the zenith of its popularity in this country, with huge crowds at the popular grounds, and outstanding quality in a schoolboy was seldom missed. The terrible anxiety of a manager with an obvious future star almost within his grasp is graphically described in Sir Stanley's own book, but he was successfully signed, at seventeen, for Stoke City. Fifty-four caps for England in all, the first at nineteen and the last at forty-two; this number could well have been doubled were it not for seven seasons during the war when no full internationals were played. Supreme performers in any sphere were recorded inadequately in the dark ages before television, but a few outstanding examples of his artistry survive on film, notably the Matthews Cup Final of 1953. In one respect, Sir Stanley Matthews is unsuitable for a Keele degree, because at football he was undoubtedly a narrow specialist, insisting on winning games from his place on the wing, rather than tackling back to help his defence like a modern automaton. Since his retirement from professional football he has travelled the world educating young footballers. He spent several years teaching the skills of the game to black children in Soweto and elsewhere in Africa. Sir Stanley Matthews has carried the name of Stoke and of England to all corners of the globe; he has been an ambassador of sporting skill and of fair play throughout his life. It is fitting that we should offer him a degree in the King's Hall, where three thousand people gathered in protest when he thought of leaving Stoke City in 1938. We are proud to have provided the occasion today to welcome him back. Chancellor, on behalf of the Senate, I present to you Sir Stanley Matthews to be admitted to the degree of Master of the University, *Honoris Causa*.

On Wednesday, 21 October there was unveiled in the new pedestrian precinct in Hanley a statue of Sir Stanley by Colin Melbourne, the accomplished Stoke sculptor. It was a cold and windy day, yet the precinct was packed, with the loyal and the curious. Old ladies who remembered him from when he was a lad – and they were younger and gay – were there in their bonnet hats, calling him 'duck' and shaking hands and crying a bit and looking happy and saying it was lovely to see him. Workmen, busy completing some new office block, stopped work and lined the scaffolding in rows of several dozen, in their protective helmets looking like yellow pigeons waiting for the corn. The Ceramic City Brass Band played a merry tune to keep minds off the cold, and at eleven o'clock Sir Stanley, a little bowed of leg and shoulder, shyly pushed his way through the throng with Lady Mila, to mount the podium for the unveiling. There had been criticism of the Highway Committee's decision to spend the money on this honour; and there would be more criticism afterwards by Conservative councillors, when it was discovered that the Labour-controlled city council had spent a tidy sum in flying Sir Stanley and his wife from Canada for the ceremony. Yet, as Mr Fowler in the oatcake shop in Waterloo Street observed, the television coverage and publicity of the event throughout the Midlands for a new shopping area would more than have justified the council's carefully calculated budget, if justification be needed. There are some occasions upon which you cannot put a price.

There were children there from his old Wellington Road School, dressed in the red and white of Stoke, and they sang songs and recited verses. The streets of the Potteries have changed little, in spite of modernization, over the sixty years since Stanley's childhood, and in this little gathering there was a Dickensian touch of homeliness, a sense of people in tune with their roots and with each other. Melbourne's sculpture caught Stanley in that familiar pose, weight forward slightly to the left, chin over the ball, arms out in that tightrope walk towards the full-back. Some complained that the baggy shorts were missing: but

Stanley had been insistent. *This* was the kit he wore when he came back, this was the veteran whose magnetism had rekindled the crowd's enthusiasm for the game when he was almost fifty.

When Melbourne had first discussed the proposed work, Stanley had been full of doubt. 'Why a footballer?' he asked reticently. It should be some doctor, maybe, or Reg Mitchell, the local-born engineer whose Spitfire had saved England. 'How many times did you save England?' Melbourne had asked him.

Melbourne's father saw Stanley in his first match as a fifteen-year-old with the reserves: an enthusiast and a regular at the Victoria Ground. 'He always said to me that Stanley was good enough to play for England from the moment he first appeared in the reserves,' Melbourne says. 'All that happened after that was that he became *stronger*. It's this that makes me think that so much of his game was spontaneous, instinctive. If there was a calculated link between brain and feet, it was different from everyone else's.'

The first time his father took Melbourne to see Stanley, he challenged him to pick him out from among the others:

It was easy, I didn't know what he looked like, but I'd been told what he was going to do, that people couldn't handle him [Melbourne says]. He was a nervous and shy man, but he was utterly ruthless with the full-backs, until they would either lose their temper, or try to get lost, to disappear into a position where *he* couldn't find *them*. Pre-war, everybody worked Saturday mornings, and to watch the match you had to get home, wash, and have a quick lunch before getting to the ground. The friendliness was something special. At Stoke, people always seemed *surprised* if you had a big crowd. There was so much excitement if you'd won, you'd walk home rather than take the bus, just to be able to talk about it. I remember an extraordinary feeling on one occasion. We'd played Sheffield Wednesday, and Stan had a brilliant game. It was foggy and getting dark as I made my way home, and with the gas lamps glistening in the fog, and me being so happy, it felt just like Christmas. There was a lot of talk of Finney in due course. I found it offensive! Stan always turned it on against Preston, and even after Tom had been picked for England, it seemed Stoke still beat them. In those days, when Stan was at his peak before the war, it wasn't a ninety-minute game, it was a four-hour game – getting there, the bus, the queues, the talk, and always the debate about Stan.

Melbourne was studying sculpture at night school when Alan King, the tutor, predicted he would go to the Royal College of Art. He had never heard of it. King assured him that he could win a place to the RCA if he would take extra lessons at the art school on Saturday afternoons and Sundays. Melbourne told him he agreed, except for the Saturday afternoons. He was studying for entry in 1946, with thousands of applicants for one hundred and fifty places. He won one of two scholarships, worth £500 a year, which was more than his own father was earning. He recalls:

> I thought Stanley played like an artist, he was in parallel with what I was trying to achieve: change of pace, change of mind. I never dared speak to him when there was a chance, if he was in a group surrounded by people. They usually seemed a flash lot. How would I speak without sounding silly? When he left in '47, the city lost its heart. Some people felt let down. The hero had walked out. They didn't think of blaming the club. When he came back in '61, Stan lined up on the same spot, and I was in the same seat. I could see he was nervous. Stoke is a defeatist sort of place. It hasn't got much money or glamour, but it's got a lot of quality. We tend to be the second best, or third best, and we settle for that. Our motorways here don't have bridges over them like other motorways. It's just that we know we won't win. In sport, there's always a result, a winner and a loser. To have Stoke having a winner, that was really something fantastic.

There are others who felt, that October day in 1987, the same as Colin Melbourne. Cliff Cox had made a five-hundred-mile return journey from Paignton in Devon for the unveiling. He had been eight when he first saw Stanley, paying sixpence at the Boothen End. Now he was sixty-seven. Then, he'd been on the cross-bar of his father's bike. The inscription on the statue's mounting, which Melbourne had invited me to compose, says: 'Sir Stanley Matthews, CBE. Born Hanley, 1 February 1915. His name is symbolic of the beauty of the game, his fame timeless and international, his sportsmanship and modesty universally acclaimed. A magical player, of the people, for the people.' The following day the *Independent* thought fit to use the inscription as their headline.

Stanley pulled the cord for the unveiling; and standing there for all time is a reminder, even for those who never saw him play, of someone who achieved distinction: for himself, for his town and for his country, and indeed for a great many beyond his country who loved the game. The city council had asked me to make a short address before the unveiling, and this is what I said:

> Stanley Matthews has been to football in the twentieth century what Johann Strauss was to music in the nineteenth. He has given pleasure and entertainment to millions, who followed him like a Pied Piper wherever he played. He put a dance into a dull life. He was as well known abroad as in Britain. There was a joke when I was a boy,

round about the time England beat Italy 4–0 in Turin: the England team was said to have had an audience with the Pope; when the group appeared on the Vatican balcony, an Englishman in the crowd in St Peter's Square asked the Italian next to him which was the Pope. 'I'm not sure,' the Italian said, 'but the fellow on the right is Stan Matthews.' It has always been the practice of nations to honour their heroes. Great events in history, and those who made them, are given permanent public recognition by monuments: Nelson, Livingstone, Churchill. While portrait paintings are common, statues take a little longer.

It needs time for the gratitude of the people to take root, and this is as true of sporting heroes as in other walks of life. We now have the Grace Gates at Lord's Cricket Ground, and a bronze bust of Herbert Chapman in Highbury's marble hall. Yet it is something special when a man is heralded in this way during his own lifetime. Three years ago Wimbledon graced the achievement of Fred Perry, that incomparable three times tennis champion, with a statue at the All England Club grounds. Today we are gathered here in honour of a man who is unique in the history of English sport, indeed perhaps unique in the whole world of sport: Sir Stanley Matthews, the only professional footballer knighted while still playing. Stan won no wars, discovered no foreign land, made no scientific invention. What he did was, in its way, bigger than that. He touched the heart of the nation, because he was simultaneously exceptional and ordinary, internationally famous yet humble, spectacular yet shy and unpretentious. Most of all, playing this simplest of games, he had a special affinity with ordinary people, with his own roots. He was from these Potteries streets where we now stand.

He loved his home town and its traditions. When England were playing in the World Cup – disastrously as it happened – in Rio in 1950, the British Ambassador said to Walter Winterbottom, the team manager, that he would like to ask Matthews a question. Stan was introduced. 'Do you know what that is?' the Ambassador asked with a rather knowing smile, pointing to a huge Ali Baba vase. Stanley blew the wind right out of the Ambassador's sails. 'Yes,' he said. 'There are only about fourteen of them left in the world. It's a rare Wedgwood.'

Stanley's father Jack Matthews was a local hero, 'the fighting barber of Hanley,' a fine professional and a fitness disciplinarian, who established in his third son the personal principles which would make him a most remarkable footballer. As a fifteen-year-old apprentice with Stoke City, young Stanley walked or ran from Seymour Street, where he was born, to the Victoria Ground and back again twice a day. He was only allowed the bus fare if it was snowing. As a schoolboy, he practised his formidable skills on the rough waste ground beside Meakins pottery, or up against the two-foot wall in front of his house, until he could dribble like no one else could before or since. Yet if genius was born in him, it was dedication and self-discipline, to a degree almost unknown to many of the present generation, which allowed it to flower until, incredibly, his fiftieth year.

He won two Second Division championships – thirty years apart: in 1933, aged eighteen, and in 1963, aged forty-eight. In between, his career cut in half by the war, he played eighty-four times for England, a total that might otherwise have far exceeded one hundred. He tormented full-backs until they wished they could leave the field, and how the crowds adored him for it: even the crowds of the opposition. When it seemed he might leave Stoke in 1938, three thousand protestors packed King's Hall; and when, after three Cup Final appearances with Blackpool, after the war, he returned to Stoke, the Potteries crowds jumped by thirty thousand in recognition of his still potent magic. Famous players flocked to join him in Stoke City's rebirth and a return to the First Division. He had truly come home.

Stanley was a great sportsman in manner as well as performance, never booked or reprimanded for unfair conduct, despite often being brutally kicked. Last month he received the 1987 award of the International Fair Play Committee for his services to sport. Never again will football witness such a career, either for endurance or spellbinding entertainment. The public thronged through the turnstiles, during four decades, to enter a life of fantasy, as J. B. Priestley wrote, 'away from clanking machinery and into a splendid kind of life, hurtling with Conflict yet passionate and beautiful in its Art'. It has been Matthews the sorceror who more than any other in my lifetime has created that fantasy which made fathers take young boys who were almost babes in arms to some of his last matches, so that they, too, might say in later years, 'I saw Stan Matthews.'

APPENDIX

Matthews' International Record of 84 Appearances for England (including 2 appearances for Great Britain)

DATE	PLACE	OPPONENT	RESULT
September 1934	Cardiff	Wales	4–0
November 1934	Highbury	Italy	3–2
December 1934	Tottenham	Germany	3–0
April 1937	Hampden	Scotland	1–3
November 1937	Middlesbrough	Wales	2–1
December 1937	Tottenham	Czechoslovakia	5–4
April 1938	Wembley	Scotland	0–1
May 1938	Berlin	Germany	6–3
May 1938	Zurich	Switzerland	1–2
May 1938	Paris	France	4–2
October 1938	Cardiff	Wales	2–4
October 1938	Highbury	Rest of Europe	3–0
November 1938	Newcastle	Norway	4–0
November 1938	Old Trafford	Northern Ireland	7–0
April 1939	Hampden	Scotland	2–1
May 1939	Milan	Italy	2–2
May 1939	Belgrade	Yugoslavia	1–2
November 1939	Cardiff	*Wales	1–1
December 1939	Newcastle	*Scotland	2–1
April 1940	Wembley	*Wales	0–1
May 1940	Hampden	*Scotland	1–1
May 1941	Hampden	*Scotland	3–1
October 1941	Wembley	*Scotland	2–0
October 1941	Birmingham	*Wales	2–1
January 1942	Wembley	*Scotland	3–0
April 1942	Hampden	*Scotland	4–5
October 1942	Wembley	*Scotland	0–0
October 1942	Wolverhampton	*Wales	1–2
February 1943	Wembley	*Wales	5–3
April 1943	Hampden	*Scotland	4–0
May 1943	Cardiff	*Wales	1–1
September 1943	Wembley	*Wales	8–3
October 1943	Maine Road	*Scotland	8–0
February 1944	Wembley	*Scotland	6–2
April 1944	Hampden	*Scotland	3–2
September 1944	Anfield	*Wales	2–2
October 1944	Wembley	*Scotland	6–2
February 1945	Villa Park	*Scotland	3–2
April 1945	Hampden	*Scotland	6–1
May 1945	Cardiff	*Wales	3–2
May 1945	Wembley	*France	2–2
September 1945	Belfast	*Northern Ireland	1–0
October 1945	West Bromwich	*Wales	0–1

January 1946	Wembley	*Belgium	2–0
May 1946	Stamford Bridge	*Switzerland	4–1
May 1946	Paris	*France	1–2
August 1946	Manchester	*Scotland	2–2
April 1947	Wembley	Scotland	1–1
May 1947	Hampden	*Rest of Europe (v GB)	6–1
May 1947	Zurich	Switzerland	1–0
May 1947	Lisbon	Portugal	10–0
September 1947	Brussels	Belgium	5–2
October 1947	Cardiff	Wales	3–0
November 1947	Goodison Park	Northern Ireland	2–2
April 1948	Hampden	Scotland	2–0
May 1948	Turin	Italy	4–0
September 1948	Copenhagen	Denmark	0–0
October 1948	Belfast	Northern Ireland	6–2
November 1948	Villa Park	Wales	1–0
December 1948	Highbury	Switzerland	6–0
April 1949	Wembley	Scotland	1–3
July 1950	Rio	Spain (World Cup)	0–1
October 1950	Belfast	Northern Ireland	4–1
April 1951	Wembley	Scotland	2–3
October 1953	Wembley	FIFA	4–4
November 1953	Goodison Park	Northern Ireland	3–1
November 1953	Wembley	Hungary	3–6
June 1954	Basle	Belgium (World Cup)	4–4
June 1954	Basle	Uruguay (World Cup)	2–4
October 1954	Belfast	Northern Ireland	2–0
November 1954	Wembley	Wales	3–2
December 1954	Wembley	West Germany	3–1
April 1955	Wembley	Scotland	7–2
May 1955	Paris	France	0–1
May 1955	Madrid	Spain	1–1
May 1955	Oporto	Portugal	1–3
August 1955	Belfast	Rest of Europe (v GB)	1–4
October 1955	Cardiff	Wales	1–2
May 1956	Wembley	Brazil	4–2
October 1956	Belfast	Northern Ireland	1–1
November 1956	Wembley	Wales	3–1
November 1956	Wembley	Yugoslavia	3–0
December 1956	Wolverhampton	Denmark (World Cup)	5–2
April 1957	Wembley	Scotland	2–1
May 1957	Wembley	Eire (World Cup)	5–1
May 1957	Copenhagen	Denmark (World Cup)	4–1

*War-time International (no cap).

PICTURE ACKNOWLEDGEMENTS

The author and publishers wish to thank the following sources for permission to reproduce the pictures listed below, which are credited in order of appearance:

Jack Matthews, the Fighting Barber of Hanley (*Stanley Matthews*).

Jack Matthews sparring with Jim Washington (*Stanley Matthews*).

Ada Matthews and young Stanley (*Express Newspapers*).

At Wellington Road School (*Staffordshire Sentinel Newspapers Limited*).

Stanley captains Hanley Schools, aged 12 (*Stanley Matthews*).

Ground staff attempt to de-frost the Victoria Ground Pitch (*Hulton-Deutsche*).

Stanley in plus-fours sets off for a meeting (*Staffordshire Sentinel Newspapers Limited*).

On holiday at Llandudno with Betty and daughter Jean (*Hulton-Deutsche*).

Jean, aged four, tries out her birthday tricycle (*Hulton-Deutsche*).

Stanley junior takes a ride (*Express Newspapers*).

The family enjoys a day at the races, Ayr (*Stanley Matthews*).

Off to Paris with the RAF XI (*The Associated Press Limited*).

Relaxing in Brighton, 1947 (*Express Newspapers*).

Mortensen puts Blackpool temporarily in front, 2–1, in the FA Cup Final of 1948 (*Popperfoto*).

King George VI is introduced to the Blackpool team (*The Press Association Limited*).

The Blackpool goal under pressure (*Popperfoto*).

Stanley meets his new racehorse, Parbleu (*The Press Association Limited*).

A lifetime of fitness earned on the beach (*Express Newspapers*).

The 1953 FA Cup Final (*The Press Association Limited*).

Perry scores the injury-time winning goal from Matthews' pass
(*The Associated Press Limited*).

The young Queen presents Stanley with his Cup Winner's Medal (*Express Newspapers*).

Jubilant Blackpool in the 1953 FA Cup Final (*Syndication International*).

Stanley, aged 42, trains at Highbury (*Mail Newspapers plc.*).

Coaching in Kenya, 1956 (*Express Newspapers*).

Nilton Santos is taken on, England v. Brazil, 1956 (*Mail Newspapers plc.*).

. . . and is left floundering (*Popperfoto*).

Marche tackles Stanley at State Colombe in Paris (*Express Newspapers*).

Stanley, aged 50, in his Testimonial Match (*Syndication International*).

After the last game (*Syndication International*).

An invitation indoor tournament, 1971 (*Syndication International*).

Eddie McCreadie of Chelsea is beaten by Stanley, 1963 (*Popperfoto*).

The Matthews' swerve, here against Scotland, 1949 (*Express Newspapers*).

At the unveiling of his statue in Hanley (*Staffordshire Sentinel Newspapers Limited*).

Mother and son after Stanley has received the Freedom of Stoke (*Express Newspapers*).

Mila and Stanley in Canada (*Stanley Matthews*).

BIBLIOGRAPHY

THE following books were used as reference:

John Arlott, *Soccer – The Great Ones* (Pelham); Wally Barnes, *Captain of Wales* (Stanley Paul); Charles Buchan, *A Lifetime of Football* (Sportsmans Book Club); Jack Cox, *Don Davies – An Old International* (Stanley Paul); Terence Delaney, *A Century of Soccer* (Heinemann); Maurice Edelston and Terence Delaney, *Masters of Soccer* (Heinemann); Bob Ferrier, *Soccer Partnership* (Heinemann); Tom Finney, *Finney on Football* (Nicholas Kaye); Tom Finney, *Football Round the World* (Museum); Trevor Ford, *I Lead the Attack* (Stanley Paul); Neil Franklin, *Soccer at Home and Abroad* (Stanley Paul); Leslie Frewin, *The Saturday Man* (Macdonald); Brian Glanville and Jerry Weinstein, *World Cup* (Robert Hale); Brian Glanville, *Soccer – A Panorama* (Eyre & Spottiswoode); Geoffrey Green, *Great Moments in Sport* (Pelham); Geoffrey Green, *Soccer: The World Game* (Phoenix); Geoffrey Green, *Soccer in the Fifties* (Ian Allen); Eddie Hapgood, *Football Ambassador* (Sporting Handbooks); Johnny Haynes, *It's All in the Game* (Arthur Barker); Alan Hoby, *One Crowded Hour* (Museum); Arthur Hopcraft, *The Football Man* (Collins); Brian James, *England v. Scotland* (Pelham); Harry Johnston, *The Rocky Road to Wembley* (Museum); Tommy Lawton, *Football is my Business* (Sporting Handbooks); Tommy Lawton, *My Twenty Years of Soccer* (Heirloom); J. P. W. Mallalieu, *Sporting Days* (Sportsmans Book Club); Stanley Matthews, *Feet First Again* (Nicholas Kaye); Stanley and Mila Matthews, *Back in Touch* (Arthur Barker); Joe Mercer, *The Great Ones* (Oldbourne); David Miller, *Cup Magic* (Sidgwick and Jackson); Stanley Mortensen, *Football is My Game* (Sampson Low); John Moynihan, *Soccer Syndrome* (MacGibbon and Kee); Don Revie, *Soccer's Happy Wanderer* (Museum); Stanley Rous, *Football Worlds* (Faber); Ivan Sharpe, *Soccer Top Ten* (Stanley Paul); Ivan Sharpe, *Forty Years of Football* (Hutchinson); Frank Swift, *Football from the Goalmouth* (Sporting Handbooks); Billy Walker, *Soccer in the Blood* (Soccer Book Club).

INDEX

NOTE:
Names in team formations and lesser known foreign players are not listed in the index.